Using Picture Storybooks to Teach Literary Devices

Recommended Books for Children and Young Adults

by Susan Hall

ORYX PRESS
1990

The rare Arabian Oryx is believed to have inspired the myth of the unicorn. This desert antelope became virtually extinct in the early 1960s. At that time several groups of international conservationists arranged to have 9 animals sent to the Phoenix Zoo to be the nucleus of a captive breeding herd. Today the Oryx population is nearly 800, and over 400 have been returned to reserves in the Middle East.

The Oryx Press
2214 North Central at Encanto
Phoenix, AZ 85004-1483

Published simultaneously in Canada

Printed and Bound in the United States of America

The paper used in this publication meets the minimum requirements of American National Standard for Information Science—Permanence of Paper for Printed Library Materials, ANSI Z39.48, 1984.

Library of Congress Cataloging-in-Publication Data

Hall, Susan, 1940–
Using Picture Storybooks to Teach Literary Devices / by Susan Hall.
p. cm.
Bibliography: p.
Includes index.
ISBN 0-89774-582-5
1. Children's stories—Bibliography. 2. Picture-books for children—Bibliography. 3. Style, Literary—Study and teaching. 4. Figures of speech—Study and teaching. 5. Children's stories--Study and teaching. 6. Children—Books and reading. I. Title.
Z1037.H23 1990
[PN1009.A1] 89-8574
016.0883'9—dc20 CIP

Contents

Introduction

The genesis for this research grew out of a startling comment made by respected children's book reviewer Barbara Elleman during a speech at a *Booklist* Open Forum at the 1983 American Library Association annual conference. She had been asked to highlight the use of picture books with school subjects. One of her suggestions seemed particularly intriguing: She could see no reason why picture books could not be used to "intensify children's awareness of literary elements."[1]

Peggy Sharp, a librarian's educator, concurs. "Picture books effectively illustrate many literary devices found in more difficult novels and should be considered by teachers working with students of all ages."[2] Indeed, why not use quality picture books to teach literary devices? Knowledge of such elements may begin as early as second or third grade when, for example, children learn to recognize simile and may continue through junior high school or until students have a comfortable understanding of those devices commonly found in the literature they read.

Examples of full studies using picture books to demonstrate the teaching of literary devices are hard to find. One study used Tomie de Paola's *Quicksand Book* with fourth and seventh graders to learn whether students at various age levels could recognize and understand satire. Results indicated that students gleaned information about the story's satrical devices through aspects of both its artwork and its text.[3]

Jerry Watson believes that students can only begin to move beyond the literal interpretation of a story and to its symbolic level through progressive practice in exploring how literary devices function. Unsophisticated readers may never achieve discriminating appreciation for profound literature unless they have first been well grounded in recognizing these devices in books exhibiting simple, clearly illustrated examples of them such as picture books afford.[4]

Regardless of age and grade level, students, even older ones, need careful step-by-step learning experiences when comprehending a new concept. Because picture storybooks are relatively short, they can easily be read and analyzed in one class session. Their pictures serve to expand a limited text so that working together, words and illustrations clarify ideas with a literary punch not possible in any other fictional genre. By selectively choosing the simpler vehicle of picture storybooks to illustrate a particular concept such as *metaphor* or *pun,* students may not only more easily comprehend the device, but may also readily understand its operation as it occurs in more challenging literature.

Sometimes students fail to grasp difficult aspects of critical reading because complicated concepts are being taught in the context of short stories or novels too esoteric for them to recognize the targeted literary device, let alone to internalize its meaning well enough to enable future recognition of it in other pieces of literature. Consider the plight of the struggling eighth-grade student attempting to recognize irony in a story regarded to be on grade level, "The Monkey's Paw" by W.W. Jacobs. This tale of three free wishes is a variation on the theme of "There's no such thing as a free lunch." An old couple comes into possession of a talisman. Since they need 200 pounds as final payment on their home, for their first wish, they request exactly that amount. Their beloved son scoffs at the faith they put in the talisman saying, "Well, I don't see the money . . . and I bet I never shall." How right he is!

The couple is warned that the granting of the wishes may seem so natural as to appear coincidental. Soon after, they receive the grievous news that their son has been killed in a mutilating factory accident. Although the firm disclaims all liability, it offers a certain sum as compensation for the son's valued services—an amount of 200 pounds.

Irony is frequently useful to comment on the unpredictable nature of life. It also demonstrates how events turn out to be the opposite of what is expected. Both of these characteristics are present in "The Monkey's Paw," but the supernatural elements in this tale and the aspect of fate ruling people's lives complicates recognition of the literary device. Unless both the situation irony and the dramatic irony are pointed out to the average eighth grader, he or she is kept busy enough identifying the themes and messages in this story.

How much more easily and quickly the concept of irony unfolds in a carefully selected picture storybook such as Margaret Gordon's *The Supermarket Mice* (Dutton, 1984). In this delightfully funny blend of text and illustration, some mice enjoying the good life in a supermarket find their night activities of unhampered foraging in jeopardy when a cat is brought in to eliminate them. However, these resourceful mice soon ply the willing cat not only with the remains from their own snacks, but anything else they can lay paw to because they discover that this guard cat will devour absolutely everything. The cat fattens on these forced feedings, and the mice thrive peacefully in the style to which they have been accustomed. The market manager is happy; since he no longer finds slightly knawed cracker boxes in the morning, he assumes the cat must be successfully getting rid of those nasty mice. Students of all ages can readily see the irony in this cat and mouse situation. And the story is as appealingly humorous to a twelve-year-old as it is to an eight-year-old.

Deceptively simple, picture storybooks have the advantage of teaching complex literary elements in an accessible format to students of all ages. Flashback, inference, and rich imagery occur in the art and text of the picture storybook as frequently as they occur in more mature fictional literature. Recognition of such devices on the part of any reader improves, at the least, comprehension of a book's message and may, at best, ultimately lead to enhanced reading pleasure and discriminating literary tastes, objectives which surely must find advocates among those working in the educational setting!

Astutely introduced to older students in ways that demonstrate their educational value, picture storybooks ought to be able to serve the school curriculum as well as any resource material. Readability studies[5] indicate that the level of reading difficulty found in many picture storybooks may reach sixth grade or beyond. Note this passage from Eve Bunting's wistful *How Many Days to America?* (Clarion Books, 1989).

> Boats bobbed in the dark water off the quay and men talked behind their hands while gold passed from one pocket to another.

Possibly the reason more picture storybooks are not now regularly employed in the teaching of literary concepts is because teachers are unaware that they can be useful in this manner. Clearly neither the Media Center subject card index nor the list of suggested sources found in the back of literature texts is alone sufficient to fully address the relationship picture storybooks have with literary devices.

There would appear to be demonstrable need for picture storybook titles to be organized under the literary devices they exhibit and for the list to be accessible to educators who desire it. Hence, this guide to picture storybooks which evince particular literary devices has been developed. Part One, "Using Picture Storybooks to Teach Literary Devices," discusses picture storybooks as literature, showing how they can be used to teach elements of literature. Part Two, "Literary Devices in Picture Storybooks—A Source List," presents 30 literary terms, ranging from alliteration to hyperbole to parody to understatement. Each term is defined and followed by a list of appropriate picture storybooks which incorporate the term listed. Each book listed is described and, in most cases, an example that illustrates the particular literary device is presented. See Chapter 5, "Bibliographical Selection Process," for a sample entry and more information about how the 275 books listed in this guide were selected.

NOTES

1. Barbara Elleman, "Picture Books: More Than a Story," *Booklist*, 80 (1 October 1983), 292.
2. Peggy Agnostino Sharp, "Teaching with Picture Books Throughout the Curriculum," *The Reading Teacher,* 38 (November 1984), 133–34.
3. Shelley McNamara, "Children Respond to Satire in Picture Books," *Reading Improvement*, 21 (Winter 1984), 301–23.
4. Jerry J. Watson, "Picture Books for Young Adolescents," *Clearing House*, 51 (January 1978), 209.
5. Adrianne Hunt and Janet Rueter, "Readability and Children's Picture Books," *Reading Teacher*, 32 (October 1978). 23–27.

PART ONE

Using Picture Storybooks to Teach Literary Devices

■ 1 ■

The Picture Storybook Audience

In a 1984 study using the informal open-ended interview technique to describe fifth-grade students' reactions to picture books, one researcher discovered that because these middle school subjects had limited opportunities to experience picture books after their primary school years, their response to them was arrested. They tended to regard them with nostalgic feelings as reading material for young children. This study concluded, however, that among other positive benefits, certain appropriate picture books can contribute to fifth graders' literary and artistic awareness.[1]

British children's book reviewer and librarian Elaine Moss, a long-time advocate of sharing picture books with older students, deplores the fact that children between nine and thirteen generally lack the opportunity to see plenty of picture books all the time as a matter of course. Educators operate on the erroneous notion, she says, that "five-year-olds begin with picture books and 'progress' towards unillustrated novels at the age of eleven."[2]

The long-held, widely accepted opinion that picture books are suitable only for very young children is a difficult tenet to dislodge. The world somehow suspects "that a book of pictures is too pleasant, too easy to be really adult. . . . Poring over a page of print is seen as an inherently more valuable experience than poring over a page of drawings or photographs."[3] Nevertheless, the picture storybook can exhibit mature intellectual and emotional depth. If a story told in picture and text fulfills the criteria of good literature, that book can be read and enjoyed by any age group.

The subtleties of language, art, and, at times, the subjects found in a number of picture books are beyond the comprehension and appreciation of the very young child. Especially does the humor expressed in some picture books escape the youngest child's notice. While Mother Goose rhymes are generally within the interest range only of pre-schoolers, for example, *The Chas Addams Mother Goose* (Harper & Row, 1967), with the ghoulish illustrations of Charles Addams, is clearly directed at teenagers or adults.

Another rhyming book, *Granfa Grig Had a Pig* (Little, Brown, 1976) by Wallace Tripp, is enjoyable for its comic illustrations alone, but is sprinkled with several visual puns and famous personages not expected to catch the attention of the child at whose age this fare is normally pitched. For example, in the illustrations for the rhyme "There Was a Mad Man and He Had a Mad Wife," among the fiends pictured in a chicken-like creature with a body caricature of Adolf Hitler.

One of the all-around funniest picture storybooks to appear in a long time concerns a subject of interest to children both young and old, dinosaurs. Hudson Talbott's *We're Back! A Dinosaur's Story* (Crown, 1987) calls forth sophisticated scientific allusions grounded in a sound understanding of dinosaur lore when it refers to someone who used to "hang around the tar pool." And a bedtime story designed just for dinosaurs concerns a little trilobite who wants nothing so much as to climb up out of the ocean. The tone of this rollicking tale told by Rex the dinosaur much better suits the youngster (or adult) who has lived long enough to garner an appreciation for wit, not to mention some facts on paleontology. It seems apparent that picture storybooks can, in part, "fill the older child's need for humor, sophisticated word play, social comment, and fantasy."[4] Successful author/illustrator Marcia Brown puts it this way: "Many books seem to be put out for oversized children in adult skins."[5]

Although the format of large-size and numerous illustrations has prevented many intermediate and teenaged children from looking at picture books, which they perceive as 'babyish,' there are in this genre a number of books that possess sophisticated theme, plot, and illustrations of such universal appeal that they address even the interests of adults. Ann Turner's *Dakota Dugout* (Macmillan, 1985) is such an example. This account of one woman's struggles and successes to survive, with her husband, a pioneer life out West, uses crisp textual imagery and mood-evoking pen drawings of life on the prairie to create a satisfying volume of cross-generational picture storybook literature.

An interesting and desirable development emerging within the last several years is a deliberate use of the picture storybook medium to explore serious subjects. Sobering comments on such weighty topics as nuclear weapons, wars, and even what constitutes satisfyingly meaningful vocations appear in modern picture storybooks. *Hiroshima no Pika* (Lothrop, 1980) by Toshi Maruki first broke ground with its stark depiction of the aftereffects on one Japanese family following the atomic bomb.

Christobel Mattingley's *The Angel with a Mouth Organ* (Holiday House, 1986), a spare account of World War II refugee anguish, is more likely to touch the psyche of the older reader than that of the very young child. Roberto Innocenti's haunting view of a German child's interpretation of Nazi Germany's treatment of her village in *Rose Blanche* (Creative Education, 1985) is a powerful set of intricately painted images strung together to depict war's random cruelty. This literary gem possesses allusions and inferences well beyond the comprehension of the usual picture book audience. For example, a disguised reference in the book's title to the former underground German youth peace organization known as the White Rose requires more knowledge of history than is generally found in elementary or junior high school social studies texts.

Charles Keeping's *Sammy Streetsinger* (Oxford, 1984) is a values tale about a simple street singer turned big rock star, turned back into a humble street singer. Carefully orchestrated art parallels the changing fortunes of the main character. The message projected through this insightful story can hardly be aimed at second graders only.

One hopes that authors/illustrators will continue to explore and develop this promising trend toward "all ages" picture storybooks and that reviewing journals will correspondingly note their universality with comments like the following that refer to Jane Yolen's *Piggins* (Harcourt, 1987): "The book is clearly not for the preschool crowd, who are presumably ignorant of lavaliers, much less Edwardian dinner parties....[6]"

Elaine Moss reiterates that the allure of picture books need not end when a child can read. This special genre enables older readers to examine various aspects of life openly, controversially, and often humorously to a degree that younger children would not find possible.[7]

Like all vital things, the modern picture book continues to evolve. Its audience can range from infants to adults. So powerful can its message impact be that the picture book fits perfectly today's visually oriented society. It has come into its own.

NOTES

1. Diane Driessen, *A Description of a Select Group of Six Fifth Grade Students Response to Picture Books*, (ERIC ED 250 707), p. 8.

2. Elaine Moss, "'Thems for the Infants, Miss,'" First of two-part article, *Signal; Approaches to Children's Books,* 26 (May 1978), 66.

3. Patty Campbell, "The Young Adult Perplex," *Wilson Library Bulletin,* 55 (October 1980), 136.

4. Moss, p. 67.

5. Marcia Brown, "My Goals as an Illustrator," *The Horn Book*, 43 (June 1967), 308.

6. Cited in *The Horn Book*, 63 (July/Aug. 1987), 459.

7. Moss, pp. 66–72.

2

Analyzing the Picture Book

PICTURE BOOK CHARACTERISTICS

What is a picture book? This supposedly simple literary form turns out to be technically and artistically an extremely precise medium which depends for its success upon many integrated factors, from the inception of an inspired idea to its salable finished package. The process is composed of artistic, literary, technical, and commercial talent to a degree not required in any other form of literature.

Some author/illustrators in the field like to view the well-executed picture book as a sort of seamless entity in which the attention of a good illustrator can collaborate, expand and illuminate discreetly so that the end product seems to be "tossed off casually complete and whole."[1]

Picture storybook aficionados argue about the proper relationship between the author and the illustrator. Is it better for the book if the two roles of writer and artist are combined in one person or separated into two? The bottom line must be the quality of the finished product. If excellent text and pictures interlock harmoniously, the issue of how it came about is not important. The craft of distinctive picture book creation can be accomplished just as well by a partnership team of artist and author working together as it can by one person doing both tasks. And sometimes only superior work can be achieved by team effort.

Traditional means of identifying picture books usually refer concretely to their physical elements. Such books may be profusely illustrated, possess less text than a juvenile illustrated story, have generally, but not always, a larger typeface, be either smaller or larger than a standard size book, and have between 32 and 48 pages. On the more abstract level, a picture book is "text, illustrations, total design; an item of manufacture and a commercial product; a social, cultural, historical document; and, foremost, an experience for a child."[2]

Picture books have been variously compared to poetry and drama. Sarah Ellis, commenting on the picture book's similarity to stage writing says, "The words are written to be spoken aloud. Pacing is essential, each page heralding a new scene."[3] William Scott, continuing in this vein but including the picture book's art, compares picture books to much condensed one-act plays. He notes that each double-page spread of words and pictures is like a scene in a play, contributing one more significant action to the development. "As in a play, the timing and pace of the actions are subtle, but tremendously important, structured ingredients in a good picture book."[4]

Picture book creators recognize that the scant text provides only the skeleton for the story and that embellishing, dramatizing, elucidating, and expanding illustrations, while never obliterating the story's idea, do, nevertheless, flesh it out. A cooperative relationship between the two enables full realization of the picture book potential, a composite verbal-visual narrative achievement.

Most illustrators and critics agree that the illustrations should not copy exactly what is written in the text. The idea is to leave space in the text to juggle picture and word—the rhythm of one foremost and then the other. This requires a supple text that stops and waits for shrewdly interspersed pictures. Judicious editing can improve the product. When Jacqueline Briggs Martin wrote her mouse tale *Bizzy Bones and Uncle Ezra* (Lothrop, Lee & Shepard, 1984), she originally described in careful detail the appearance of the carousel that Uncle Ezra made as a surprise for little Bizzy. But during the editing process, this lengthy description was cut out in favor of illustrator Stella Ormai's double-page painting of the carousel including Bizzy's wide-eyed appreciative view of it. No words were necessary. The effect on the story's plot is visually stunning. Occasionally the illustrator may have something more important to say than the writer.

Editing of picture books requires a very sound instinct about what is best expressed in verbal language and what is best left for visual description and elaboration. In this literary genre, illustrations play a major role in filling out and carrying the brief written text, allowing wide possibilities of interpretation. They provide "visual clues which can take the reader beyond the confines of the printed word."[5]

Perry Nodelman discusses the mechanical relationship between the text and pictures. Like a movie which is a collection of still pictures arranged to create the illusion of motion, many pictures that isolate moments in time tend to close the distance of isolation, thus running them together and downplaying the inevitable jumpy rhythm of a picture storybook. By interfering with the forward thrust of the words, the pictures create small moments of suspense that enable us to see one moment in clear detail—much greater detail than the sparse text implies. Good picture books "concentrate our attention on a series of carefully perceived moments of stopped time."[6]

One begins to see the picture book genre as both simple and immensely complex—a combination of text and art fused into a totality which must be carefully conceived from its inception to its conclusion. The picture book must contain a simple but skillfully composed narrative which says best what accompanying pictures cannot. It must retain reader/listener interest through repeated exposures. It must exhibit artwork appropriate to the textual mood and subject matter and be paced exactly into an integrated whole with the narrative. Like a perfect poem or one-act play, every tightly, precisely executed page must add its bit to the whole effect. If either element, the art or the text, is weak, the book's quality is flawed and its value diminished.

FUNCTION OF PICTURES IN PICTURE BOOKS

The illustrated portion of a picture book serves several purposes in relationship to the text. Pictures set the mood of the story, reinforce facts in the text, counterpoint textual material, belie textual content, or actually tell another story altogether alongside the textual version.

The capacity of illustrations to participate in mood setting is seen as a byproduct of artists being unable to avoid interpreting the things they depict. By adding their stamp of special expression to the story, they provide emotional depth to incidents and events. The most successful illustrations will leave a "residue of atmosphere and feeling, lingering long after the book has been read."[7]

Apparently, the different ways pictures make us feel about the same information is a matter of style—not what is depicted, but how it is depicted. For example, in the book *The Visitors Who Came to Stay* (Viking Kestrel, 1984) by Annalene McAfee, the words themselves do not alone elicit the stark, prim, barrenness of a lonely child's life with her divorced father. Anthony Browne's illustrations, however, leave no doubt about the nature of Kathy's orderly, predictable, rather sad existence. It is obvious to the reader that a zestful excitement for life is missing from the daily routine of these two characters.

Once her father's guests, a woman and her son, arrive in the household, events quickly turn zany, exhaustingly disruptive, and with each passing scene, more illogical and surrealistic. The reader understands Kathy's reactions to the intruders not only from the spare prose but even more from the mood-producing art that is revealed through her point of view. This book's art exhibits a good deal of sophistication, contributing depth to the book's central message of emotional growth and change, thereby raising the maturity level of the story beyond the confines of its simple text alone. Here is an example of superb author/illustrator collaboration working to produce something better than each could accomplish alone—a special creation which exactly suits those unique characteristics of the picture book genre.

Picture books demonstrate interesting methods of textual and artistic interaction. One common effect requires a narrative and a closely corresponding and corroborating art. In this situation the illustrations contribute to the sequence and mood that pushes the story ahead. For example, in Robert McCloskey's *Blueberries for Sal* (Viking, 1948), the text and pictures join to support one another scene by scene as the story progresses. What is said is shown, albeit enhanced, by the accompanying pictures.

In other books another condition operates. Here what the pictures show is not in support of but rather is in contrast to what is being said in the text. The story's meaning actually depends upon the juxtaposition of illustrations that say something opposite to the meaning of the words in the story. The truth is what the pictures say, not what the words indicate. For example, in Ellen Raskin's *Nothing Ever Happens on My Block* (Atheneum, 1967), a kid stands on his home sidewalk with his back to the houses. He bemoans the fact that his street is dull; nothing goes on. While he laments this state of boredom, many things are actually happening behind him, out of his sight—fires, burglaries, growing things, a witch's actions, etc. The reader knows something the book character does not. For its effect and its irony the story depends upon the contrast between what the words say and what the pictures actually show to be true.

Another example of text and enlightening illustration working together is Pat Hutchins' *Rosie's Walk* (Macmillan, 1968). The words make no mention of a villain stalking the blissfully unaware hen. Only the reader knows how close the fox comes to snapping her up. It is left to the pictures to inform the reader what the text does not say. What producers of good picture books understand is that their product can really deal with two story lines at once, the visual and the verbal. Each can be separately phased so as to reinforce, anticipate, contrast, counterpoint, or expand one another.

A good example of counterpointing is what author/illustrator John Burningham does with his Shirley series. Especially in his *Come Away*

From the Water Shirley (Crowell, 1977) each double-page spread is divided into the left side, the parental reality of tedious, cautionary, well-meaning patter, and the right side, Shirley's fantasy world of high adventure. These two side-by-side plates become the story's essence—a child's armament against her parents' wearisome rustle of words. Here, again, is this deviation of the illustrated message from the textual message. Although there is illustration on the left page—the text side—the right page, Shirley's private fantasy world, provides counterpoint to dull reality. Often it is the distance between the story the words tell and the story the pictures tell that makes a book interesting. Pleasure derives from our consciousness of this distance. Thus, parallel or contrasting visuals either correlate or contrast with text so that illustrations tend to make the printed word more concrete and facilitate reader comprehension.

One other function illustrations perform in picture books is their ability to provide clues to a more interesting story than the one going on in the text. Books by Richard Scarry and Mitsumasa Anno require the reader to pore over the pictures looking for interesting details. Anno especially uses physical objects in original ways. For example, he might use street signs to instruct, amuse, and puzzle. One sign might be a bottle that gradually empties as pages are turned; another is the opening bars of a Beethoven symphony. Information emanates from the sign shapes themselves.

Numerous picture book authors are known for their ability to take an idea and elaborate on it with illustrations. Tomie de Paola, in his series of picture books on scientific topics, presents basic information on the topic, then richly enhances the text with a parallel story told in pictures that expand the central idea. Examples of his books which do this so well are *The Quicksand Book,* (New York, Holiday, 1977),[8] *Charlie Needs a Cloak* (New York, Prentice-Hall, 1974),[9] *The Cloud Book* (New York, Holiday, 1975),[10] and *The Popcorn Book* (New York, Holiday, 1978).[11]

In *The Quicksand Book* a self-important young fellow takes time to present a scientifically correct lecture about the nature of quicksand while a friend is meanwhile slowly sinking in it and is desperately trying to secure his help. As he finally condescends to throw her a rope, he says, "Jungle girl, this is your lucky day. I'm here to help you." He sniffs that she should have watched where she was going. Of course, the tables turn on him. He trips over a turtle and suddenly finds himself struggling in the bog and hollering for help. His friend now enjoys the lecture activity while he attends to the quicksand inconvenience. She tells him to keep calm and float on his back. She'll pull him out when her tea is finished. The reader takes time to examine picture details and delight in discoveries—the whole point of such stories-within-a-story.

Sometimes the illustrations support the text; sometimes they contrast the text; sometimes they parallel the textual story with a story of their own. Always they set the mood of the story and serve to tell portions of the tale that are not told by the text. In this way the text and the illustrations complement one another by performing a different but cooperating venture to get the story told.

NOTES

1. Walter Lorraine, "An Interview with Maurice Sendak," in *Only Connect: Readings on Children's Literature,* 2nd ed., edited by Sheila Egoff et al., (New York: Oxford University Press, 1980), p. 328.

2. Barbara Bader, *American Picturebooks from Noah's Ark to the Beast Within,* (New York: Macmillan, 1976), p. 1.

3. Sarah Ellis, "News from the North," *The Horn Book,* 61 (May/June 1985), 342.

4. William R. Scott, "Some Notes on Communication in Picture Books," *Elementary English,* 34 (February 1957), 72.

5. Barbara Kiefer, "Looking Beyond Picture Book Preferences," *The Horn Book,* 61 (November/December 1985), 705–06.

6. Perry Nodelman, "How Picture Books Work," in *Proceedings of the Eighth Annual Conference of Children's Literature Association,* March 1981, edited by Priscilla A. Ord (University of Minnesota, 1982), pp. 62–63.

7. Ethel L. Heins, ed., "Art and Text and Content," *The Horn Book,* 60 (April 1984), 158.

8. Tomie de Paola, *The Quicksand Book,* New York: Holiday, 1977.

9. ———, *Charlie Needs a Cloak,* New York: Prentice-Hall, 1974.

10. ———, *The Cloud Book,* New York: Holiday, 1975.

11. ———, *The Popcorn Book,* New York: Holiday, 1978.

3

Picture Storybooks, Illustrated Story Books, and Picture Books

While most authorities willingly recognize a distinction between picture storybooks and other kinds of picture books, they are hard pressed to define the difference, which they all perceive exists, between picture storybooks and illustrated story books. The two contain similar elements but are technically different literary genres.

PICTURE STORYBOOKS AND ILLUSTRATED STORY BOOKS

Author/illustrator Uri Shulevitz feels the distinction is important. He contends that understanding the fundamental difference between illustrated story books and picture storybooks and applying this knowledge intelligently can be of considerable help in creating better books of both kinds. In a true picture storybook, Shulevitz says, pictures provide information not contained in the words. Both pictures and words are "read," which means fewer words are needed to tell the story.

In other words, in an illustrated story book the text alone makes sense of the story. The illustrations are not integral to the basic meaning of the story and most likely serve only to repeat particular details of an occasional key sentence between intervening pages of text.

The picture storybook, on the other hand, is a blend of text and illustration in which the two elements are of equal importance and "work together to produce an artistic unit stronger than either the words or pictures would be alone."[2] Pictures are actually necessary to tell the story; without pictures the story would be incomplete. In this sense, a true picture storybook could not, for instance, be read over the radio. The meaning would be unclear without the necessary accompanying illustrations.

The mere inclusion of many pictures is not sufficient to distinguish the picture storybook from the illustrated story book, according to purists, who contend that illustrations that don't supply a necessary harmonious function with the text become mere decoration. *Peter Rabbit* then, would not fit the true picture storybook definition, since the story is complete by the text alone without the adornment of Beatrix Potter's cunningly, charming miniatures.

Having thus drawn rather severe lines of distinction between the domains of the picture storybook and the illustrated story book, one quickly discovers the necessity of backing off from such a stringently narrow differentiation in order to successfully operate in the real world of the picture book craft. Few children's book authorities would deny the category of "picture storybook" to the tiny tales of Beatrix Potter with their pleasingly, delightful watercolors simply because they read complete without the decorative art.

Despite purist views to the contrary, illustrated story books do, as a matter of practice, often seem to differ from the picture storybook genre precisely in relation to the amount of illustrations per text. The more pictures there are, the more likely a book will be, for all practical purposes, designated a picture storybook whether the pictures are essential to the story's meaning or not. The pictures in an illustrated story book are not usually profuse, as would be the case with a picture storybook. The print will definitely overshadow the illustrations in an illustrated story book. Even though text and illustration are of partnership importance in picture storybooks, these elements do vary in prominence from book to book because of the incredible range and diversity of the picture book. If the question "Do the text and illustrations together tell the story?" can be answered affirmatively, then the book probably may be classified as a picture storybook even though controversy may rage on among the experts. In the real world, many illustrated story books end up getting shelved successfully as picture storybooks because of the number of pages and their many illustrations.

THE PICTURE STORYBOOK AND THE PICTURE BOOK

The picture storybook is also distinctly recognizable from its close relative, the picture book. In addition to the basic elements of the picture book, the picture storybook must also attend to the creation of character, place, and action. These ingredients are the essentials of storytelling and are not present in the visualization of an abstraction without the presence of narrative suspense. The picture book doesn't contain a story line demonstrating a recognizable problem, conflict, and resolution.

There is a caution here not to ascribe picture storybook status to those books that possess an organized series of events from beginning to end but which really have only a minimal story line if at all. Such books describe environment, feeling, and action to the extent that they create a memorable impression, but they do not tell a story, that is, presenting a beginning problem situation, leading to a climax and concluding with some sort of resolution. Rather, they fall into the category of mood pieces, regardless of their impressive art characteristics. Ann Jonas creates extravagant and technically superb artistic productions that wondrously delight the eye but which cannot be categorized as picture storybooks. (In a couple of her picture books, after reaching the last page, the reader can turn the book upside down and read it backwards. A second text accompanies each page from back to front. The illustrations take on new meaning observed again from this different perspective. One is taken with the mechanics of the book, but the story is really nonexistent.

The Caldecott-winning *A Tree is Nice* (Harper & Row, 1956) by Janice Udry also is a picture book. It illustrates everything there is of interest about the concept *tree* but does not involve trees in a story.

Other non-story books with concepts such as counting, alphabet, shapes, or emotions (anger, sadness, joy) as their theme, or any such teaching picture books, serve purposes other than telling a story.

Mary Lou White, writing in a journal for elementary school educators, lists nine features of the picture storybook to distinguish it from the illustrated story book and the picture book:

1. It must be an imaginative product of the author's thinking.
2. It must contain only one story in the entire book. Collections aren't considered picture storybooks.
3. It must be an original story, not a retelling. Folktales would not be included under these circumstances unless reworked as a deliberate parody.
4. It must have a recognizable plot consisting of a set of discernible actions arranged in a logical pattern leading to a climax and denouement. This would eliminate concept books intended to develop an idea or instructional theme.
5. It must contain a minimum of approximately one illustration on every other page. Books with more text than pictures, such as Russell Erickson's *A Toad for Tuesday* (Lothrop, Lee & Shepard, 1974), are considered to be illustrated story books rather than picture storybooks.
6. It must consist of pictures and text closely related to a story-line so that one must 'read' both text and pictures in order to gain all information intended in the story. Books that depend more on pictures than text or vice versa do not meet picture storybook criteria.
7. The general interest level must be pre-school to grade three.
8. It must impose no vocabulary restrictions. Thus, books following the Dolch-controlled vocabulary guidelines are not included in the picture storybook category. (The Dolch-controlled vocabulary restrictions were compiled by Dr. Edward Dolch in the 1940s. Dolch built a list of the 220 most commonly used words in all pre-primer, primer, first-grade, second-grade, and third-grade basal reading texts. Book companies used this list for years to establish reading levels for their books.)
9. It must be written in prose form but may contain occasional refrains that are lovely enough to be "poetic," such as in Wanda Gag's *Millions of Cats* (Coward-McCann, 1928)[3]

Hundreds of cats
Thousands of cats
Millions and billions and trillions of cats.

White developed her picture storybook criteria in the mid 1970s. More recently, authorities have slowly begun to recognize that this format can be used creatively to design stories for older children and even adults. Thus, number 7 is rejected as a picture storybook criterion for the purposes of this guide, since it does not fully reflect current application of this evolving genre.

Number 9 also needs to be slightly amended. Story poems, such as *The Ghost-Eye Tree* (Holt, Rinehart & Winston, 1985) by Bill Martin and John Archambault are picture storybooks in every sense of the word except that the dialogue and text happen to be in rhyme:

I dreaded to go. . .
I dreaded the tree. . .
Why does mama always choose me
When the night is so dark
And the mind runs free?

It seems unnecessarily wasteful to eliminate such stories from consideration as picture storybooks simply because they are in verse rather than prose.

Books included in this guide are, as nearly as is possible to classify them, only picture storybooks. The same literary devices that function in mature fictional literature will similarly be observed to operate in the simpler picture storybook format. It is fair then to apply equally the same principles of literary standards to the picture storybook as are applied to the short story or novel.

NOTES

1. Uri Shulevitz, "What Is a Picture Book?" *Wilson Library Bulletin,* 55 (October, 1980), 101.

2. John Warren Stewig, *Children and Literature* (Chicago: Rand McNally, 1980), p. 97.

3. Mary Lou White, "A Structural Description of Picture Storybooks," *Elementary English,* 52 (April 1975), 495–96.

4

Literary Quality in Picture Storybook Literature

There are not a few authorities who view the picture storybook as undeserving of the claim to literature. To them, literature starts where picture books end. The very trait that gives the picture storybook genre its unique character, its integral art, is often singled out as precisely the reason why literature status should be denied it.

As one writer puts it, to the degree that it dilutes the opportunities for a child to respond to a word story the modern picture storybook becomes a nonliterary commodity limiting a child's interest in real books and even imparting a neutral or a negative attitude toward words.[1] This author goes on to decry the fact that "a child can scarcely find words because of the forest of giant often overpowering illustrations."[2] He worries that excessive visual experiences might serve to remove the child from the values of written literature. This view sees the text running a poor second to the art, reduced to merely providing caption for a series of illustrations.

Echoing this uneasiness about the picture storybook's heavy reliance upon illustrations, Kenneth Marantz goes on to assert that rather than be considered a literary work to be read, the picture storybook ought to be recognized as an art object to be experienced. It is not literature, i.e., a word-dominated thing, but rather, a form of visual art.[3]

To these observers, "true" reading cannot be fostered from a diet of picture books or picture storybooks. The very essence of reading is the formation of a series of pictures in the imagination that result from words. "Modern children are bombarded on every side by the visual image; meanwhile they may be suffering from language impoverishment.[4] The best that can be said about the picture book and picture storybook genre so far as these writers are concerned is that they serve as a "halfway house between the seductions of TV, film, or animated cartoon and the less blatant charms of the full-page text."[5]

Many such authorities apparently equate heavily illustrated stories with necessarily having also a poor or inadequate text. These "milk-and-cookie-table"[6] books have their counterpart in the like-named adult market coffee table, photographic extravaganzas from which no one expects to find any textual depth.

Some picture storybook critics doubt whether today even Randolph Caldecott, the father of this special genre, could earn the award named after him. He did not illustrate material merely to display his artistic ability but, rather, to enhance a lively text for a good story. He would have been the last to want to see his works framed and enjoyed in museums. His illustrations were designed for specific books, and they worked in close conjunction with the text.[7]

While overblown, expensively illustrated picture storybooks lacking literary quality unquestionably do exist, the same condemnation of poor literary standards may be made against particular examples of all other kinds of literature. Each creation must necessarily stand on its own merit.

The charge that picture storybooks in general lack a well-designed text containing observable literary quality must be countered by evidence to the contrary. Actual picture storybook text and reviewers' comments about the text of the picture books they review demonstrate abundantly that many picture storybooks can readily stand up to high literary standards.

In a recent reviewing journal, a book titled *Wanda Gag's The Earth Gnome* (Coward, 1985) elicited such comments as: ". . .direct yet poetic language. . .opening lines are especially lovely, yet filled with foreboding."[8] Good writing need not be forfeited in picture storybooks. Another review in this same issue of *School Library Journal* discusses a book by Mavis Jukes titled *Blackberries in the Dark* (Knopf, 1985). Referring to its text, the reviewer had this to say: "The simple actions and genuine emotions are accentuated by subtleties of language and intertwining of phrases. Skillfully succinct descriptions shape the composition and the characterizations."[9] With careful selection, it is possible to find examples of picture storybooks that exhibit not only fine illustrations but appropriately matching excellent text. Being a picture storybook does not automatically preclude its having literary quality. That picture storybooks have always demonstrated sophisticated, fine language is attested to by this passage from Valens Evans's *Wildfire* (World, 1963).

> Daylight revealed charred ruins of the valley sunk beneath a haze of sour smoke. A slow snow of ash drifted down among the high black tombstones that marked the death of firs and cedars.

Carefully crafted language exists, as well, in recently published books. This passage from Cynthia Rylant's *When I Was Young in the Mountains* (Dutton, 1983) is vivid with imagery.

> When I was young in the mountains, we sat on the porch swing in the evening, and Grandfather sharpened my pencils with his pocket-knife. Grandmother sometimes shelled beans and sometimes braided my hair. The dogs lay around us, and the stars sparkled in the sky. A bobwhite whistled in the forest.

Fine language exhibiting imagery and metaphor are present in another story that creates a poetically observant mood for a child's experiences on a rainy day walk. Taken from a book by James Skofield titled *All Wet! All Wet!* (Harper & Row, 1984) are these muted reflections.

> Skunk passes spiders, sitting like black stars, motionless, at the hub of diamond webs. . . . He sniffs and grouches off back to his hollow log.

Picture storybooks must individually face the same canons of judgement by which other forms of literature are measured. Although the language in picture storybooks can be characterized by extreme economy, this is not to say that such literature is exempt from good style. Good writing is good writing at any level. Beatrix Potter in *Peter Rabbit* wrote that Mr. McGregor went to "fetch a sieve to pop upon the top of Peter." This sounds infinitely more interesting than if she had simply written, "to put a sieve over his head." At another juncture in that story she discusses a cat watching the goldfish in a pond: "The tip of her tail twitched as if it were alive." How dull and colorless it would have sounded if Potter had portrayed this typical cat behavior with "Her tail waved back and forth."

Perhaps a part of the difficulty in accepting picture storybooks as viable literature lies in a basic misunderstanding of the relationship between text and illustrations. In this genre, since the two operate as a combined unit, the illustrations may at times serve as part of the story line so that any notion of text must be expanded to include all sequences of pictures, too. The narrative may be expressed occasionally with character and action in the art alone.

Sometimes a story may even begin on the flyleaf page or the title page with lead-in illustrations. For example, in a little book titled *Fix It* (Dutton, 1984) by David McPhail, the playful roughhousing of a cat chasing a mouse behind the family TV set accidentally unplugs the set. These early illustrations are crucial to alert the reader as to what is actually wrong with the TV and how it happened, but no text is employed to get across the message. Nevertheless, the story must be said to begin with these pre-text pictures regardless of their physical placement in the body of the book and the fact that no text accompanies them. The traditional configuration—cover, title page, end papers, and frontispiece—can merge in new and creative ways by using text and art together to present the story.

Acceptance of the growing importance of the illustrative portion of the picture storybook is a fairly recent awakening. Prior to the late 1970s, authorities were still of the opinion that "the story is the tune, the illustration its accompaniment."[10] What an about-face is this new recognition that the text may exist as a kind of musical accompaniment that anticipates, coincides with, and may even follow the illustration.

Far from condemning an excess of art in modern picture storybooks, some writers express quite the opposite view. Blair Lent and Arnold Lobel praise the unique contribution of the illustrative portion of the text. "A child will learn to understand even more words when the words and pictures weave in and out of one another.[11] The issue becomes not a question of whether the word or the image dominates a particular picture storybook but, rather, how best to exploit their interaction. In a good picture storybook, "the pictures and ideas are so interwoven they become one."[12]

Picture storybooks ought no more to be penalized for their interdependence of illustrations and words than should poetry be for its brevity and incomplete sentence structure. In both forms of literature the reader comes away with an impression which is more than the sum of the parts.

A practical dilemma regarding literary devices as they operate in picture storybooks does exist and must be resolved to the educator's satisfaction so that this genre can truly be a useful resource for teaching purposes. Sometimes a literary device will occur only within the picture portion of the story but not at all in the text. If the device is not expressed in words, must it be denied usability, discounted, ignored? Literary devices are readily observed in picture storybooks, but some are lodged only in the illustrations. For example, in the story *The Chocolate Chip Cookie Contest* (Lothrop, Lee & Shepard, 1985) by Barbara Douglass, there is a visual allusion to a Charles Dickens-era chimney sweep, complete with black swallow coattails and stovepipe hat. The reader "reads" this allusion in the picture. Reference to it is never mentioned in the text. Is the chimney sweep, then, any less a bona fide example of allusion because it is presented visually rather than in written description? If one accepts the premise that in the picture storybook genre the illustrations and text work together to synthesize the literary creation, then all literary concepts must be acknowledged wherever they happen—text alone, pictures alone, or together as a combined unit of information.

At times the impact is more effective when a literary device does appear only in the illustration. In particular, understatement is powerfully demonstrated through a juxtaposition of text and picture. Babette Cole skillfully employs this technique in her *The Trouble With. . .* titles. A deliciously grotesque story line in illustrations counterpoints a rather straight text and belies the reality of the trouble with mom (who is really a witch), and dad (who makes fantastic robot creations), and Grandma (who is an outer space alien).

Today's picture storybooks also purposely employ art and text together to evince metaphor and other figurative language. In Sarah Wilson's *Beware the Dragons!* (Harper & Row, 1985), fog was perceived as "dragon smoke" all over Spooner Bay on the morning Tildy was to take the boat out alone. By sunup the "smoke" had cleared.

Picture storybooks can directly make the illustrations communicate part of the mood-creating mechanism. Large size, for example, indicates power and strength and ferociousness in some illustrations. In Maurice Sendak's *Where the Wild Things Are* (Harper, 1963), Max is huge when he's king of the royal parade and small when he is just a child in his own room.

In the aforementioned *Hiroshima No Pika,* which exposes the wrenching effects of atomic holocaust, the art clearly matches the family's changing fortunes. An ordinary morning begins peacefully enough with a breakfast routine that one can imagine does not vary much from day to day. There is in the art a sense of flowing serenity. Colors are cool blue and muted browns. Events suddenly smash this family scene headlong into instant turmoil. Colors are smeared. Outlines lose their distinctness. An artistic firestorm of expressionistic madness is dominated by colors of frightening red, yellow, orange, and smokey gray. An occasional detail, such as a dead cat floating in the river, is obscenely thrust into sharp perspective. The story's ending parallels the same sense of calm that existed when the book opened, but peaceful quiet results now from the the absence of activity that follows utter desolation. The atmosphere in this story is achieved by a masterful combination of simple factual text augmented by powerfully evocative art. No one young or old who experiences this picture storybook is unaffected by its message.

By slightly amending her list, we may use Donna Norton's eight evaluative questions (see below) to ascertain the merit of a picture storybook. Both illustrations and text must be considered as a unit in any examination. Current thinking suggests that numbers 5 and 8 ought not to imply that picture storybooks are created only for young children.

1. Are illustrations accurate and do they correspond to the content of the story?
2. Do the illustrations complement the setting, plot, and mood of the story?
3. Is characterization enhanced through the illustrations?
4. Do both text and illustrations avoid stereotypes of race and sex?
5. Is the plot one that will appeal to children [or a broader audience range]?
6. Is the theme worthwhile?
7. What is the purpose of sharing this book with children or recommending that they read it?
8. Is the author's style and language appropriate for children's interests and age levels [or for whatever intended audience]?[13]

NOTES

1. Patrick Groff, "The Picture Book Paradox," *PTA Magazine,* 67 (March 1973), 28.

2. Groff, p. 28.

3. Kenneth Marantz, "The Picture Book as an Art Object: A Call for Balanced Reviewing," *Wilson Library Bulletin,* 52 (October 1977), 150–51.

4. David Fletcher, "Pictures in the Mind," *The Horn Book,* 35 (December 1959), 466.

5. Selma Lanes, *Down the Rabbit Hole,* (New York: Atheneum, 1977), p. 18.

6. Karla Kuskin, "Books for Children," *Saturday Review of Education,* 55 (19 August 1972), 59.

7. Anita Silvey, "Could Randolph Caldecott Win the Caldecott Medal?" *The Horn Book,* 62 (July/Aug 1986), 405.

8. Cited in *SLJ/School Library Journal* (December 1985), 72.

9. Cited in *SLJ/School Library Journal.*

10. Bettina Ehrlich, "Story and Picture in Children's Books," (*The Horn Book,* October, 1952). Rpt. in Elinor Whitney Field, ed. *Horn Book Reflections on Children's Books and Reading Selected from Eighteen Years of the Horn Books Magazine 1949–1966,* (Boston: The Horn Book, 1969), p. 88.

11. Blair Lent, "There's Much More to the Picture than Meets the Eye," *Wilson Library Bulletin,* 52 (October 1977), 161.

12. Arnold Lobel, et al., "Children's Book Illustrators Play Favorites," *Wilson Library Bulletin,* 52 (October 1977), 168.

13. Donna Norton, *Through the Eyes of a Child: An Introduction to Children's Literature,* (Columbus, OH: Charles Merrill, 1983), p. 137.

5

Bibliographical Selection Process

Since the purpose of this guide is to present literary devices found in fictional literature, only picture storybook material will do. A large portion of the total picture book population must necessarily be rejected because of its failure to qualify as story material.

Not appropriate to this list are picture concept books, with their emphasis on elements of an abstract idea, such as "disobeying," "purple," "weather," "body parts," or such mathematical terms as "round." Also not included are counting and alphabet books and word definitions such as up/down, inside/outside, etc. Mood pieces such as Alvin Tresselt's *Hide and Seek Fog,* (Lothrop, 1965), are also excluded due to lack of plot and character development. Self-help books that explore emotions and behavior, such as Dorothy Chlad's *Safety Town* series or Joy Wilt Berry's *Let's Talk About* series (whining, tattling, lying, etc.), are not included because their purpose is primarily not the telling of an original story having a plot, setting, and characters. While themes of personal safety or emotional growth may occur in many stories, formula books which set out purposely to teach these elements are not included here.

Controlled vocabulary "beginning reader" books, regardless of their subject content, are also rejected due to their narrow textual scope. The breadth of language necessary to shape literary content is extremely limited in this form of literature. Again, the purpose of this type of book is not strictly a story for its own sake but, rather, a carefully crafted tale that will fit certain prescribed parameters.

For much the same reasons, toy books—those which are manipulative or have special effects, such as textures, holes, smells, shapes, or pop-ups—were also categorically eliminated from this bibliographical search. Needless to say, so are wordless picture books, since they have no interaction with text even though some may exhibit mature fictional subject matter.

Three other kinds of picture storybooks were also not considered, although they do qualify as stories and are often found shelved among other picture storybooks. These are traditional fairy tales such as "Cinderella," traditional hero folktales such as those about Johnny Appleseed, legends that account for the beginnings of something (sun, moon, zebra's stripes, etc.), and multiple-story story books such as a book of bedtime tales.

Tales by the Grimm brothers and such other authors have over the years entered into the common domain of numerous adaptations, and no longer possess one standard, unaltered-from-the-original text. Unlike *Peter Rabbit,* for example, the "Cinderella" tale has been reworked into a version for readers of nearly every nationality on earth.

Ageless folktales, of course, never did have a single literary text, since they evolved orally over the generations. Notwithstanding latter-day artist/adaptors who have chosen to embellish strategic segments of these stories with written text and interpretative illustrations, the fact remains that such stories are perfectly understandable without any adornment at all. They are actually heavily illustrated story books rather than picture storybooks. So far as is possible, only original picture storybooks are included in this guide. "New" folktales are included but not traditional ones, unless reworked strictly as parodies of the original, as for example, *Snow White in New York* (Oxford Press, 1986) by Fiona French. In this version Snow White is taken down into the heart of New York City and abandoned. She finds her way into a cafe where she meets seven jazz musicians. She is poisoned by the cherry in her drink at a party. And her prince is a news reporter. This obviously novel rendition is an original spoof worthy of examination for literary devices.

The special integral relationship between carefully orchestrated pages of text and corresponding illustrations that results in the picture storybook totality is absent in the multiple-story story book. Precise page-by-page movement that creates small moments of suspense is a luxury of space the multiple-story book cannot afford. The picture storybook format is missing. Only single stories between two covers are included here.

Finally, drawing a firm line that includes only picture storybooks and excludes all books designated as illustrated story books amounts to an arbitrary judgement call. To a certain extent, books were included based on amount of text per illustration and total number of book pages. In some cases, literary merit outweighed a dubious genre label. Books published up to, and including, 1989 have been selected.

In summary, original picture storybooks which tell in prose, or occasionally in verse, a story possessing a recognizable opening situation, a conflict, and a resolution were included in this guide.

SELECTION OF LITERARY TERMS

The first step in this research involved creating a manageable list (reproduced in Part Two, "Literary Devices in Picture Storybooks—A Source List") of common literary devices most often found in the prose fiction read by children from primary through junior high grades. Several publishing firms' literature textbooks for grades six to nine were examined to discover which concepts were deemed important for students to comprehend at particular grade levels. Below grade six literary terms were not singled out in a special glossary. Presumably, in grades five and below, the occasional literary concept is more likely incorporated, as needed, within an individual lesson rather than systematically taught as one device among many others covered during that specific grade. It would be unfair to imply, however, that literary devices are not nor should not be introduced to students before sixth grade just because no formal list of them exists in the back of reading textbooks.

Early on it was discovered that the various publishers did not agree upon which terms ought to be taught at any given grade level. Satire, for example, might be introduced in one series at seventh-grade level and in another at ninth-grade level. Therefore, a list was compiled of all terms that appeared at some time in each of the companies' texts. Terms that are included in this master list were those that appeared in at least one grade level of all companies' series.

Suggested grade levels associated with the teaching of any term are thus not offered here, since no purpose would be served by delimiting their use in this arbitrary manner. It is left to the instructor to select, as the need arises, appropriate picture storybooks from any category on the list, whether that need occurs in fifth grade or eighth grade or even second grade. In fact, the recent trend toward a "whole language" approach in language arts instruction emphasizes using trade books to teach reading and writing skills rather than relying exclusively upon textbook fare. A wide variety of resources would be expected to include picture storybooks in this teaching scheme.

Almost all texts defined and included the basic fictional elements of plot, character, setting, and style. These terms are omitted from this bibliographical list because all picture storybooks, as well as other forms of fiction, possess to some degree each of these basics. To list all picture storybooks under all these headings would negate the purpose for creating a bibliography of literary devices whose purpose is to discriminate certain concepts by highlighting evidence of their presence.

A similar case against the inclusion of atmosphere and tone might also be made, since all fiction including the picture storybook must be said to exhibit these elements too. However, these terms are included on the bibliographical list because certain book examples demonstrate an especially striking instance of their effect. It would be advantageous in such circumstances to point out to students how atmosphere and tone operate within the context of the story's overall impression.

DEFINITIONS FOR LITERARY DEVICES

Using the list of terms gleaned from the school texts, the next step was to formulate precise, simple, working definitions for each literary device so that educators who consult this resource might determine whether a specific term is indeed the one they might wish to employ in a particular lesson. Four reputable standard literary dictionaries were consulted in order to derive the best, clearest definition possible. Combinations of several definitions were sometimes necessary to create the end result of each defined term. The four sources consulted were the following:

Beckson, Karl and Arthur Ganz. *Literary Terms, A Dictionary.* New York: Farrar, Straus & Giroux, 1977.

Cuddon, John A. *A Dictionary of Literary Terms.* Garden City, NY: Doubleday, 1977.

Holman, C. Hugh. *A Handbook to Literature.* 4th ed. Indianapolis, IN: Bobbs Merrill, 1980.

Yelland, H.L., S.C. Jones, and K.S.W. Easton. *A Handbook of Literary Terms,* Rev. ed. London: Angus & Robertson, 1983.

Notable for its absence in these literary dictionaries was the term "picture book" or any reference to it. The genre was simply not acknowledged, although other forms of fictional literature such as the mystery novel, science fiction, and even the romance novel were included and defined.

In some instances it was noted that among the four dictionary sources a mix of different terms was identified for the same literary concept. "Parallel story," "story-within-a-story" and even "subplot" were each variously listed to mean a second story operating independently within and alongside the book's main story. The term chosen in such cases was the one that the majority of the textbooks used for the concept. In this case, "parallel story" was selected.

Certain literary concepts connected only to picture storybooks and which, therefore, would apparently have no further carry-over into other mature forms of fictional literature were neither found defined in these dictionaries nor included here. Emphasizing those traits found exclusively in picture storybooks would serve no useful function under the stated goals of pointing out literary devices in picture storybooks which *are* commonly found in mature fiction. A term such as "cumulative tale" for example, which refers to the repetition of events only slightly altered from one episode to the next and which so often occurs in picture storybook plots such as *Epaminondas and His Auntie* by Sara Bryant, is just the sort of picture-book-only device excluded from this bibliography.

Some literary terms have, with general use, become almost interchangeable with one another. Although they may have referred to separate concepts in the past, their meanings have now blurred together. "Atmosphere" and "mood" are such a pair. Mood is not defined as a separate entity by Cuddon, Yelland, or Beckson. It is incorporated instead into the definition of atmosphere as one of its aspects. Common usage referring to the mood of a piece of literature is technically a comment upon the work's atmosphere.

Tone, on the other hand, is a term frequently misused for atmosphere. Although they both rely upon descriptive words and details chosen by the author and, in the case of picture storybooks, by the illustrator also, to arouse the reader's emotions and sensory perceptions, atmosphere refers to the general mood of the piece—humorous, pensive, joyous, melancholy, etc., while tone refers to the author/illustrator's attitude toward his or her characters and also toward the reader. He or she may be purporting to present a sober topic but may in fact adopt a tongue-in-cheek mock-serious attitude that belies his or her true feelings about the characters or their actions. The counterpart to literary tone is one's tone of voice in speech—detached and clipped like a report, droll, condescending, satirical, bantering, etc.

It is possible to find instances in which the atmosphere and tone are quite different from each other in the same story. Atmosphere is light, humorous banter in James Marshall's *The Cut-Ups* (Viking Kestrel, 1984) and in the *Cut-Up* sequels, but the tone is satirical in his treatment of the two main characters, two troublesome schooboys, who richly deserve their just rewards. Marshall's special talent for humorous understatement and droll comments (his tone) combines with bright, cartoon-like exaggerated sketches and funny situations (his atmosphere) to convey his message of atonement, which, incidentally, does not leave adults unscathed either. As Rebecca Lukens observes, "Any kind of tone can be found in any kind of children's literature."[1]

Despite careful delineation between atmosphere and tone, it still takes practice to recognize the difference between them. Sometimes the clue to a discordant tone that doesn't quite match the story's atmosphere lies in personal asides to the reader. In Nancy Willard's *The Marzipan Moon* (HBJ, 1981), an ostensibly straight period story, the author steps out of the narration to speak to the reader directly. Immediately, from the first sentence in the story, "Now then, the story begins," the reader is alerted to a tone which is at odds with such respectable establishments of society as churches and church officers. Quickly, a satirical attitude is created by such comments as the following, which refers to typical Christmas gifts left for the poor parish priest.

> The cakes and marzipan went quickly enough, but a man can wear only one muffler at a time and mufflers rarely wear out.

Speaking directly to the reader, this comment is offered concerning the nature of marzipan: "It's a diet likely to kill you if you stick to it long enough." And finally, at the story's conclusion is this direct message to the reader.

> But the clay crock, now that's the one you want to get hold of. And if you do, remember the priest's story. Wish for something sensible.

The reader's serious frame of mind is jolted by this lighthearted dissonance toward a subject normally presented with quiet dignity—the poverty of a kindly priest living among simple people in a nondescript parish community. Events are now perceived as humorous ridicule.

Despite an abundance of terms to meet practically any literary condition evident in literature, there is still not a satisfactory definition for a rather common mix-up situation often found in humorous writing. In lieu of a precise definition, a close one was finally chosen. *Ambiguity* means "details of language that are effective in several ways at once"—double meanings. This term unfortunately possesses some of the same connotations as does double entendre, which implies a sly secondary meaning of an indecent or suggestive nature. To rid the concept of this perjorative aspect, some authorities advocate substituting either "multiple meaning" or "plurisgnation" for conditions of "ambiguity." As none of the dictionaries did use either of these terms for a replacement, *ambiguity,* with its attendant fault, remains the accepted term for referring to a statement which may be interpreted by two characters in different ways.

An application of *ambiguity* illustrates its literary usefulness and also points to a need for correctly defining it with an appropriate term. In Mavis Jukes's *Like Jake and Me* (Knopf, 1984), there is a scene in which the child is watching an interesting female spider crawling along his stepfather's shirt collar and comments idly, without mentioning what he is referring to, how pretty she is, how big her stomach is, and how fuzzy her legs are. The macho stepfather meanwhile, as is carefully shown in the illustration, is looking out the cabin window into the yard, where his pregnant wife in leg warmers is standing beside a pear tree. He assumes the boy at his side is also watching the woman, and he agrees with the boy's observations which, on the surface, certainly fit either the woman or the spider. They proceed to chat together for some time in apparent mutual agreement until something happens and the misunderstanding is exposed.

By this time the spider has disappeared into the man's clothes and reduces this self-assured adult into a wildly scrambling caricature of a comedian as he frantically searches for the tiny beast he clearly cannot abide. Just what such highly effective humor is called eludes lexicographers, but it's the stuff of which stage comedy is made. Until a better term defines it, ambiguity will have to inadequately suffice for the condition in which two people seem to be, but actually are not at all, talking on the same wave length.

MATCHING PICTURE STORYBOOKS TO LITERARY DEVICES

The final step in this project entailed matching to this list of literary terms examples of appropriate picture storybooks that were selected from specific samples showing evidence of the concepts in question. Issues of *The Horn Book Magazine* from 1980 to 1989 were examined for picture storybook reviews in order to select a viable list of useful titles. Promising books were then located, examined, and added to the guide if they were found to exhibit one or more of the targeted concept terms.

Horn Book was chosen as a source of titles because it alone among the reviewing journals presifts picture books from all its other trade books for young people and puts them under a special heading called "Picture Books: Infancy Through Older Readers." This acknowledgement that picture books can exist as a classification exclusive of age-designated categories was a major factor favoring *Horn Book.* To know that beginning-readers and illustrated story books would not be included was also no small advantage.

BIBLIOGRAPHIC ENTRY INFORMATION

The literary terms in this guide are arranged alphabetically, and within each literary category all the picture storybooks are also arranged alphabetically by author's last name. Each entry includes the following information:

1. Complete book citation.
2. Brief summary of the story plot (taken when available and when suitable, from Cataloging in Publication information on the verso of the book's title page or elsewhere in the book).
3. In most cases, a notation under the section called Examples, showing how the literary device functions in the book (unless the device can be shown in the above story summary).
4. Notation in the section called Other Devices listing any additional literary terms operating in the same book (to which categories one may also refer to obtain the full entries). If none existed, this section was eliminated.

Any selection of a particular picture storybook depends upon the educator's perception of his/her students' needs regardless of their age level. For this reason there is no suitable or suggested grade or age level indicated. There are enough books in each category from which to make a selection so that almost all needs may be addressed successfully. Shown below as a sample of the format used is a typical entry for a book under the category "Alliteration":

Cole, Brock. *The Winter Wren.* New York: Farrar, Straus & Giroux, 1984. [*Bibliographic Citation*]
Two children in a modern folktale set out to discover why an overlong winter won't give up to spring. [*Story Summary*]

Examples:
*s*owing the earth with *s*leet; threw down his *s*ack of *s*leet and *s*tomped away; *w*hispered the *w*inter *w*ren; *c*reep up *c*lose; who *p*lants where I *p*rune; *b*lowing *b*lossoms [*Examples of Literary Device Operating in Book*]

Other Devices:
Personification; Foreshadow; Simile; Imagery
[*Other Literary Devices to Refer to Elsewhere in the Source List*]

NOTE

1. Rebecca Lukens, *A Critical Handbook of Children's Literature,* 2nd ed., (Glenview, IL: Scott, Foresman, 1982), p. 150.

Source Notes

Bader, Barbara. *American Picture Books from Noah's Ark to the Beast Within.* New York: Macmillan, 1976.

Brown, Marcia. "My Goals as an Illustrator." *The Horn Book,* 43 (June 1967), 305–16.

Campbell, Patty. "The Young Adult Perplex." *Wilson Library Bulletin,* 55 (October 1980), 136–37, 158.

Chapman, Diane. "The New Look of Children's Picture Books." Paper delivered at International Reading Association, St. Louis, MO, May 5, 1980.

Driessen, Diane. *A Description of a Select Group of Six Fifth Grade Students' Response to Picture Books.* ERIC ED 250 707.

Ehrlich, Bettina. "Story and Picture in Children's Books." (*Horn Book,* October, 1952). Rpt. in Elinor Whitney Field, ed. *Horn Book Reflections on Children's Books and Reading Selected from Eighteen Years of the Horn Books Magazine–1949–1966.* Boston: The Horn Book, 1969, pp. 86–93.

Elleman, Barbara. "Picture Books: More than a Story." *Booklist,* 80 (October 1, 1983), 292–94.

Ellis, Sarah. "News from the North." *The Horn Book,* 61 (May/June 1985), 342–45.

Fletcher, David. "Pictures in the Mind." *The Horn Book,* 35 (December 1959), 465–68.

Groff, Patrick. "The Picture Book Paradox." *PTA Magazine,* 67 (March 1973), 26–29.

Heins, Ethel L. "Art and Text—and Contrast," editorial. *The Horn Book,* 60 (April 1984), 158–59.

Hunt, Adrianne and Janet Reuter. "Readability and Children's Picture Books." *Reading Teacher,* 32 (October, 1978), 23–27.

Hurst, Carol O. "Picture That." *Early Years,* 14 (March 1984), 30–34.

Kiefer, Barbara. "Looking Beyond Picture Book Preferences." *The Horn Book,* 61 (November/December 1985), 705–13.

Kuskin, Karla. "Books for Children." *Saturday Review of Education,* 55 (19 August 1972), 59–61.

Lanes, Selma. *Down the Rabbit Hole.* New York: Atheneum, 1971.

Lent, Blair. "There's Much More to the Picture than Meets the Eye." *Wilson Library Bulletin,* 52 (October 1977), 161–64.

Lobel, Arnold, et al. "Children's Book Illustrators Play Favorites." *Wilson Library Bulletin,* 52 (October 1977), 165–73.

Lorraine, Walter. "The Art of the Picture Book." *Wilson Library Bulletin,* 52 (October 1977), 144–47.

Lorraine, Walter. "An Interview with Maurice Sendak." In *Only Connect, Readings on Children's Literatures.* 2nd ed. Ed. by Sheila Egoff et al. New York: Oxford University Press, 1980, pp. 326–36.

Lukens, Rebecca J. *A Critical Handbook of Children's Literature.* 2nd ed. Glenview, IL: Scott, Foresman, 1982.

McNamara, Shelley G. "Children Respond to Satire in Picture Books." *Reading Improvement,* 21 (Winter 1984), 301–23.

Marantz, Kenneth. "The Picture Book as an Art Object: A Call for Balanced Reviewing." *Wilson Library Bulletin,* 52 (October 1977), 148–51.

Marantz, Sylvia, and Kenneth Marantz. "An Interview with Anthony Browne." *The Horn Book,* 61 (November/December 1985), 696–704.

Moss, Elaine. "'Them's for the Infants, Miss.'" First of two-part article. *Signal: Approaches to Children's Books,* 27 (September 1978), 144–49.

Nodelman, Perry. "How Picture Books Work." In *Proceedings of the Eighth Annual Conference of the Children's Literature Association.* March 1981. Ed. Priscilla A. Ord. University of Minnesota, 1982, pp. 57–67.

Norton, Donna. *Through the Eyes of a Child; an Introduction to Children's Literature.* Columbus, OH: Charles Merrill, 1983.

Polette, Nancy. *E Is for Everybody.* 2nd ed. Metuchen, NJ: Scarecrow Press, 1982.

Richards, Olga, and Donnarae MacCann. "Picture Books for Children." *Wilson Library Bulletin,* 53 (June 1979), 708–11.

Rovenger, Judith. "Picture Books for Older Children." *School Library Journal,* 33 (May 1987), 38–39.

Scott, William R. "Some Notes on Communication in Picture Books." *Elementary English,* 34 (February 1957), 67–72.

Sharp, Peggy Agostino. "Teaching with Picture Books throughout the Curriculum." *The Reading Teacher,* 38 (November 1984), 132–37.

Shulevitz, Uri. "What Is a Picture Book?" *Wilson Library Bulletin,* 55 (October 1980), 99–101.

Silvey, Anita. "Could Randolph Caldecott Win the Caldecott Medal?" *The Horn Book,* 62 (July/August 1986), 405.

Stewig, John Warren. *Children and Literature.* Chicago: Rand McNally, 1980.

Watson, Jerry J. "Picture Books for Young Adolescents." *Clearing House,* 51 (January 1978), 208–12.

Weiss, Ava. "The Artist at Work: The Art Director." *The Horn Book,* 61 (May/June 1985), 269–79.

White, Mary Lou. "A Structural Description of Picture Storybooks." *Elementary English,* 52 (April 1975), 495–98, 502.

PART TWO

Literary Devices in Picture Storybooks— A Source List

ALLITERATION

Repeated consonant sound occurring at the beginning of words and within words as well; used to establish mood.

Example: Miserable, mizzling, morning drizzle.

Sources

Allison, Diane Worfolk. *In Window Eight, the Moon Is Late.* Boston: Little, Brown, 1988.
At the end of a summer day, a little girl goes through the house saying good-night to the various members of her family.

Examples:
sunny sweet; sun-splashing; down the dark stairs; bucking broncos; swallows soar; satin jacket soft; black branches; where sofas are sewn; hush in the house; basket in bed; watch out the window and wait.

Other Devices:
Internal Rhyme

Carlstrom, Nancy White. *Wild Wild Sunflower Child Anna.* Illus. by Jerry Pinkney. New York: Macmillan. 1987.
Spending a day outdoors, Anna revels in the joys of sun, sky, grass, flowers, berries, frogs, ants, and beetles.

Examples:
sifts the soil; burr babies; skipping/slipping.

Other Devices:
Atmosphere; Imagery: Internal Rhyme

Cole, Brock. *The Winter Wren.* New York: Farrar, Straus, & Giroux, 1984.
Two children in a modern folktale set out to discover why an overlong winter won't give up to spring.

Examples:
sowing the earth with sleet; threw down his sack of sleet and stomped away; whispered the winter wren; creep up close; who plants where I prune; blowing blossoms.

Other Devices:
Foreshadow; Imagery; Personification; Simile

Kellogg, Steven. *Chicken Little.* New York: William Morrow, 1985.
A traditional story of irrational fear is set in a modern culture.

Examples:
flattened the fleeing fox; simmered in spices and sauce; Gosling Gilbert; foolish fowl; Hippo Hefty

Other Devices:
Parody

Lobel, Arnold. *The Rose in My Garden.* Illus. by Anita Lobel. New York: Greenwillow Books, 1984.
A variety of flowers and creatures grow near a rose with a sleeping bee on it. Disruption sets in on this peaceful cumulative tale when a mouse chased by a cat enters the scene.

Examples:
shudders the sunflowers; quivers the pansies placed in a clump; pushes the peonies pleasingly plump; mangles the marigolds

Other Devices:
Imagery; Inference

Mayne, William. *The Patchwork Cat.* Illus. by Nicola Bayley. New York: Knopf, 1981.
A cat braves frightening experiences to retrieve her favorite sleeping quilt, which her mistress has unthinkingly decided to throw away.

Examples:
crush the patchwork quilt or crunch her bones.

Other Devices:
Internal Rhyme; Metaphor; Point of View

Root, Phyllis. *Soup for Supper.* Illus. by Sue Truesdell. New York: Harper & Row, 1986.
A wee woman catches a giant taking the vegetables from her garden and finds that they can share both vegetable soup and friendship.

Examples:
Soup for supper—eat it with a scoop; parsnips, peas; blinked at the bushes; sprinkled sparsely.

Other Devices:
Caricature

Stevenson, James. *What's Under My Bed?* New York: Greenwillow Books, 1983.
Grandpa tells his two young houseguests a story about his own childhood when he was scared at bedtime.

Examples:
Grandpa describes the many creatures after him at night: things smelly or shaky like jelly; creatures that pinched, poked, snapped, stomped, squished, etc.

Other Devices:
Flashback; Internal Rhyme; Theme

Willard, Nancy. *The Voyage of the Ludgate Hill.* Illus. by Alice and Martin Provensen. New York: HBJ, 1987.
A poem inspired by Robert Louis Stevenson's letters describes how the author and his wife survived a stormy ocean voyage with a cargo of exotic animals.

Examples:
"Oh buckets and brushes and bales!; buttons and bobbins and lace; goat made a meal; Oh, the monkeys with muttering maws; a comforting chat with the shipmaster's cat; scours the pads of her paws; let them thump and twitter and thrum."

Other Devices:
Internal Rhyme; Imagery

ALLUSION

A reference in one literary work which calls forth within the reader an appropriate association to another work of literature, a well-known person, an event from history, or a place; used to enrich surface meanings.

Example: having the patience of Job (biblical character)

met his Waterloo (historical site of Napoleon's defeat)
Black Monday (event: stock market collapse)
sour grapes (Aesop fable: work of literature)

Sources

Aliki. *Use Your Head, Dear.* New York: Greenwillow Books, 1983.
Charles, a young alligator, means well but gets things mixed up until his father gives him an invisible thinking cap for his birthday.

Examples:
Story characters are alligators so, of course, Charles' teacher is named "Miss Crock." A visual reference to the author/illustrator's previous book *Keep Your Mouth Closed, Dear* occurs when Charles receives a copy of it for a birthday gift.

Other Devices:
Inference

Armitage, Ronda and David Armitage. *Grandma Goes Shopping.* London: André Deutsch, 1984.
This slight, cumulative tale has grandmother going out one Friday on a shopping trip. After making many purchases, she arrives back home in time for tea.

Examples:
Each two-page spread alludes by means of an illustration somewhere on the page to a familiar nursery rhyme or, in one instance, to a fairy tale. Examples that can be identified from the illustrations are "Owl and the Pussy Cat," "Hey Diddle Diddle," "Ride a Cock Horse to Banbury Cross," "Humpty Dumpty," "Little Miss Muffet," "Mary Mary, Quite Contrary," "See-Saw Margery Daw," "Old King Cole," "Little Red Riding Hood," "Baa, Baa Black Sheep," "Frog Went A-Courting," and "Old Mother Hubbard."

Baker, Jeannie. *Where the Forest Meets the Sea.* New York: Greenwillow Books, William Morrow, 1987.
On a camping trip in an Australian rain forest with his father, a young boy thinks about the history of the plant and animal life around him and wonders about the environment's future.

Examples:
The motorboat used to get to the camping site is called Time Machine. Just as does the device in the science fiction book of the same name by H.G. Wells, the boat also serves to displace its occupants in time. For a brief, enjoyable day, they step back into a period of ecological balance and simplicity on an island not, as yet, developed by humankind.

Other Devices:
Theme

Brighton, Catherine. *Five Secrets in a Box.* E.P. Dutton, 1987.
Galileo's small daughter relates, in her simple and innocent way, the magical world she observes in her father's scientific lab.

Examples:
Galileo's work with gravity is alluded to when the child finds a feather in a special box on her father's desk. A "book slips to the floor. The feather floats after it. He says the feather is important to his work."

Other Devices:
Inference; Point of View

Douglass, Barbara. *The Chocolate Chip Cookie Contest.* Illus. by Eric Jon Nones. New York: Lothrop, Lee, & Shepard, 1985.
A boy and his young helper prepare to enter a cookie baking contest. The winner is a surprise to everyone—except the reader.

Examples:
A visual image of a stereotypical "chimney-sweep," as depicted in illustrations from Charles Dickens' literature shows a child wearing the traditional stovepipe hat and black swallow-tail coat.

Other Devices:
Inference

Hearn, Michael Patrick. *The Porcelain Cat.* Illus. by Leo and Diane Dillon. Boston: Little, Brown, 1987.
A sorcerer's apprentice has to complete several difficult tasks before dawn in order to obtain a missing ingredient for one of his master's spells.

Examples:
At the end of the story when the living porcelain cat shatters to pieces, out of its "ashes" arises a beautiful "Phoenix," a porcelain bird.

Other Devices:
Irony; Pun

Kellogg, Steven. *Ralph's Secret Weapon.* New York: E.P. Dutton, 1983.
When eccentric Aunt Georgiana decides that nephew Ralph shows promise as a sea serpent charmer, Ralph is ready with a secret weapon.

Examples:
Book is dedicated to "Kevin"; a bust in Aunt Georgiana's music room is a boy's head—"Kevin the Great," along with "Lovable Ludwig," "Wow, It's Wolfgang," and "Jolly Gioacchino" (G. Rossini, 1792–1868, author of "William Tell" overture and "The Barber of Seville"). Other signs scattered throughout the illustrations evoke visual jokes.

Other Devices:
Foreshadow

Locker, Thomas. *The Boy Who Held Back the Sea.* Retold by Lenny Hort. New York: Dial, 1987.
A boy banished to his room for a misdeed hears from his grandmother a tale about a misbehaving lad like himself who saved his town from a flood.

Examples:
An unspoken allusion to the fable "The Boy Who Cried Wolf" is noted in the person of Jan who had too often falsely annoyed townsfolk with enemy soldiers tales in order to arouse the guard.

Other Devices:
Inference

Mahy, Margaret. *Jam, a True Story.* Illus. by Helen Craig. Boston: Atlantic Monthly Press, 1985.
When Mrs. Castle finds a job as an atomic scientist, it's Mr. Castle who stays home to look after the children—and make plum jam.

Examples:
Mother describes her husband as a "born artist . . . the Picasso of jam makers."

Other Devices:
Inference

Maiorano, Robert. *A Little Interlude.* Illus. by Rachel Isadora. New York: Coward, McCann, & Geoghegan, 1980.
In the interlude before Bobby's important ballet appearance, he sees a man playing piano and chats away his pre-performance jitters.

Examples:
The piano player is called "Jiminy Cricket"; like little Pinocchio's little conscience, he serves as a sounding board for the new dancer.

Other Devices:
Atmosphere; Inference

Nesbit, Edith. *The Deliverers of Their Country.* Illus. by Lisbeth Zwerger. Natick, MA: Picture Book Studio, 1985.
Two children set out to rid their land of a nasty plague of dragons.

Examples:
Alluded to are: St. George, the dragonslayer; St. Andrew, who was awakened over the engineer's strike; St. Denis, who discussed a very pretty looking-glass that shows all the world and what is going on in it; a monument as high as "Nelson's."

Other Devices:
Imagery; Simile; Stereotype/Reverse Stereotype; Tone

Noble, Trina Hakes. *Meanwhile Back at the Ranch.* Pictures by Tony Ross. New York: Dial, 1987.
Looking for some diversion, a bored rancher drives to the town of Sleepy Gulch, little knowing that some amazing things are happening to his wife and ranch during his absence.

Examples:
Rancher Hicks lived out west. As far as the eye could see there was nothing, "not even a roaming buffalo" (This alludes to the expression in the song "Home on the Range."). A glamorous "cow palace" was built for all the cows (This alludes to the famous nightblub of the same name.). The President waves out of his helicopter holding a Stetson hat. (After the dust settles from its take-off, a poster photo lying on the ground shows a caricature of Ronald Reagan.).

Parker, Nancy Winslow. *The Christmas Camel.* New York: Dodd, Mead, 1983.
A boy receives a unique gift which possesses one special trait at Christmas time.

Examples:
Camel reverts to one of the Magi camels on Christmas Eve and flies back to the event of the holy birth of Jesus.

Other Devices:
Inference

Peet, Bill. *No Such Things.* Boston: Houghton Mifflin Co., 1983.
A description in rhyme of a variety of fantastic creatures such as the blue-snouted Twumps, pie-faced Pazeeks and the fancy Fandangos.

Examples:
Spooky-tailed Tizzy alludes to the like-appearing Prewitt Peacock developed in an earlier tale by author Peet. Also, Flubduds bear resemblance to the Wumps in his *The Wump World.*

Other Devices:
Paradox; Pun

Peppé, Rodney. *The Mice and the Flying Basket.* New York: Lothrop, Lee, & Shepard, 1985.
A family of mice decide to make an airplane out of a big basket and learn to fly.

Examples:
As they plan their scheme to participate in an air show, they seek advice from two brothers named Orville and Wilbur. The flying fiend is Baron von Rathoven.

Sadler, Marilyn. *Alistair's Time Machine.* Englewood Cliffs, New York: Prentice-Hall, 1986.
Alistair's entry in a science competition takes him to many places and time periods, but unfortunately, he can't prove this to the judges.

Examples:
During one of his trips back in time, Alistair seems to be in a "King Arthur" setting.

Other Devices:
Understatement

Schwartz, Amy. *Oma and Bobo.* New York: Bradbury Press, 1987.
Bobo the dog learns to stay, sit, and with the help of Oma, to fetch.

Examples:
Grandma Oma watches Bobo stubbornly refuse to fetch and sarcastically says he's a "real Rin Tin Tin," the famous dog star of television movies. Clearly Bobo is never going to learn any of the tricks that made Rin Tin Tin a star.

Other Devices:
Foreshadow; Inference; Stereotype/Reverse Stereotype

Talbott, Hudson. *We're Back! A Dinosaur's Story.* New York: Crown, 1987.
In this very funny picture book, creatures from prehistoric time travel to the twentieth century and create excitement at New York's Museum of Natural History.

Examples:
The dinosaur narrating the story is named "Rex." By his appearance he is a Tyrannosaurus Rex. The contact person at the Museum of Natural History is Dr. Miriam Bleeb, who looks very much like the famous anthropologist Dr. Margaret Mead. During the annual Thanksgiving Day parade, the displaced dinosaurs see a balloon-shaped rubber fellow floating in the air and attached with strings to parade walkers. They wonder if he isn't "That allosaurus who used to hang out by the tar pool." In an effort to divert the police from the dinosaurs in her "diorama," Dr. Bleeb tells the officers she can't imagine who they saw run in there. "Perhaps it was a publicity stunt for some movie or the *Enquirer.*" The bedtime story that Dr. Bleeb reads speaks of a "little trilobite" from "early Paleozoic era who wanted more than anything to walk on land."

Other Devices:
Point of View; Tone; Understatement

Tennyson, Noel. *The Lady's Chair and the Ottoman.* New York: Lothrop, Lee, & Shepard, 1987.
An ottoman has spent as long as he can remember trying to get close to a lady's chair. Though fortune separates them and they seem to come to unhappy ends, a marvelous coincidence reunites them in a very happy way.

Examples:
The used-furniture store's repairman is a person called "Duncan Fiefe" (an allusion to the respected American cabinetmaker Duncan Phyfe, 1768–1854).

Other Devices:
Personification; Pun; Simile

Van Allsburg, Chris. *The Wreck of the Zephyr.* Boston: Houghton Mifflin Co., 1983.
A boy who reaches beyond his abilities ignores advice and ends up wrecking a boat. He feels compelled to tell his tale to any who will listen.

Examples:
The boat's name alludes to the fast-flying train of the past named Zephyr.

Other Devices:
Flashback; Foreshadow; Inference; Theme

Wallace, Barbara Brooks. *Argyle.* Illus. by John Sandford. Nashville, TN: Abingdon, 1987.
A Scottish sheep's unusual diet causes him to produce multicolored wool, which changes his life and the fortunes of his owners.

Examples:
The "Argyle" sheep ate colored flowers, which made his wool rainbow hued. The plaid socks which resulted from these colors became the famous "argyle sock."

Walsh, Jill. *Lost and Found.* Illus. by Mary Rayner. London: André Deutsch, 1984.
This story describes a series of episodes through time which involve things lost in the same general location in one generation that are found by someone in a future generation.

Examples:
Terminology for the same phenomenon changes to fit each time era. In the earliest episode, a Stone Age child runs down a hill below the "Great King's Tomb." In another time, a child from the Middle Ages goes down a hill below "Old Henga's Tump," (Old English for a 'mound'). In the 1700s a child goes past "Henny's Hump," (mystical folklore for the unexplained topography). Finally, in modern times, a child goes past a "barrow" (English term for a mound over the remains of the dead).

Other Devices:
Aphorism; Flash-Forward

Wild, Jocelyn. *Florence and Eric Take the Cake.* New York: Dial, 1987.
A brother and sister lamb accidentally cause a major mix-up between a delicious cake and a beautiful hat.

Examples:
When Muriel dresses up for her evening at the opera, she goes to the "Baa Baa of Seville," an allusion to the "Barber of Seville."

Other Devices:
Ambiguity; Personification; Pun

Willard, Nancy. *The Marzipan Moon.* Illus. by Marcia Sewall. New York: Harcourt Brace Jovanovich, 1981.
The almonds in an old, mended, but magic crock produce a delicious, nourishing marzipan moon nightly for a poor parish priest, until a visiting bishop decides the miraculous almonds need a more fitting home.

Examples:
The magic that provides the priest with his daily ration of marzipan seems custom-designed to work only in his humble parish. The bodies of the "spirit angels," who concoct the marzipan for him, are really composed of all the things that surround him and which are unique to his life. Their bodies are flour sacks, "always empty" at the parish. Their legs are the mufflers he always gets for Christmas gifts. Their arms are firewood, the fuel he can't afford for his fireplace. Their queer animal heads are the nave gargoyles. Their height is described as being similar to the pampered "bishop in his miter." A special box is prepared with the likenesses of "Matthew, Mark, Luke, and John."

Other Devices:
Satire; Tone

Yolen, Jane. *Piggins.* Illus. by Jane Dyer. New York: Harcourt Brace Jovanovich, 1987.
During a dinner party, the lights go out and Mrs. Reynard's beautiful diamond necklace is stolen, but Piggins the butler quickly discovers the real thief.

Examples:
Names of characters correspond to the animals they are: "Piggins" is, of course, the butler pig; "Reynard" is the fox surname; "Professor T. Ortoise" is a turtle; "Lord & Lady Ratsby" are rats; "Inspector Bayswater" is a hound dog; "Pierre Lapin" the famous explorer is a rabbit. Also, similarities may be observed in the style of detective work attributed to the fictional sleuth Sherlock Holmes and that used by capable Piggins. For

example, when the legitimate officer on the scene can find no clues to the theft, Piggins makes perfect sense out of obscure facts which he ties together to make his startling announcement of the guilty offenders.

Yorinks, Arthur. *Bravo, Minski.* Illus. by Richard Egielski. New York: Farrar, Straus, & Giroux, 1988.

The greatest scientist who ever lived creates today's modern marvels. But he is not content to stop with these feats. He perseveres until he accomplishes the act which tops them all, his famous singing.

Examples:

The famous Minski's achievements span a remarkable period of time. There are allusions to Ben Franklin's invention of electricity, Galileo's and Isaac Newton's discovery of gravity, Thomas Edison's creation of the light bulb, Alexander Bell's invention of the telephone, and Leonardo da Vinci's experiements with rockets. Finally, even "Caruso couldn't croon clearer" than Minski.

Yorinks, Arthur. *It Happened in Pinsk.* New York: Farrar, Straus, & Giroux, 1983.

A complaining man wishing always to be someone else suddenly loses his head and becomes mistaken for other people after his wife makes a pillowcase head for him.

Examples:

Irv's trusted friend doesn't recognize him and mistakes him for Leo Totski, "You vermin. You low-life."

Other Devices:

Ambiguity; Irony; Satire; Understatement

AMBIGUITY

Alternative reactions to the same piece of language: same expression which conveys more than one meaning simultaneously.

Example: "Who" is on third base. (Could be a question or a statement that someone with the last name of WHO is on third base.)

Sources

Cazet, Denys. *You Make the Angels Cry.* Scarsdale, NY: Bradbury Press, 1983.

When rain begins to fall after his mother scolds him, Albert is convinced that he really made the angels cry.

Examples:

Albert mistakes one of his mother's sayings for literal fact. In her frustration over the crash of the cookie jar she sees messing her floor, Mother says, "You make the angels cry!" Rain falls. Albert thinks he is responsible. Later, after he makes peace with the "angels" by going out into the storm to tell them that it was the wind, not he, who upset the cookie jar, he tells his mother what he did. She is moved to say, "You make the sun shine." Albert looks out the window and sees the sun breaking through the rain clouds. "I know," he says.

Jukes, Mavis. *Blackberries in the Dark.* Illus. by Thomas Allen. New York: Knopf, 1985.

In a sensitive gentle story, a young boy and his grandmother must forge a new relationship together without Grandpa.

Examples:

The grandmother tells the boy there is something for him in the corner cupboard. The boy assumes his grandmother is describing the doll she wants him to have. She is, however, talking about the knife: ". . .belonged to someone special for many years. . .not really something for a boy to have but still and all I want it to be yours. Promise you'll handle it carefully. . .not something to play with. . . ." The boy takes the doll that was handed down through the generations instead of the knife his grandmother meant him to find. She is surprisingly pleased that he thought she meant the doll but tells him the knife is also his.

Other Devices:

Theme

Jukes, Mavis. *Like Jake and Me.* Illus. by Lloyd Bloom. New York: Knopf, 1984.

Alex feels that he does not have much in common with his macho stepfather Jake until a fuzzy spider brings them together.

Examples:

Both the boy and man converse together in apparent agreement about her fuzzy legs and her big size and how pretty she is. But the boy is talking about a spider crawling on the man's shirt collar, and the man is talking about his pregnant wife in leg warmers.

Pomerantz, Charlotte. *The Half-Birthday.* Illus. by DyAnne DiSalvo-Ryan. New York: Clarion Books, 1984.

Daniel can't think of a half-gift for his little sister's six-month birthday until he spots the half moon outside his window and offers her that half moon.

Examples:

At the party, Daniel listens to two guests, Grandma and Mr. Bange, talk about how "the best things come last." They ostensibly are referring to the gift Daniel has yet to give to his little sister. But one can see from the illustration that the two also mean their own relationship blooming in their later years.

Other Devices:

Pun

Say, Allen. *The Lost Lake.* Boston: Houghton Mifflin, 1989.

A young boy and his father become closer during a camping trip in the mountains.

Examples:

A boy clips magazine pictures and pins them on his wall. Then he fears that his dad will be angry since he saves magazines for his work. But Dad responds, "I'm having this place painted soon anyway." The boy is worried about the damaged magazines, while Dad's concern is the pin marks on the wall.

Other Devices:

Inference

Stolz, Mary. *Storm in the Night.* Illus. by Pat Cummings. New York: Harper & Row, 1988.

While sitting through a fearsome thunderstorm that has put the lights out, Thomas hears a story from Grandfather's boyhood, when Grandfather was afraid of thunderstorms.

Examples:

"Think of that. . . . " said Thomas. (Said in amazement.)

"That's what I'm doing," said Grandfather. (Said literally.)

"Where was I?" (Grandfather asks as he loses track of his place in the

telling of the story.)
"Under the bed." (Thomas reminds him, speaking literally about the story plot.)

Other Devices:
Hyperbole; Imagery; Inference; Pun; Simile

Turner, Ann. *Nettie's Trip South.* Illus. by Ronald Himler. New York: Macmillan, 1987.
A ten-year-old northern girl encounters the ugly realities of slavery when she visits Richmond, Virginia and sees a slave auction.

Examples:
Having heard that slaves are 3/5 of a person, the little girl literally tries to see which part they are missing, hand, eye, something inside? (The figurative 3/5 was set by the Constitution for southern states to use in population counts.) There is also a misunderstanding about what "stinks." The fine ladies and gentlemen around Nettie, who put their handkerchiefs to their noses, think it is she when she vomits. Nettie says, "It's not me who stinks." She refers to the slave auction, which she believes is the worse stink.

Other Devices:
Atmosphere; Simile

Wild, Jocelyn. *Florence and Eric Take the Cake.* New York: Dial, 1987.
A brother and sister lamb accidentally cause a major mix-up between a delicious cake and a beautiful hat.

Examples:
The objects in question look like a cake and like a hat. They are identical, one edible, one not. Each ends up in the wrong calamitous situation.

Other Devices:
Allusion; Pun

Yorinks, Arthur. *It Happened in Pinsk.* New York: Farrar, Straus, & Giroux, 1983.
A complaining man wishing always to be someone else suddenly loses his head and becomes mistaken for other people after his wife makes a pillowcase head for him.

Examples:
Irv spots his head in a hat shop being used to display a hat. He tells the shopkeeper, "I'll take that." The shopkeeper replies, "I don't think that's your size, sir." Irv, of course, means the head; the shopkeeper means the hat. When Irv snatches back his head, the shopkeeper tells him, "Sir, take hold of yourself." That's literally what Irv has done though the shopkeeper meant that Irv should get hold of his emotions.

Other Devices:
Allusion; Irony; Satire; Understatement

ANALOGY

An illustrative example of something familiar to explain and clarify something unfamiliar by comparing the likeness of the known thing to the unknown thing.

Example: "Revolution" can often come upon us like a storm. At first only a series of dark, lowering clouds on the horizon, it is heralded by the rising wind of discontent, and soon the gale and the rain are upon us, sweeping everything before them, heedless of the irretrievable destruction they may cause.

Sources

Goffstein, M.B. *A Writer.* New York: Harper & Row, 1984.
A writer uses sophisticated metaphors to show how the creative process of writing is like growing plants.

Examples:
A writer sometimes creates a "garden" (story/article) of "flowers," (good paragraphs/sentences) and "weeds," (paragraphs/sentences needing revision). A "slender tree," (promising idea/thought) and such complex creations as "pansies" (literary gems) require more planning. A rabbit (possibly, the teacher/editor) eats two small "green leaves" (words/phrases/ideas).

Other Devices:
Metaphor

Jonas, Ann. *The Trek.* New York: Greenwillow Books, 1985.
A little girl sees jungle animals in the natural shapes and environment of her cityscape as she and a friend walk the blocks to her school.

Examples:
Illustrations cleverly show how a child with a vivid imagination can see jungle animals in a cityscape. She sees physical similarities between the appearance of ordinary objects and the animals they resemble. Shrubs become emus, sheep, lions, and porcupines; a stone walkway becomes an alligator; a chimney becomes a giraffe; giant trees seem to take on characteristics of elephants; garbage bags crouch like rhinos; steps lounge like hippos; clothing in a laundromat machine turns into swimming sea creatures; and vines growing on building walls become crawling lizards.

Steig, William. *Rotten Island.* Boston: David R. Godine, 1984.
Rotten Island has always been a paradise for nasty creatures until one awful day a beautiful flower begins to grow threatening to spoil the island's character forever.

Examples:
The island and its terrible inhabitants stand for a foul political or social or religious system which can be turned around by one brave new idea.

Other Devices:
Imagery

Steig, William. *Yellow & Pink.* New York: Farrar, Straus, & Giroux, 1984.
Two wooden marionettes lying on a newspaper begin to speculate about how they came to be and invent a logical story for their existence which is, nevertheless, quite wrong.

Examples:
With great seriousness, trying and discarding a number of hypotheses, two dolls come to erroneous conclusions about how they came to exist, as man tries to account for life through scientific methodology.

Other Devices:
Personification; Satire

APHORISM

A brief statement expressing some general truth; sometimes putting a twist into an old saying. Means same as "maxim" or "proverb."

Example: The proper study of mankind is man.
Don't count your Boobies before they've hatched.

Sources

Blaustein, Muriel. *Lola Koala and the Ten Times Worse Than Anything.* New York: Harper & Row, 1987.
Two sisters realize they can be brave about different things when Lola, the younger sister, is timid about scary movies and high places and her big sister is terrified of the amusement park rides.

Examples:
"Big and little sisters can be brave about different things" reexpresses "Everyone is afraid of something."

Other Devices:
Poetic Justice

Blos, Joan W. *Old Henry.* Illus. by Stephen Gammell. New York: William Morrow, 1987.
Henry's neighbors are scandalized that he ignores them and lets his property get run down, until they drive him away and find themselves missing him.

Examples:
The townspeople's emotions evolve in the story so that they come to the understanding: "Having him gone doesn't make us more right" and they really "don't have to make such a terrible fuss because everyone isn't exactly like us."

Other Devices:
Irony; Paradox

Garfield, Leon. *King Nimrod's Tower.* Illus. by Michael Bragg. New York: Lothrop, Lee, & Shepard, 1982.
During the construction of a tower to God, a boy and his small dog learn how to relate to each other.

Examples:
The boy and puppy have trouble understanding each other. After the mix of languages, they understand each other well; the boy wants only to be the dog's friend and to take him home. God says: "My Kingdom of Heaven is better reached by a bridge than by a tower."

Other Devices:
Parody

Gedin, Birgitta. *The Little House from the Sea.* Pictures by Petter Pettersson. Trans. by Elisabeth Dyssegaard. New York: Farrar, Straus, & Giroux, 1988.
A little house on a rocky island never moves but longs to be a ship that can travel over the ocean to see the Other Side.

Examples:
When asked by the house, "Are there many horizons?" the cormorant remarks sagely, "Each of us has his own." Again, when the house declares itself a boat, the cormorant says, "No doubt about it. You know yourself best."

Other Devices:
Paradox; Personification

Levitin, Sonia. *Nobody Stole the Pie.* Illus. by Fernando Krahn. New York: Harcourt Brace Jovanovich, 1980.
The annual lollyberry festival in Little Digby is marred because everybody sneaks a little taste of pie meant to be shared together at the celebration.

Examples:
"It's one thing to take a taste, a speck, a piece—but the whole pie! That is a terrible crime." (Or is the crime actually taking the first taste itself?)

Other Devices:
Theme

Lindbergh, Anne. *Next Time, Take Care.* Illus. by Susan Hoguet. San Diego, CA: Harcourt Brace Jovanovich, 1988.
While making friends outdoors, Ralph manages to lose all the caps made for him by his constantly knitting Aunt Millicent.

Examples:
Practical, observant, but until recently, uninvolved, Aunt Millicent pronounces: "If half the world unraveled what the other half knits, there would be no order left at all."

Other Devices:
Foreshadow; Inference; Pun; Stereotype/Reverse Stereotype

Lionni, Leo. *Nicolas, Where Have You Been?* New York: Knopf, 1987.
Nicolas and his mouse friends are angry because birds have taken the best berries. When he sets off to get berries that birds haven't found, his adventures lead him to see that not all birds are his enemies.

Examples:
It is Uncle Raymond who inadvertently plants the idea of all birds being bad, but he is also the one who summarizes their experiences with the birds later when he remarks "One bird doesn't make a flock."

Other Devices:
Stereotype/Reverse Stereotype; Theme

Martin, Rafe. *Foolish Rabbit's Big Mistake.* Illus. by Ed. Young. New York: G.P. Putnam's Sons, 1985.
A jungle version of the sky-is-falling theme.

Examples:
A story of fear and rumors. If one stops to see what is so frightening, it may turn out to be nothing important.

Other Devices:
Parody

Miller, Moira. *The Proverbial Mouse.* Illus. by Ian Deuchar. New York: Dial, 1987.
During his nightly quests for food in a toy shop, a hungry mouse learns a number of proverbs from the toys and eventually devises one himself for the cat that tries to catch him.

Examples:
Each situation sets up and illustrates a familiar proverb: "Look before you leap"; "All that glitters is not gold"; "You cannot have your cake and beat [eat] it"; "Don't count your chickens before they hatch"; "No use crying over spilt milk."

Other Devices:
Pun

Morris, Winifred. *The Magic Leaf.* Illus. by Ju-Hong Chen. New York: Atheneum, 1987.
When a foolish man believes he has become invisible by possessing a magic leaf, he sneaks into the mayor's private garden to view the peonies.

Examples:
The author tells the reader that, "he was no longer interested in clever plans, and he no longer thought of himself as a very smart man. So maybe

he was smarter than he had been before." We gain wisdom when we stop believing we know it all.

Other Devices:
Paradox; Satire

Snyder, Zilpha Keatley. *The Changing Maze.* Illus. by Charles Mikolaycak. New York: Macmillan, 1985.
A shepherd boy braves the evil magic of a wizard's maze to save his pet lamb.

Examples:
Granny's remark that "if you touch a wizard's gold, it stays forever in your hand, an evil golden wizard-brand," can be translated into the truth, "Greed taints the owner and alters him forever."

Other Devices:
Atmosphere; Flash-forward; Imagery; Inference; Internal Rhyme; Personification; Symbol

Stevens, Kathleen. *Molly McCullough and Tom the Rogue.* Illus. by Margot Zemach. New York: Thomas Crowell, 1982.
Tom Devlin roams the countryside, charming the farmers' wives and tricking the farmers out of fruits and vegetables until he meets his match in a plain-faced, sharp-tongued, farmer's daughter.

Examples:
As the story progresses, several truths are noted in passing regarding the richest farmer around: "Rich with land, or rich with happiness?" "In my mind, it's pleasure in living that makes a man rich." As remarked by the sharp-tongued farmer's daughter: "Stupid men merit sharp tongues. I've saved my soft words for a man clever enough to deserve them." As Tom notes: "My eyes were dull indeed when they failed to see the softness a smile would work on that face."

Other Devices:
Foreshadow; Irony; Poetic Justice; Theme

Turner, Ann. *Dakota Dugout.* Illus. by Ronald Himler. New York: Macmillan, 1985.
A woman describes her experiences living with her husband in a sod house on the Dakota prairie.

Examples:
At the close of her reminiscence about the first prairie home she had, she remarks: "Sometimes the things we start with are best."

Other Devices:
Atmosphere; Flashback; Imagery; Inference; Metaphor; Simile

Walsh, Jill. *Lost and Found.* Illus. by Mary Rayner. London: André Deutsch, 1984.
This story describes a series of episodes through time which involve things lost in one generation that are found by someone in a future generation.

Examples:
Things all turn out for the best and illustrate the truth: "All things in their time."

Other Devices:
Allusion; Flash-forward

ATMOSPHERE

Prevailing mood or feeling developed through descriptions of setting and details about how things look, sound, feel, taste, and smell in order to create an emotional climate that establishes a reader's expectations and attitudes.

Example: Referring to the celebrated jumping frog of Calaveras County: "like a solid gob of mud" (light, humorous).

Sources

Aitken, Amy. *Wanda's Circus.* New York: Bradbury Press, 1985.
Children use their fantasy to plan and execute a backyard circus.

Examples:
Illustrations are in black and white before the big event occurs. Color is used when the performance begins, and the acts appear professional. Animals are real and the scene very circus-like. As the story concludes, the art reverts to a black and white ordinary, humdrum world.

Aylesworth, Jim. *Shenandoah Noah.* Illus. by Glen Rounds. New York: Holt, Rinehart, & Winston, 1985.
Work is something Noah doesn't care for, but he is forced to go to the trouble of taking a bath when he catches fleas from his hounds.

Examples:
"All his kin are farmers in the valley, but Shenandoah Noah doesn't like farming. Farming means plowing, and plowing means walking behind a mule in the hot sun, and walking behind a mule in the hot sun means work, and work is something that Shenandoah Noah doesn't care for."

Other Devices:
Caricature; Stereotype/Reverse Stereotype

Baylor, Byrd. *The Best Town in the World.* Illus. by Ronald Himler. New York: Charles Scribner's Sons, 1982.
A nostalgic view of the best town in the world, where dogs, chickens, waterholes, cooks, wildflowers, and food are remembered as being best.

Examples:
The town had "caves to find," "honey trees," "giant rocks to climb." "You could swing on the wild grapevines." "All the best cooks in the world lived there." They would "call you in and give you sweet potato pie or gingerbread. . . and smile at you while you were eating." "All plants liked to grow there." "Chickens in that canyon laid prettier brown eggs than chickens twenty miles on down the road." The town had "smarter dogs," "best blackberries," and the "summer days were longer there than they are in other places."

Other Devices:
Hyperbole

Berger, Barbara Helen. *When the Sun Rose.* New York: Philomel Books, 1986.
An imaginative little girl spends a happy day with her playmate who arrives with a pet lion.

Examples:
Bright color, especially shades of gold, extends the dreamlike quality of the story giving it substance and credibility. Simple, pure, direct text tells with beauty and sensitivity a perception of the miraculous within the ordinary.

Other Devices:
Pun; Symbol

Bunting, Eve. *The Man Who Could Call Down Owls.* Illus. by Charles Mikolaycak. New York: Macmillan, 1984.
A stranger, thinking he can make owls come to him by wearing the owl caller's clothing, kills the owl caller and tries to assume his position. The owls drive him off.

Examples:
Folklore-like style; mysterious, ethereal; sense of foreboding; eerie reminder of good and evil: "Owls everywhere. And the man in the middle, his cloak drifting about him like marsh mist, and Con, always Con, and the man with the Owls around him."

Other Devices:
Foreshadow; Poetic Justice; Simile; Theme

Carlstrom, Nancy White. *Wild Wild Sunflower Child Anna.* Illus. by Jerry Pinkney. New York: Macmillan, 1987.
Spending a day outdoors, Anna revels in the joys of sun, sky, grass, flowers, berries, frogs, ants, beetles.

Examples:
Warm exuberance and high spirited pleasure are evident in the lilting poetry and colorful illustrations as Anna's uninhibited joy in the garden is related. She rolls down a hill till she's dizzy, runs barefoot, splashes with frogs, climbs a tree, finds insects under rocks, watches a spider, picks flowers and berries, and falls asleep.

Other Devices:
Alliteration; Imagery

Cazet, Denys. *A Fish in His Pocket.* New York: Franklin Watts, Inc., Orchard Books, 1987.
All through school Russell is worried about the little orange fish in his pocket until he figures out how to return it to its pond.

Examples:
This is a gentle book about a sensitive, tender-hearted boy who is responsible for the accidental death of a pond fish. Being the type of person who is in touch with his environment (he keeps time to the music coming from a nearby house by exhaling puffs of warm air into the frosty morning), he believes he must return the fish to nature in a proper, dignified manner. After brooding over how to make it up to the fish, he is finally inspired to return it to the pond in a little paper casket barge dubbed the "Take Care."

Demi. *Chen Ping and His Magic Axe.* New York: Dodd, Mead, 1987.
Chen Ping's honesty in his encounter with a stranger causes his axe to acquire magical powers. His greedy master's attempt to reap the same reward comes to a different end.

Examples:
When Chen Ping's axe falls into the water, friendly beasts are pictured playing at the scene; the water is shown laden with fish. When his master Wing Fat tries to get the gold axe by throwing his axe in the water, the scene is full of slimy snakes, lizards, and rodents, and the sea roils with threatening dragons.

Other Devices:
Poetic Justice

Dragonwagon, Crescent. *Jemima Remembers.* Illus. by Troy Howell. New York: Macmillan, 1984
Just before leaving for the winter, Jemima visits one last time her favorite places on the farm, recalling the wonderful summer she spent with her aunt.

Examples:
Juxtaposed are images of summer then and fall now as the girl remembers the physical and emotional landscapes of her happy summer. Awareness of

time passing as seasons cycle again and again and her aunt's love makes her leave-taking endurable.

Other Devices:
Imagery; Simile

Fields, Julia. *The Green Lion of Zion Street.* Illus. by Jerry Pinkney. New York: Margaret K. McElderry, 1988.
The stone lion on Zion Street, proud and fierce, instills fear and admiration in those who see it in the cold city fog.

Examples:
The staccato poetic rhythm of the sentences and the mood-building phrases all create a shivery, tension-filled feeling of approaching fear and dread. With the lifting of the fog, the lion is demystified a little and recognized for the inert thing that it is.

Other Devices:
Imagery; Simile

Fleischman, Paul. *Rondo in C.* Illus. by Janet Wentworth. New York: Harper & Row, 1988.
As a young piano student plays Beethoven's Rondo in C at her recital, each member of the audience is stirred by memories.

Examples:
A nostalgic mood of personal reverie grips everyone individually as they listen, recalling specific experiences that the piano selection evokes.

Other Devices:
Metaphor

Gould, Deborah. *Grandpa's Slide Show.* Illus. by Cheryl Harness. New York: Lothrop, Lee, & Shepard, 1987.
Whenever they visit Grandpa, Sam and Douglas always watch a slide show. After Grandpa dies, they watch the show to remember him.

Examples:
Every detail is gentle, believable, and sensitive with natural homey touches in both the text and art. "The first slide beamed vacation sunlight into the nighttime room. Sometimes in the first slide Douglas, Sam, and Mom sat smiling at a picnic table. Other times Grandma and Grandpa stood together at a mountain lookout, or Uncle Carl and his girls waved from a Ferris wheel."

Hearn, Michael Patrick. *The Porcelain Cat.* Illus. by Leo & Diane Dillon. Boston: Little, Brown, 1987.
A sorcerer's apprentice has to complete several difficult tasks before dawn in order to obtain a missing ingredient for one of his master's spells.

Examples:
This traditional fantasy is laced with tongue-in-cheek irreverence for magic as is evident in the behavior of a tactless sorcerer. Regarding the porcelain cat, the sorcerer says, "It had been a gift from his aunt, a witch of great abilities but little taste." The sorcerer desires to bring the cat to life so that it will deal with a rat problem he's having. But it lands on the floor and shatters when it makes its first pounce. The sorcerer says, "I never liked the cat anyway" and goes back to his books.

Other Devices:
Allusion; Irony; Pun

Innocenti, Roberto. *Rose Blanche.* Mankato, MN: Creative Education, 1985.
Matter-of-fact reporting of the effect upon one German village and one little girl living there during World War II.

Examples:
Illustrations are photographic in detail. Colors are somber military browns and greens except for the striking red Nazi armband and the little girl's red hair ribbon. The text is unadorned and composed of factually short

statements that seem to be deliberately devoid of emotion while expressing war's random cruelty. "A little boy jumped from the back of the truck and tried to run away. But the mayor was standing there in the middle of the street. He grabbed the little boy by the collar and brought him back to the truck. . . . The sky was gray."

Other Devices:
Inference; Point of View; Symbol; Tone

Keeping, Charles. *Sammy Streetsinger.* Oxford: Oxford University Press, 1984.
A young street musician's career is told full circle, from his start on sidewalks, to big rock star video personality, back to simple street singer.

Examples:
The illustrations show the changing mood of this rising 'success' story: the higher up he ascends, the more bizarre and psychodelic become the lines and colors. Thrusts back to reality are simple brown tones and lines.

Other Devices:
Flashback; Satire; Theme; Tone

McAfee, Annalena. *The Visitors Who Came to Stay.* Illus. by Anthony Browne. New York: Viking Kestrel, 1984.
Katy's ordered predictable life is turned upside down when her father brings home a zany woman and her practical joker son to live with them.

Examples:
Almost surrealistic is the way Katy sees the world with the visitors in it. After they leave, the empty humdrum of ordinary life is no longer satisfying until she and Dad go to visit them. She even joins the boy's practical joking world by buying a trick to pull on him. The art mirrors Katy's internal world of emotions.

Other Devices:
Paradox; Pun

Maiorano, Robert. *A Little Interlude.* Illus. by Rachel Isadora. New York: Coward, McCann, & Geoghegan, 1980.
In the interlude before Bobby's important ballet appearance, he sees a man called Jiminy Cricket playing a piano, and the two share a brief companionship.

Examples:
A momentary, private, uninhibited slice of life between two strangers is gently shown. Jiminy Cricket says, "Well, if you believe old Jiminy Cricket can dance, then maybe I can. Come have a seat and let's share a little music." Bobby learns a little piano, and Jiminy Cricket learns a little ballet.

Other Devices:
Allusion; Inference

Mattingley, Christobel. *The Miracle Tree.* Illus. by Marianne Yamaguchi. San Diego, CA: Harcourt Brace Jovanovich, Gulliver Books, 1985.
Separated by the explosion of the atomic bomb, a husband, wife, and mother carry on with their lives in the ruins of Nagasaki. They are eventually reunited one Christmas by a very special tree.

Examples:
Stark pain, numbness, and, eventually, blossoming hope are expressed in the language: "No one is beautiful who has suffered atomic blast"; "Taro's heart was broken like the myriad pieces of broken lives he loaded each day into baskets to be cleared away."

Other Devices:
Inference; Irony; Metaphor; Simile; Symbol

Murphy, Jill. *Five Minutes' Peace.* New York: G.P. Putnam's Sons, 1986.
All Mrs. Large (elephant) wants is five minutes' peace from her wonderful, rambunctious children. But chaos follows her all the way from the kitchen to the bathroom and back again.

Examples:
Illustrations show mother's futile efforts to get off by herself. Text reinforces her long-suffering patience. "She poured herself a cup of tea and laid back with her eyes closed. It was heaven. . . .'Can I play you a tune?' asked Lester."

Other Devices:
Inference; Understatement

Parnall, Peter. *Winter Barn.* New York: Macmillan, 1986.
A dilapidated old barn shelters a wide variety of animals during the sub-zero winter temperatures in Maine while they wait for the first signs of spring.

Examples:
The tense waiting time is shown through the beauty of the language, the tight togetherness and deep silence shown in the illustrations, and the suspension from life's regular routines told with a minimum of detail. A letting go of held breath is symbolized when a single dripping icicle heralds the end of winter's grip, and a chickadee sips each falling drop.

Other Devices:
Imagery; Personification; Simile

Rogers, Paul. *From Me to You.* Illus. by Jane Johnson. New York: Orchard Books, Franklin Watts, 1987.
A grandmother shares her memories of three generations with a young granddaughter and presents her with a precious gift.

Examples:
A poignant message of love comes through the matter-of-fact sentences: "Tess became a lady and had us all to tea." "And Father spanked us one by one. I saw Harry cry." "When Grandad turned to me in church, you should have seen his face." "With that same lace I trimmed the crib where your mother lay." "She was asleep under a tree when your Grandad went away."

Other Devices:
Inference; Point of View; Theme

Rylant, Cynthia. *The Relatives Came.* Illus. by Stephen Gammell. New York: Bradbury Press, 1985.
The visit of relatives from the hill country is humorously described in detailed text and illustrations.

Examples:
The bouncy, active, round pictures depicting pleasure in common human interaction among family members illustrates enjoyment of simple life.

Other Devices:
Caricature

Sheldon, Dyan. *A Witch Got on at Paddington Station.* Illus. by Wendy Smith. New York: E.P. Dutton, 1987.
It's a rainy afternoon rush hour. The bus is crowded. Everyone feels grumpy, tired, and in need of a lift. Who should oblige but the cheeriest, sweetest witch imaginable. Frowns change to smiles as out of her bag spills enough magic to transform a trying experience into a fantastic one.

Snyder, Zilpha Keatley. *The Changing Maze.* Illus. by Charles Mikolaycak. New York: Macmillan, 1985.
A shepherd boy braves the evil magic of a wizard's maze to save his pet lamb.

Examples:
A sense of menacing environment and lurking harm is present in the text as people enter the maze to seek the gold reward. "The hedge grew thick and wondrous fast, higher and higher, but when at last it towered above the gardners' heads, they one by one fell deadly ill. So the gardners died and the secret, too. But the king still knew. And the maze still grew."

Other Devices:
Alliteration; Aphorism; Flash-forward; Imagery; Inference; Internal Rhyme; Personification; Symbol

Tejima, Keizaburo. *Fox's Dream.* New York: Philomel Books, 1987.
Wandering through a winter forest, a lonely fox has an enchanting vision and then finds the companionship for which he has been longing.

Examples:
In a faraway forest, near a faraway mountain, a fox is alone in the depth of bitter winter: shadows stretch across the frozen snow, frozen trees glitter in the moonlight. In the morning light a female fox's fur shines; they nuzzle in the early sunshine. A desolate, lonely fox faces another cold day but with a friendly vixen.

Other Devices:
Imagery

Turner, Ann. *Dakota Dugout.* Illus. by Ronald Himler. New York: Macmillan, 1985.
A woman describes her experiences living with her husband in a sod house on the Dakota prairie.

Examples:
The stark harshness of prairie life is simply and unemotionally evoked, through text and illustration, more by what is not said than by what is. "Built from sod, you know. . . Matt cut them into bricks, laid them up. . . that was our first home. I cried when I saw it." "First summer we watched the corn grow, strode around the field clapping hands. We saw dresses, buggies, gold in that grain until one day a hot wind baked it dry as an oven, sst-sst, sst-sst."

Other Devices:
Aphorism; Flashback; Imagery; Inference; Metaphor; Simile

Turner, Ann. *Nettie's Trip South.* Illus. by Ronald Himler. New York: Macmillan, 1987.
A ten-year-old northern girl encounters the ugly realities of slavery when she visits Richmond, Virginia and sees a slave auction.

Examples:
Through crisp unadorned sentences, the bleak, ugly business of slavery is described. Brother hustles them out of the slave auction: "I've seen all I need to see!"; she "couldn't wear her lace collar; she felt too raw and ill"; the person "could be sold by a fat man in a white hat in a tight white suit"; "shack run-down with heaps of rags in a corner for beds."

Other Devices:
Ambiguity; Simile

Van Allsburg, Chris. *The Polar Express.* Boston: Houghton Mifflin Co., 1985.
A magical train stopping right outside of a child's house on Christmas Eve picks up a boy and whisks him and other children to the North Pole city where one child is picked to receive a gift personally from Santa.

Examples:
A hushed, sacred feeling is evoked by the soft illustrations and clipped text. A majesty of moment belies the state of fantasy.

CARICATURE

Use of exaggeration or distortion (physical characteristic, eccentricity, personality trait, or exaggeraged act) to make a figure appear comic or ridiculous.

Example: "Droll little mouth drawn up like a bow. . . belly, that shook like a bowl full of jelly." ("Night before Christmas" Santa description.)

Sources

Aylesworth, Jim. *Hush Up!* Illus. by Glen Rounds. New York: Holt Rinehart & Winston, 1980.
Jasper is rudely awakened from his nap through a chain of events set off by a mean horse fly.

Examples:
Jasper Walker of Talula County is the laziest of hill country men doing nothing in particular and napping with his chair tilted back and feet propped up. All the barnyard animals are also lazily disjointed nappers.

Other Devices:
Stereotype/Reverse Stereotype

Gammell, Stephen. *Git Along, Old Scudder.* New York: Lothrop, Lee, & Shepard, 1983.
In this tall tale, Old Scudder doesn't know where he is until he draws a map and names the places on it.

Examples:
In first-person narration, the mountain man's Western speech dialect is exaggerated humorously. "You kin get t' feeling spookity, alone in the mountains, and so one day I plumb didnt' know whar I was at. So I drew m'self a map."

Nixon, Joan Lowery. *Fat Chance, Claude.* Illus. by Tracey Campbell Pearson. New York: Viking Kestrel, 1987.
Two zany Texans, Shirley and Claude, grow up and meet out in the gold mining hills of Colorado.

Examples:
Shirley's antics put one in mind of a tall-tale heroine such as Slewfoot Sue. Claude is someone reminiscent of a Pecos Bill. "Shirley never was one to get into a head-on argument with a copperhead snake. . . ." She dumps boiling stew on the snake "frizzling him so dead she changed whatever he had in mind." Claude's brothers "weren't much for farming." It is up to Claude to earn college expenses for them. "So he worked twice as hard and sent one brother to Harvard and the other brother to Yale."

Other Devices:
Flashback; Inference; Irony; Satire; Simile; Stereotype/Reverse Stereotype; Understatement

Root, Phyllis. *Soup for Supper.* Illus. by Sue Truesdell. New York: Harper & Row, 1986.
A wee woman catches a giant taking the vegetables from her garden and finds that they can share both vegetable soup and friendship.

Examples:
A name-calling, spunky, little woman talks to an imposing but gentle giant. "'Here, stop that!' cried the wee small woman, running out from behind the bush and flapping her wide, wide, apron. . . . 'Give me back my vegetables—you potato nose!'. . ."

Rounds, Glen. *Washday on Noah's Ark.* New York: Holiday House, 1985.
When the forty-first day on the ark dawns bright and clear, Mrs. Noah decides to do the wash, and having no rope long enough, devises an ingenious clothesline.

Examples:
"She'd noticed that there were thousands of snakes hiding in dark corners all over the Ark. . . her string of snakes was long. . . tossed the kite into the air. . . hung wet clothes, piece by piece, on the strange clothesline. . . ."

Other Devices:
Parody

Rylant, Cynthia. *The Relatives Came.* Illus. by Stephen Gammell. New York: Bradbury Press, 1985.
Description of a mountain family get-together.

Examples:
The illustrations depict the typical family characteristics among relatives such as the jolly uncles, good-cook-grandmas, dirty-faced tots.

Other Devices:
Atmosphere

Yoeman, John. *The Wild Washerwomen.* Illus. by Quentin Blake. New York: Greenwillow Books, 1979.
In this modern fairy tale, seven washerwomen sick of their work go on an uncontrollable rampage, only to meet their match in seven very dirty woodcutters.

Examples:
The women are tired of filthy sheets, grubby hankies, horrid socks, and ghastly towels. Stereotypes of capable tough women and tough, capable but uncivilized men, about whom the women say "they rather liked the look of" after they are tamed.

FLASHBACK

Interruption of present action to insert an episode that took place at an earlier time for the purpose of giving the reader information to make the present situation understandable or account for a character's current motivation.

Example: Orson Welles dies in the opening scene of the classic film *Citizen Kane.* The remainder of the story covers events prior to his death.

Sources

Abolafia, Yossie. *Yanosh's Island.* New York: Greenwillow Books, 1987.
Vicky and David take their broken mechanical turtle to Yanosh, who can fix anything. In the turtle's mechanism Yanosh discovers just the part he needs to finish an airplane he's been secretly working on. What follows is a zany adventure that brings Yanosh back to a familiar place.

Examples:
The author describes two incidents that occur out of sequence. One goes back to the fixit-man's childhood to an experience that figures as a cause for his present action. The next incident describes a period of time which accounts for action that just occurred but to which the children were not privy.

Cooney, Barbara. *Miss Rumphius.* New York: Viking Press, 1982.
Great Aunt Alice Rumphuis was once a little girl who loved the sea, longed to visit faraway places, and wished to do something to make the world more beautiful.

Examples:
The story begins with the Lupine lady (Great Aunt Alice Rumphuis), little and old. But it quickly backs up to her youth and then follows her life until it catches up to the present again.

Friedman, Ina R. *How My Parents Learned to Eat.* Illus. by Allen Say. Boston: Houghton Mifflin Co., 1984.
A little girl narrates the story sequentially in the beginning and ending but in between goes back in time to tell the story of how her mixed ethnic parents learned to eat in one another's native style. As a result, their daughter can eat Japanese and American style equally well.

Examples:
"In our house, some days we eat with chopsticks and some days we eat with knives and forks. For me, it's natural. When my mother met my father, she was a Japanese schoolgirl and he was an American sailor. His ship was stationed in Yokohama. . . .That's why at our house some days we eat with chopsticks and some days we eat with knives and forks."

Other Devices:
Irony

Keeping, Charles. *Sammy Streetsinger.* Oxford: Oxford University Press, 1984.
The rise and fall of a superstar is examined in relation to his current state so that the reader may see how he got to his present situation and why he is happy being a simple street singer again instead of the big rock star he had beome.

Examples:
"Most days you will find Sammy Streetsinger there, dancing and singing to his one-man band. . .remembers the time he left the subway to seek fame and fortune. This is how it happened."

Other Devices:
Atmosphere; Satire; Theme; Tone

Levinson, Riki. *Watch the Stars Come Out.* Illus. by Diane Goode. New York: E.P. Dutton, 1985.
A child hears a bedtime story from her grandma, who describes the little girl's greatgrandma's tale of her journey to America as an immigrant child.

Examples:
"Grandma's mama would come to her room and tell her a special story. . . When I was a little girl, my big brother and I went on a boat to America."

Macaulay, David. *Why the Chicken Crossed the Road.* Boston: Houghton Mifflin Co., 1987.
By crossing the road, a chicken sets off a series of wild reactions which eventually return full circle and threaten to repeat the whole sequence.

Examples:
The ending reveals why the chicken was crossing the road at the beginning of the story. Thus, all the story's events are now put into perspective. The ending is actually the story's beginning.

Other Devices:
Inference; Pun; Understatement

Marshall, James. *Rapscallion Jones.* New York: Viking, 1983.
A would-be writer fox can't think of anything to write to earn rent money until he recalls an incident from his youth which turns into the story he is looking for.

Mattingley, Christobel. *The Angel With a Mouth-Organ.* Illus. by Astra Lacie. New York: Holiday House, 1986.
Just before the glass angel is put on the Christmas tree, Mother describes her experiences as a little girl during World War II when she and her family were refugees. She recounts how the glass angel came to symbolize a new beginning in the lives of her family members.

Other Devices:
Inference; Metaphor; Point of View; Understatement

Nixon, Joan Lowery. *Fat Chance, Claude.* Illus. by Tracey Campbell Pearson. New York: Viking Kestrel, 1987.
Two zany Texans, Shirley and Claude, grow up and meet out in the gold mining hills of Colorado.

Examples:
Story opens with Shirley's growing-up years. As she is ready to leave for the West, the story switches to show the growing-up years of Claude, as he gets ready to embark on his own fortunes out West.

Other Devices:
Caricature; Inference; Irony; Satire; Simile; Stereotype/Reverse Stereotype; Understatement

Pryor, Bonnie. *The House on Maple Street.* Illus. by Beth Peck. New York: William Morrow, 1987.
During the course of 300 years, many people have passed by or lived on the spot now occupied by a house numbered 107 Maple Street.

Examples:
Starting out in the present, the story goes back in time to account for the finding of a toy tea cup with an arrow head in it.

Stevenson, James. *What's Under My Bed?* New York: Greenwillow Books, 1983.
Grandpa tells his two young houseguests a story about his own childhood, when he was scared at bedtime.

Examples:
As grandpa retells the strange sounds of nighttime when he was a child, the children account for what probably actually made the noises.

Other Devices:
Alliteration; Theme

Turner, Ann. *Dakota Dugout.* Illus. by Ronald Himler. New York: Macmillan, 1985.
A woman describes her experiences living with her husband in a sod house on the Dakota prairie.

Examples:
A woman walking on a city street with a young girl refers back to an earlier time as she describes how she and her new husband began married life alone on the empty land.

Other Devices:
Aphorism; Atmosphere; Imagery; Inference; Metaphor; Simile

Van Allsburg, Chris. *The Wreck of the Zephyr.* Boston: Houghton Mifflin Co., 1983.
A boy disobeys advice on trying out a new skill and lives to regret his behavior.

Examples:
Story opens with an old man in the present telling his tale through memory of a past incident. He returns to the present to end the story.

Other Devices:
Allusion; Foreshadow; Inference; Theme

FLASH-FORWARD

Sudden jump forward in time from chronologically narrated events to a later time in which the story usually progresses to its conclusion.

Examples:
Martha angrily threw the toy locomotive, and although it missed her brother Albert, a tiny piece of mama's precious mantel clock disappeared. One dainty leg was gone. The clock listed clumsily.

Martha tenderly touched the rough place where the missing leg had been. Carefully rewrapping the clock in its tissue, she laid it back into the old trunk as her grandchildren slammed the kitchen door. Someday she would share her memories with them.

Sources

Johnston, Tony. *The Quilt Story.* Illus. by Tomie de Paola. New York: G.P. Putnam's Sons, 1985.
A pioneer mother lovingly stitches a beautiful quilt which warms and comforts her daughter Abigail. Many years later another mother mends and patches it for her little girl. The illustrations show the time lapse.

Martin, Charles E. *Island Rescue.* New York: Greenwillow Books, 1985.
When Mae breaks her leg, she is taken by boat off the island where she lives to a mainland hospital.

Examples:
At first Mae is in the hospital and her island friends visit. The next page jumps to the end of vacation when Mae returns to her island healed and feeling better.

Snyder, Zilpha Keatley. *The Changing Maze.* Illus. by Charles Mikolaycak. New York: Macmillan, 1985.
A shepherd boy braves the evil magic of a wizard's maze to save his pet lamb.

Examples:
As the boy tells of his experience in the maze, he and the lamb are rushing to the gate toward freedom; suddenly, in the next paragraph he is in the cottage kitchen talking to his granny about their narrow escape.

Other Devices:
Aphorism; Atmosphere; Imagery; Inference; Internal Rhyme; Personification; Symbol

Walsh, Jill Paton. *Lost and Found.* Illus. by Mary Rayner. London: André Deutsch, 1984.
This story describes a series of episodes through time which involve things lost in the same general location in one generation that are found by someone in a future generation.

Examples:
A Stone Age child is sent by his mother on a delivery errand. Along the way the child loses the item he is supposed to take to his grandfather but finds something else which the grandfather finds even more valuable. In a later era, another child is sent over this route; he loses his delivery item but finds the Stone Age child's lost item and picks it up instead. So goes the tale constantly flashing forward.

Other Devices:
Allusion; Aphorism

FORESHADOW

Clues to alert the reader about events that will occur later in the narrative; serves to build suspense.

Example: Nothing could go wrong on such a perfect day. Or so I, in my childlike innocence, thought.

Sources

Agee, Jon. *The Incredible Painting of Felix Clousseau.* New York: Farrar, Straus, & Giroux, 1988.
Who would dare enter a portrait of a duck in the Grand Contest of Art? When the painting quacks, Clousseau, the artist is suddenly hailed a genius. And that is only half of it.

Examples:
Felix Clousseau's paintings are alive (literally) with excitement. Trouble erupts and the paintings must be confiscated, "all except one." When a jewel thief attempts to steal the king's crown, a painting of a dog hanging on the wall next to the crown can be seen. On the next page, the thief is being held "caught in the grasp of a ferocious dog" sitting within the framed picture.

Other Devices:
Pun

Allard, Harry. *Miss Nelson Has a Field Day.* Illus. by James Marshall. Boston: Houghton Mifflin Co., 1985.
The notorious Miss Swamp reappears at the Horace B. Smedley School, this time to shape up the football team and make them win at least one game.

Examples:
As Miss Nelson and Mr. Blandworth overhear students discuss how they need substitute Viola Swamp to get the football team in shape, each remarks "Hmmm" and sets off to make Mis Swamp appear on the scene. Later Miss Nelson reveals she had "made an important phone call" to someone who remarked, "I'll be right there."

Other Devices:
Inference; Pun; Understatement

Arnold, Tedd. *No Jumping on the Bed!* New York: Dial, 1987.
Walter lives near the top floor of a tall apartment building, where one night his habit of jumping on his bed leads to a tumultuous fall through floor after floor, collecting occupants all the way down.

Examples:
After Walter's dad warns about the dangers of jumping on the bed, Walter obediently lays down. The last thing he hears before going to sleep is the "soft thump thump coming from the room above." He guesses that his friend Delbert, up there, must be jumping on his bed. The reader is alerted. Later Walter hears a creak. "The ceiling cracked, and down came Delbert, bed and all. . . ."

Other Devices:
Inference; Internal Rhyme; Understatement

Balian, Lorna. *A Garden for a Ground Hog.* Nashville, TN: Abingdon Press, 1985.
Mr. O'Leary appreciates his groundhog's help in predicting the weather on Groundhog Day but tries to come up with a plan to keep him from eating all the vegetables in his garden.

Examples:
The dishes which the O'Learys eat at every meal contain zucchini. Obviously, this vegetable is in good supply. A neighborhood groundhog had spent the previous summer wantonly helping himself to carrots, beans and peas. The O'Learys decide, "We must allow him some food in exchange for his help in forecasting the weather." It is not too surprising that when the garden is divided, the groundhog is assigned not the melons or cabbages, but, of course, the zucchini!

Brett, Jan. *Annie and the Wild Animals.* Boston: Houghton Mifflin Co., 1985.
When Annie's cat disappears, she attempts friendship with a variety of unsuitable woodland animals, but with the emergence of spring, everything comes right.

Examples:
Something was wrong with Taffy, the cat: she stopped playing, ate more than usual, slept all day long, and one day disappeared. The cause? Border pictures around the illustrations hint at the birth of kittens.

Brown, Ruth. *The Big Sneeze.* New York: Lothrop, Lee, & Shepard, 1985.
A chain of events is set into motion when a fly lands on a sleeping farmer's nose on a hot lazy afternoon.

Examples:
Each event is hinted at by the illustration preceding it. Good to demonstrate cause and effect.

Bunting, Eve. *The Man Who Could Call Down Owls.* Illus. by Charles Mikolaycak. New York: Macmillan, 1984.
A stranger, thinking he can call down owls by wearing the owl caller's clothing, learns that the accoutrements alone won't gain him the power he craves.

Examples:
The description, "He had shadows on his face but not in his eyes," alerts the reader to the Owl Man's personality even before learning that "By day the man worked in his owl barn where he mended wings and legs." But the stranger, who observes the Owl Caller at work, notes, "A man who can command the birds of the air has power indeed!" When assistant, Con, tries to tell the stranger that "He does not command," the stranger "was not listening." At the next dusk, it is the stranger who is wearing the white cloak and carrying the willow wand. These things belong to the Owl Caller. Con knows he would never give them away. "The stranger's smile was cold as death."

Other Devices:
Atmosphere; Poetic Justice; Simile; Symbol; Theme

Carrick, Carol. *Dark and Full of Secrets.* Illus. by Donald Carrick. New York: Clarion Books, 1984.
A boy's first tentative experiences with pond life are carefully described.

Examples:
The dog is not allowed in the canoe. He is sent back to the house. But, while the boy is close to shore and paddling in the water, the dog leaps into the water. The dog watches as the boy drifts far out. Later, while exploring under water, the boy's face mask fills with water. The dog swims over close. In a few moments, the boy becomes in danger of drowning. No people are close to rescue him. It is no surprise that the banished dog, who has really been in the background all along, is there to save his life.

Other Devices:
Inference; Imagery; Personification; Simile

Carrick, Donald. *Harald and the Great Stag.* New York: Clarion Books, 1988.
When Harald, who lives in England during the Middle Ages, hears that the Baron and his royal guests are planning to hunt the legendary Great Stag, he devises a clever scheme to protect the animal.

Examples:
When Harald expresses shock at the unfairness of so many hunting one creature, an old man talks to him about the reality of the hunt, distracting him. When the boy climbs a tree to avoid the dogs who smell deer scent on him, it is again the old man who pulls away the suspicious dogs, thereby diverting attention away from Harald. It is not a surprise, then, when the old man later confides to Harald that he too has served as secret protector of the stag all these years.

Other Devices:
Theme

Christelow, Eileen. *Mr. Murphy's Marvelous Invention.* Boston: Houghton Mifflin Co., 1983.
Cornelius Murphy, a pig inventor, makes a unique housekeeping machine for his wife's birthday, but the entire family is shocked when they discover what the machine actually does.

Examples:
The reader is warned that "Mr. Murphy was an inventor of useful and not-so-useful gadgets." When he surprises his wife by telling her that her new birthday invention "should do almost any tiresome household chore," Mrs. Murphy "looked skeptical." The reader is primed to expect some trouble from the invention, especially when Mrs. Murphy wonders whether the machine should be left turned on "warming up" while they leave the house. It is not surprising that this turns out to be one of the "not-so-useful" gadgets.

Other Devices:
Inference; Understatement

Cole, Brock. *The Winter Wren.* New York: Farrar, Straus, & Giroux, 1984.
In this folk-tale like story, a boy and his sister go out in search of spring because winter has held the land in its grip too long.

Examples:
His sister who weighed "hardly more than a bird" later turns into a tiny brown winter wren. Spring was dressed all in green and gold just like his sister Meg, who later sits up in a "spring" surrounded bed.

Other Devices:
Alliteration; Imagery; Personification; Simile

Collins, Meghan. *The Willow Maiden.* Illus. by Lazzlo Gal. New York: Dial Books, 1985.
A young farmer, Denis, falls in love with a beautiful princess, Lisane, but must accept that she lives as a willow tree during the spring and summer months.

Examples:
There are hints that Denis cannot keep his bride: the king who follows the young couple's movements does so with "an uneasy frown"; Denis notices that Lisane's face is no longer "so sparkling and lighthearted as it had been"; Lisane gently remarks that he must learn to let her go free when she needs to.

Other Devices:
Simile

Flournoy, Valerie. *The Patchwork Quilt.* Illus. by Jerry Pinkney. New York: Dial, 1985.
In a multigenerational home, the grandmother is determined to make a quilt for her granddaughter even though family members aren't convinced it is necessary or worthwhile.

Examples:
The Grandmother's illness is hinted at when she expresses the need to rest before beginning the quilt. Her insistence on sitting near the drafty window bodes illness.

Other Devices:
Inference; Theme; Tone

Fox, Mem. *Hattie and the Fox.* Illus. by Patricia Mullins. New York: Bradbury Press, 1987.
Hattie, a big black hen, discovers a fox in the bushes. This creates varying reactions among the other barnyard animals.

Examples:
As the picture grows, nose, eyes, ears, legs, body suggest that trouble in the form of a fox is about to spring.

Gerstein, Mordicai. *The Mountains of Tibet.* New York: Harper & Row, 1987.
After dying, a Tibetan woodcutter is given the choice of going to heaven or living another life anywhere in the universe.

Examples:
Though he longs all his life to see the world, after dying, he chooses to live again exactly the same life he first lived. The reader suspects this is happening when he chooses a galaxy with one bright star that has "nine perfect planets revolving around it." He chooses to live on the one planet "like a blue-green marble." From the thousands of persons he could be, he prefers the "golden people." He selects to live in "one green valley, high in the craggy mountains."

Other Devices:
Inference; Irony

Goble, Paul. *Death of the Iron Horse.* New York: Bradbury Press, 1987.
In an act of bravery and defiance against the white men encroaching upon their territory in 1867, a group of young Cheyenne braves derail and raid a freight train.

Examples:
As the young men return to their people laden with the spoils of victory, a dark smudge of smoke appears on the horizon, foreshadowing another wave of invaders as another train approaches.

Other Devices:
Personification; Point of View

Kalan, Robert. *Jump, Frog, Jump!* Illus. by Byron Barton. New York: Greenwillow Books, 1981.

Life for a pond frog is hazardous as a number of creatures hint at successive perils to come.

Examples:

Pictures show the next problem for frog looming ahead on each page.

Kellogg, Steven. *Ralph's Secret Weapon.* New York: E.P. Dutton, 1983.

When eccentric Aunt Georgiana decides that nephew Ralph shows promise as a sea serpent charmer, Ralph is ready with a secret weapon.

Examples:

On a secret foray into the kitchen for a snack, Ralph sees a mouse get sick after nibbling on his aunt's gift to him—a banana spinach cream cake. He saves the cake in his closet. Later when he needs a secret weapon to fight the sea serpent, he brings along a bag that seems about the size to hold his cake. Clearly the demise of the serpent is the result of the special cake.

Other Devices:

Allusion

Kraus, Robert. *Come Out and Play, Little Mouse.* Illus. by Jose Aruego and Arianne Dewey. New York: Greenwillow, 1987.

Little Mouse is busy helping his family five days a week, but he gets to play with them on weekends.

Examples:

When little brother is lured out of the family mousehole by a cat who wishes to "play," it is up to older brother to save him from the cat and mouse game. A blue creature which looks like a dog is visible heading after the cat in a new version of the chase game. Later, after the cat is scared off, the blue animal is unzipped; the costume is seen to house big brother mouse.

Other Devices:

Inference

Lindbergh, Anne. *Next Time, Take Care.* Illus. by Susan Hoguet. San Diego, CA: Harcourt Brace Jovanovich, 1988.

While making friends outdoors, Ralph manages to lose all the caps made for him by his constantly knitting Aunt Millicent.

Examples:

"This cap is to keep you healthy. Go out to the park now and wear it on your head, not in your pocket." "But Ralph found it hard to keep a cap on his head when he was hanging upside down." This is the first hint of many lost caps to come.

Other Devices:

Aphorism; Inference; Pun; Stereotype/Reverse Stereotype

Martin, Bill and Archambault, John. *Knots on a Counting Rope.* Illus. by Ted Rand. New York: Henry Holt, 1987.

One cool, dark night an Indian boy sits with his grandfather, bathed in the glow of a campfire as they reminisce about the night the boy was born.

Examples:

As the two talk, mention is made of the "dark mountains" the boy must cross and whether the boy will always have to "live in the dark." The grandfather responds that the boy was born with a "dark curtain in front of his eyes," all of which, we later learn refers to his blindness.

Other Devices:

Imagery; Metaphor; Symbol

Neville, Emily Cheney. *The Bridge.* Illus. by Ronald Himler. New York: Harper & Row, 1988.

When the old wooden bridge collapses, a young boy is delighted to be able to watch the many different machines at work building the new bridge.

Examples:

No one notices how a heavy truck causes the old bridge to "rattle- rattle-cr-ack," presaging a total collapse when the truck makes its return trip across the bridge.

Other Devices:

Inference

Pittman, Helena Clare. *A Grain of Rice.* New York: Hastings House, 1986.

A clever, cheerful, hardworking farmer's son wins the hand of a Chinese princess by outwitting her father the emperor, who treasures his daughter more than all the rice in China.

Examples:

Though denied the emperor's daughter, the peasant boy willingly works in the storeroom, "since he is so good with numbers." This apparently insignificant assessment of him leads to the boy's future wealth and the emperor's near bankruptcy. As a reward for services rendered, the boy humbly asks for only "one grain of rice to be doubled every day for a hundred days." The court mathematician informs the emperor after twenty days have passed, that in ten more days "there will be no rice in the palace." And in another month "he will own all the rice in China!"

Other Devices:

Irony; Paradox

Schwartz, Amy. *Oma and Bobo.* New York: Bradbury Press, 1987.

Bobo the dog learns to stay, sit, and with the help of Grandma Oma, fetch.

Examples:

Though Grandma Oma ostensibly finds Bobo offensive, it is she who takes the pot holder, Bobo's favorite chew item, out into the yard when Bobo refuses to learn the "fetch" command. She also takes it to Program Completion Night when Bobo must perform his lessons. She alone will get the dog to earn the diploma.

Other Devices:

Allusion; Inference; Stereotype

Stanley, Diane. *A Country Tale.* New York: Four Winds Press, 1985.

An ill-fated visit to the city home of the elegant Mrs. Snickers teaches an impressionable country cat a little about herself and the importance of being one's self when friendships are formed.

Examples:

Cleo clearly is smitten by the stranger in her crinoline dress, and that fine lady's notice of her results in a change in Cleo's behavior. She tries to model herself after Mrs. Snickers. But the offhand invitation for Cleo to come to see her in town "sometime" was not mentioned again. Mrs. Snickers's careless departure without a good-bye to Cleo does not bode well for a warm reception when she pays a surprise visit to the city cat.

Other Devices:

Theme

Stevens, Kathleen. *Molly McCullough and Tom the Rogue.* Illus. by Margot Zemach. New York: Thomas Y. Crowell, 1982.

Tom Devlin roams the countryside, charming the farmers' wives and doing a fruit and vegetable scam until he meets his match in a plain-faced, sharp-tongued, farmer's daughter.

Examples:

While Tom has always been more than willing to move on after bilking a farmer, just before his downfall he experiences for the first time twinges of regret as he looks at the lovely land and thinks of the roots growing in the rich soil. This provides the reader a hint that perhaps he is psychologically ready to settle down.

Other Devices:
Aphorism; Irony; Poetic Justice; Theme

Turkle, Brinton. *Do Not Open.* New York: E.P. Dutton, 1981.
An old woman and her cat, who live by the sea, find an intriguing bottle washed up on the beach after a storm. They ignore the warning on it, "Do not open."

Examples:
Captain Kid, the cat, intimates by the fearsome expression on his face that trouble is ahead when the old woman picks up the genie's bottle. He tries to prevent her from opening the bottle.

Other Devices:
Inference; Parody

Van Allsburg, Chris. *The Stranger.* Boston: Houghton Mifflin, 1986.
Farmer Bailey hits a stranger with his truck and brings him home to recuperate. The enigmatic origins of the stranger seem to have a mysterious relation to the weather.

Examples:
When the doctor tells Mrs. Bailey to throw away the thermometer because the mercury is stuck at the bottom; when the stranger blows on his soup causing a noticable "draft"; when autumn appears to be on hold and summer hangs on an extra three weeks; when colored leaves can be seen on trees at other farms but only green leaves are on the Bailey trees; when the stranger blows a leaf from green to a bright yellow color, all these hint that the stranger is Jack Frost momentarily delayed from his annual fall activity.

Van Allsburg, Chris. *The Wreck of the Zephyr.* Boston: Houghton Mifflin, 1983.
A boy disobeys advice and attempts a skill he can't achieve.

Examples:
Before the boy decides to sail by himself in the air, villagers sing a song about a man who crashed his boat when he tried to sail across land. The song warns that wind over land isn't steady or true. The boy's wreck is presaged.

Other Devices:
Allusion; Flashback; Inference; Theme

Willis, Val. *The Secret in the Matchbox.* Illus. by John Shelley. New York: Farrar, Straus, & Giroux, 1988.
Bobby Bell has a secret. And the secret is in a matchbox. No one wants to hear about his secret, especially not Miss Potts, his teacher. She takes away the box and puts it on her desk. "There's going to be trouble," Bobby warns. He is right.

HYPERBOLE

Obvious and extravagant exaggeration not meant to be taken literally.

Example: I'm so hungry I could eat a horse.

Sources

Bauer, Caroline. *Too Many Books!* Illus. by Diane Paterson. New York: Frederick Warne, 1984.
A child loves books and clutters up the house with them.

Examples:
Maralou has so many books Mom can't get out the front door and Dad can't get in the back door. After she gives some away to make room, the whole town is bulging with books.

Baylor, Byrd. *The Best Town in the World.* Illus. by Ronald Himler. New York: Charles Scribner's Sons, 1982.
This is a nostalgic view of the "best town in the world" as described by an adult looking back on it as he saw it in childhood. Dogs, chickens, waterholes, cooks, wildflowers, and food are the best, exactly right, exaggeratedly perfect.

Other Devices:
Atmosphere; Imagery

Brandenberg, Franz. *Otto is Different.* Illus. by James Stevenson. New York: Greenwillow Books, 1985.
Otto Octopus learns the advantages of having eight arms instead of only two like everyone else.

Examples:
An amusing combination of logic and absurdity is shown as Otto can brush his teeth, tie his shoes, wash his face, and blow his nose all at once; do his homework, sweep the floor, and practice the piano all at once; or play hockey all by himself.

Other Devices:
Theme

Cole, Babette. *The Trouble with Granddad.* New York: G.P. Putnam's Sons, 1988.
Granddad's enormous vegetables get him in trouble with the local police.

Examples:
When the tomato plant grew through the greenhouse roof, the fire company tried to stop it by spraying it with weedkiller; the army and Secret Service tried their weapons on it. A huge worm ate it, went into a chrysalis on the police station roof, causing it to collapse. Granddad carved out his biggest cucumber for them to use as a police station. Now they must watch for giant slugs!

Other Devices:
Inference

Domanska, Janina. *What Happens Next*? New York: Greenwillow Books, 1983.
A baron who loves tall tales promises to free the peasant who can tell him a tale that will surprise him.

Examples:
Each episode in the peasant's tall tale adventure is hyperbolic wizardry. For example, chaff is twisted into a rope to slide down; the peasant lands in a swamp and must run home to get a shovel so that he can dig himself out of the swamp.

Other Devices:
Paradox

Hutchins, Pat. *The Very Worst Monster.* New York: Greenwillow Books, 1985.
Hazel sets out to prove that she, not her baby brother, is the worst monster anywhere.

Examples:
All the details in picture and word show the absurd excesses of a monster baby. He bends iron bars with his fangs, growls early, swings from cur-

tains, scares the postman, and tries to eat the judge at the worst-baby-monster contest.

Other Devices:
Irony

McPhail, David. *Pig Pig Rides.* New York: E.P. Dutton, 1982.
Over breakfast, Pig Pig informs his mother about all the wonderful feats he intends to accomplish that day.

Examples:
He will take his racing car for a speed record; he will jump 500 elephants; he will race his horse at "Rocking Ham Park"; he will take a train to China; he will rocket trip to the moon. In reality he is going outside to ride on his two-wheeler.

Polacco, Patricia. *Meteor!* New York: Dodd, Mead, 1987.
A quiet rural community is dramatically changed when a meteor crashes down in the front yard of the Gaw family.

Examples:
As members of the community call each other to relate the momentous event, the story gets bigger with each telling. The event draws a huge response and a variety of citizens in a carnival-like holiday. As individuals touch the meteor, everyone claims special powers and abilities not evident before.

Stolz, Mary. *Storm in the Night.* Illus. by Pat Cummings. New York: Harper & Row, 1988.
While sitting through a fearsome thunderstorm that has put the lights out, Thomas hears a story from Grandfather's boyhood, when Grandfather was afraid of thunderstorms.

Examples:
"Probably at the beginning of the world, his grandfather had been a boy. As Thomas was a boy now, and always would be. Grandfather knew more stories than a book full of stories—that man was seven feet tall."

Other Devices:
Ambiguity; Imagery; Inference; Pun; Simile

Westcott, Nadine Bernard. *The Giant Vegetable Garden.* Boston: Little, Brown, 1981.
A town named Peapack engages in a huge garden effort in order to win county fair money.

Examples:
Straightforward text is juxtaposed with extravagant, absurd, outrageous-sized garden produce grown to win prize money. A giant communal cooking spree and mammoth picnic follow.

IMAGERY

Mental pictures summoned up by terms and expressions that appeal to the senses so that we see, hear, smell, feel, and taste much of what the characters experience; such images can create a writer's tone.

Example: Even the usually cool green willows bordering the pond hung wilting and dry.

Sources

Adoff, Arnold. *Flamboyan.* Illus. by Karen Barbour. New York: Harcourt Brace Jovanovich, 1988.

One sunny afternoon while everyone is resting, Flamboyan, a young girl named after the tree whose red blossoms are the same color as her hair, dreamily flies over her Caribbean island home.

Examples:

Use of sensory comparisons: hair the color of "flame-red blossoms," skin the color of the "bark of the tree," strong and round as the "branches of the Flamboyan tree," silver fish as a "shining breakfast invitation to pelicans."

Other Devices:

Tone

Alexander, Sue. *There's More. . . Much More.* Illus. by Patience Brewster. San Diego, CA: Harcourt Brace Jovanovich, Gulliver Books, 1987.

Squirrel and Sherri celebrate spring by collecting it in their May baskets.

Example

Visual things: Twig with cocoon on it; green leaf slowly unfolding; blue flower buds nestled on a tiny stem; wild strawberry beginning to blossom; baby earthworms. Smells: fresh earth; sweet flowers; grass dew. Sounds: stream rushing over rocks; wind whispering through leaves; calling birds. Physical expressions: jumping; tiptoeing; shouting; sighing.

Baring, Maurice. *The Blue Rose.* Illus. by Anne Dalton. Kingswood, England: Kaye & Ward Ltd., Windmill Press, 1982.

A wise Emperor of China sets a condition that only he who can find the Blue Rose may marry his accomplished, beautiful daughter. Less than desirable suitors respond to the condition and are rejected. The successful suitor achieves the time-honored method of earning her love.

Examples:

Eyes as brown onyxes; thousand meaningless nothings; laugh as tinkling stream; chimes of a silver bell: would die of the potent fume; mild-white in color; a living flower picked in fairyland; glory of dusty gold; twinkling like spear-heads; chatter of grasshoppers.

Other Devices;

Paradox; Theme; Tone

Baylor, Byrd. *The Best Town in the World.* Illus. by Ronald Himler. New York: Charles Scribner's Sons, 1982.

A nostalgic view of the best town in the world as recalled by an adult remembering it as it was during his youth.

Examples:

In the summertime "when the air was full of birdsong and cicadas," the boy would take his supper up into a tree to eat it alone. "No city water tasted half as good as water carried in a bucket from the well by their back door." "Wildflowers grew taller. . . not just yellow ones. There were all shades of lavender and purple and orange and red and blue and the palest kind of pink."

Other Devices:

Atmosphere; Hyperbole

Bunting, Eve. *Ghost's Hour, Spook's Hour.* Illus. by Donald Carrick. New York: Ticknor & Fields, 1987.

Scary incidents at midnight give Biff the dog and his master a frightening time, but all turn out to have good explanations.

Examples:

As a child carries his unwilling dog down stair steps to investigate the unknown dark, the situation is described: "I gathered him up, but he'd made himself heavy and he was hard to hold because of the shaking. Parts of him kept slipping as I carried him downstairs." When he finds Dad in the dark, he recognizes him by his distinctive feel and smell: "I felt the scratchiness of his cheek and smelled his Dad smell."

Other Devices:
Personification

Bunting. Eve. *How Many Days to America? A Thanksgiving Story.* Illus. by Beth Beck. New York: Clarion Books, 1989.
Refugees from a Caribbean island embark on a dangerous boat trip to America where they have a special reason to celebrate.

Examples:
"When I peered out I could see my mother's feet in their black slippers and the great, muddy boots of the soldiers." "We chugged heavily from harbor to open ocean." "Her face twisted the way it did when she closed the door of the house for the last time." ". . .whale, gray as an elephant and covered with barnacles." ". . .boat came, roaring close on wings of foam." ". . .coconut with milk that tasted like flowers."

Carlstrom, Nancy White. *Wild Wild Sunflower Child Anna.* Illus. by Jerry Pinkney. New York: Macmillan, 1987.
Spending a day outdoors, Anna revels in the joys of sun, sky, grass, flowers, berries, frogs, ants, and beetles.

Examples:
Lilting, vivid language shows Anna sifting soil, kneeling on her elbows, picking ripe juicy raspberries, pools of water trickling down her legs.

Other Devices:
Alliteration; Atmosphere

Carrick, Carol. *Dark and Full of Secrets.* Illus. by Donald Carrick. New York: Clarion Books, 1984.
A boy's first tentative experiences with pond life are carefully described.

Examples:
Pond reflects puffs of pale cloud; the fish swam and turned together as though blown by a breeze; the dog's four furry legs churned the water; explosion of water splashed over his back; pond bottom is all mucky; Ben slunk away; delicate sweep of its tail; the boat floated above a meadow of waving plants. Pictures enhance and clarify text: "something scratched his foot" is shown as pond grasses.

Other Devices:
Foreshadow; Personification; Simile

Cole, Brock. *The Winter Wren.* New York: Farrar, Straus, & Giroux, 1984.
A boy and his sister set out to find spring because winter is holding on extra long.

Examples:
Fresh green stalk of wheat; snap of his great black bill; new wheat turned yellow and rotted in furrows; air had a taste of iron.

Other Devices:
Alliteration; Foreshadow; Personification; Simile

de Paola, Tomie. *An Early American Christmas.* New York: Holiday House, 1987.
The inhabitants of an early New England village never make much fuss about Christmas until a new family moves in and celebrates the holiday with special customs they have brought with them from their country.

Examples:
Waxy berries are stirred into a black cauldron into which strings are dipped to make bayberry candles that smelled "oh-so-sweet." "Best apples, the reddest and the shiniest were set aside to be used at Christmastime." Nuts were "turned into golden fruit with the flick of a paint brush." "Cookie ladies, men, white and brown, small pretzels and large." "Now,

tulips, lovebirds, 'hands-and-heart,' peacots, and stars filled the shelves and tables of the kitchen."

Dragonwagon, Crescent. *Jemima Remembers.* Illus. by Troy Howell. New York: Macmillan, 1984.
Just before leaving for the winter, Jemima visits one last time her favorite places on the farm, recalling the wonderful summer she spent there with her aunt.

Examples:
Moving, sensuous text that shimmers with the essence of the seasons: tomato plants have fallen; zucchini brown and limp; spicy-scented leaves; green leaves gray with dust; heat glinted from the ground; cider half-frozen, icy flecks.

Other Devices:
Atmosphere; Simile

Fields, Julia. *The Green Lion of Zion Street.* Illus. by Jerry Pinkney. New York: Margaret K. McElderry, 1988.
The stone lion on Zion Street, proud and fierce, instills fear and admiration in those who see it in the cold city fog.

Examples:
The lion described as fierce, mighty, proud, smirky, vain, green, arrogant, stern, stolid, haughty, snide, jaws declarative and wide, dome of a head supercilious in the air.

Other Devices:
Atmosphere; Simile

Howe, James. *I Wish I Were a Butterfly.* Illus. by Ed Young. San Diego, CA: Harcourt Brace Jovanovich, Gulliver Books, 1987.
A wise spider helps a despondent cricket realize that he is special in his own way.

Examples:
"I am the color of dirt; you are the color of laughter." "You fly around with your whispery wings and your body all covered with jewels."

Other Devices:
Irony

Johnston, Tony. *Whale Song.* Illus. by Ed Young. New York: G.P. Putnam's Sons, 1987.
Counting as they sing, whales use their mighty voices to pass on to one another the numbers from one to ten.

Examples:
Colossal whale; mountains are of ice; great big frosty voice; big as an island; glides along; smacking their tails; rolling rainy sea; like an opera singer; like a locomotive train; turquoise seas; pod of uncle whales like a pod of peas; crusty with barnacles.

Kennedy, Richard. *Song of the Horse.* Illus. by Marcia Sewall. New York: E.P. Dutton, 1981.
Girl describes her ride on her horse.

Examples:
Describes girl's world of color, her horse's opinion of her, sounds of his reaction to her, sensations of touching him. "When he looks over the top of his stall into the sky, he sees my face in the clouds. He sees me in rainbows and shadows and hears my voice in the rain and the wind. The light of my eyes is in the stars, sun, and moon." "I yell and slap his

neck and dig my heels at his heaving sides and grip my knees to his ribs." "He snorts my name." "Now he blows through his lips, saying he is ready to run, and he stomps his feet and runs his chest against his gate."

Other Devices:
Inference; Personification; Point of View; Simile; Tone; Understatement

Lobel, Arnold. *The Rose in My Garden.* Illus. by Anita Lobel. New York: Greenwillow Books, 1984.
A variety of flowers and creatures grow near a rose with a sleeping bee on it. Disruption sets in on this peaceful cumulative tale when a mouse and cat enter the scene.

Examples:
Daisies white as snow; marigolds orange and round; bluebells with petals like lace; lilies of elegant grace; cat with the tattered ear.

Other Devices:
Alliteration; Inference

Martin, Bill and John Archambault. *Knots on a Counting Rope.* Illus. by Ted Rand. New York: Henry Holt & Co., 1987.
One cool dark night an Indian boy sits with his grandfather, bathed in the glow of a campfire as they reminisce about the night he was born. Poignant story of love, hope, and courage.

Examples:
On the night the boy was born, the grandfather describes the storm that also occurred. He says, "The wounded wind announced the boy child's birth." The wind whipped up sand "sharp as claws and crying like a bobcat." The boy knows 'blue' because his grandfather tells him it is morning. "Morning throws off the blanket of night." The boy recognizes sunrise as the "song of the birds." He knows 'sky' which "touches my face, soft, like lamb's wool." The boy says that wind is his friend. "It throws back my hair and laughs in my face." Grandfather tells the boy, "My love will always surround you with the strength of blue horses."

Other Devices:
Foreshadow; Metaphor; Symbol

Nesbit, Edith. *The Deliverers of Their Country.* Illus. by Lisbeth Zwerger. Natick, MA: Picture Book Studio U.S.A., 1985.
Two children set out to rid their land of pesky dragons.

Examples:
As the father describes the strange creature, he says," Four well-developed limbs; a long caudal appendage; five toes, unequal in length almost like on the Lacertidae, yet there are no traces of wings." " . . . dragons basking on the front-door steps of public buildings, and dragons preening their wings on the roof in the hot afternoon . . . fields greener than usual with the scaly legs and tails . . . spreading his great yellow wings, he rose into the air, rattling like a third-class carriage when the brake is hard on . . . saw the whole of England, like a great puzzle-map, green in the field parts and brown in the towns and black in the places where they make coal, and crockery, and cutlery and chemicals . . . sheets of water . . . cataracts of water . . . dragons in great green masses and scattered shoals. "

Other Devices:
Allusion; Simile; Stereotype/Reverse Stereotype; Tone

Parnall, Peter. *Apple Tree.* New York: Macmillan, 1987.
Describes the many ways an apple tree interacts with insects, birds, and other animals during a full year of its development.

Examples:
Fresher morsels of grass; beetles fuss and lurch; peeling gray, crusty bark; safe from winter claws and prying eyes; tiniest bud . . . has a little cap of snow; deer pawing great slashes in the snow; bird hammering at the frozen pulp; snow-covered branches a brilliant pink in the sun.

Other Devices:
Personification; Simile

Parnall, Peter. *Winter Barn.* New York: Macmillan, 1986.
A dilapidated old barn shelters a wide variety of animals during the sub-zero winter temperatures in Maine while they wait for the first signs of spring.

Examples:
Oak beams, hemlock boards, and cedar shingles; barn linked together with pegs and nails; icicles form a giant crystal chandelier in winter; frosty lung-burning nights; great dark cloak of hand-hewn wood; great dripping marshmallow of a barn; animals nestle in a pile of long-forgotten, rotten hay.

Other Devices:
Atmosphere; Personification; Simile

Paterson, Banjo. *Clancy of the Overflow.* Illus, by Robert Ingpen. New York: Rigby, 1982.
The ballad contrasts the life of the author/city dweller with the outback cowboy. The author longs for the country and decries the city.

Examples:
Dingy little offices; eager eyes and greedy; vision splendid of the sunlit plains; written with a thumb-nail dipped in tar; stock are slowly stringing; stingy ray of sunlight struggles feebly; language uninviting of the gutter children fighting.

Other Devices:
Symbol; Theme

Ryder, Joanne. *The Snail's Spell.* Illus. by Lynne Cherry. New York: Frederick Warne, 1982.
The reader is invited to imagine how it feels to be a snail.

Examples:
"You glide and make your own smooth sticky path to ride on . . . it feels cool and good." "Your small black eyes rest at the tip of these feelers. One eye sees the brightness above. The other feeler curls around a lettuce leaf. Now, you see the darkness there."

Other Devices:
Point of View

Rylant, Cynthia. *When I Was Young in the Mountains.* Illus. by Diane Goode. New York: E.P. Dutton, 1982.
An adult's vivid reminiscences of her simple treasured memories growing up in the rural mountains during the early 1900s.

Examples:
"Grandfather sharpened my pencils with his pocketknife"; "Grandmother sometimes shelled beans and sometimes braided my hair."

Other Devices:
Tone

Shefelman, Janice. *Victoria House.* Illus. by Tom Shefelman. San Diego, CA: Harcourt Brace Jovanovich, 1988.
An old Victorian house is moved from the country to its new location on a city street, where a family fixes it up and moves in.

Examples:
". . . where trucks brought dead cars with dented fenders and smashed windows"; "Light from a window above the stairs shone on peeling wallpaper and draped cobwebs"; "Mirrored buildings reflected the parade as it passed under bright street lights"; " dark disheveled house."

Skofield, James. *All Wet! All Wet!* Illus. by Diane Stanley. New York: Harper & Row, 1984.'
A child takes a walk in the woods during a summer shower and text is full of sights, smells, and sounds of his experiences sensitively expressed.

Examples:
The skunk "sniffs and drinks and grouches off back to his hollow log." The rain "flattens meadow grass in tangled clumps." The "soft, star-nosed mole swims through dark and damp, deep-rooted, fragrant earth." "Beside Skunk's log, on bristling thistle stalks, snails leave wet trails that glisten." ". . . each blade of grass is flashing like a jewel." "Frantic gnats swarm and dance in beams of sun." The fox watches and "paw after velvet paw, she picks her way up to the hills" where she hears "the cool, dark, green-deep voice of summer night."

Other Devices:
Metaphor; Personification; Simile

Snyder, Zilpha Keatley. *The Changing Maze.* Illus. by Charles Mikolaycak. New York: Macmillan, 1985.
A shepherd boy braves the evil magic of a wizard's maze to save his pet lamb.

Examples:
Cottage on a "sharp cold hill"; "traveled the paths of everywhere and the years he had never known"; the maze is "twisting, curving, turning, bending, crammed with corners and dead endings"; "tingly tinkle of glassy thorns."

Other Devices:
Aphorism; Atmosphere; Flash-forward; Inference; Internal Rhyme; Personification; Symbol

Steig, William. *Rotten Island.* Boston: David R. Godine, 1984.
Rotten Island has always been a paradise for nasty creatures until one awful day a beautiful flower begins to grow and threatens to spoil the island forever.

Examples:
Vivid, plentiful sensory description: seething serpents; sharp-clawed crabs; fat or scraggly; dry or slimy with scales, warts, pimples, tentacles, talons, fangs.

Other Devices:
Analogy

Stolz, Mary. *Storm in the Night.* Illus. by Pat Cummings. New York: Harper & Row, 1988.
While sitting through a fearsome thunderstorm that has put the lights out, Thomas hears a story from Grandfather's boyhood, when Grandfather was afraid of thunderstorms.

Examples:
"Lightning licking the navy-blue sky"; "rain. . . babbling in the downspouts"; "shining mandarin eyes"; "carrot-colored" flames"; "flames made a fluttering noise"; "automobile tires swished on rain-wet streets"; "siren whined"; "whooped windily brandishing branches."

Other Devices:
Ambiguity; Hyperbole; Inference; Pun; Simile

Tejima, Keizaburo. *Fox's Dream.* New York: Philomel Books, 1987.
Wandering through a winter forest, a lonely fox has an enchanting vision and finds the companionship for which he has been longing.

Examples:
Images of winter's cold and ice are contrasted with memories of warm spring and the smell of new grass and wildflowers and play with the fox's siblings. A ray of coming pleasure is hinted at in the brighter-growing light of early day.

Other Devices:
Atmosphere

Turner, Ann. *Dakota Dugout.* Illus. by Ronald Himler. New York: Macmillan, 1985.
A woman describes her experiences living with her husband in a sod house on the Dakota prairie.

Examples:
Spring-teasing slow; water booming in the lake; geese like yarn in the sky; ground was iron; like beavers in a burrow; wind scoured the dugout; paper window makes the sun look greasy; wind-empty cries in the long grass; grass whispered like an old friend.

Other Devices:
Aphorism; Atmosphere; Flashback; Inference; Metaphor; Simile

Willard, Nancy. *The Voyage of the Ludgate Hill.* Illus. by Alice and Martin Provensen. New York: Harcourt Brace Jovanovich, 1987.
A poem inspired by Robert Louis Stevenson's letters describes how the author and his wife survived a stormy ocean voyage with a cargo of exotic animals.

Examples:
Light as a cork; buttermilk sky; ape in a gabardine cape; lavendar haze; my socks too involved with my toes; rumbling a clatter and stumbling; muttering maws; retractable claws; scours the pads of her paws; thrump and twitter and thrum; moon changes seats with the sun.

Other Devices:
Alliteration; Internal Rhyme

Yolen, Jane. *Owl Moon.* Illus. by John Schoenherr. New York: Philomel Books, 1987.
One winter's night under a full moon, a father and daughter trek into the woods to see a Great Horned Owl.

Examples:
"Our feet crunched over the crisp snow and little gray foot prints followed us; My short round shadow bumped after me; Tops of my cheeks felt cold and hot at the same time; Shadows stained the snow, mouth felt furry; My eyes got cloudy with the cold; We watched silently with heat in our mouths, the heat of all those words we had not spoken."

Other Devices:
Metaphor; Simile

INFERENCE

Reasonable conclusions drawn by the reader about characters or events based upon certain limited clues or facts presented in the story by the author; allows readers to make their own discoveries without direct comment from the author.

Example: It rained heavily and steadily for three full days. Mark had set out hours ago to cross the hundred-year-old weakened wooden bridge. Susan was startled when the phone rang; her faced paled as she listened to the caller.

Sources

Aliki. *Use Your Head, Dear.* New York: Greenwillow Books, 1983.
Charles, a young alligator, means well, but gets things mixed up until his father gives him an invisible thinking cap for his birthday.

Examples:
Just why son Charles seems to be so unusually scatterbrained and absent-minded is revealed in the illustrations whenever Father is in a scene. As Father hands a gift of an invisible thinking cap to Charles and remarks that he's worn his own for years, he is standing with one foot in the gift box.

Other Devices:
Allusion

Allard, Harry. *Miss Nelson Has a Field Day.* Illus. by James Marshall. Boston: Houghton Mifflin Co., 1985.
The Notorious Miss Swamp reappears at the Horace B. Smedley School, this time to shape up the football team and make them win at least one game.

Examples:
The identity of Viola Swamp is implied by the illustration and text on the last page.

Other Devices:
Foreshadow; Pun

Allen, Jeffrey. *Nosey Mrs. Rat.* Illus. by James Marshall. New York: Viking Kestrel, 1985.
Mrs. Rat makes a career out of spying on her neighbors, but the tables are unexpectedly turned on her.

Examples:
At the end, Shirley Rat promises not to snoop anymore, but her eye gets a roving gleam when she says "Well, perhaps for special occasions. . . . "

Other Devices:
Poetic Justice; Understatement

Allen, Pamela. *Hidden Treasure.* New York: G.P. Putnam's Sons, 1987.
After claiming the treasure that he and his brother haul out of the ocean, Herbert spends the rest of his life fearfully guarding it from possible thieves.

Examples:
The title implies that the brother who has no treasure really has the best treasure of all: he is surrounded by a loving family. Harry is able to sleep and is happy and contented. Herbert, on the other hand, must guard his treasure, can't sleep, and has no peace.

Other Devices:
Theme

Arnold, Tedd. *No Jumping on the Bed!* New York: Dial, 1987.
Walter lives near the top floor of a tall apartment building, where one night his habit of jumping on his bed leads to a tumultuous fall through floor after floor, collecting occupants all the way down.

Examples:
Walter and his friend Delbert, from the apartment above, like to jump on their beds. After Walter's dad warns him about the danger of this behavior, he obediently lays down. Walter wakes up from a nightmare about his bed breaking through the floor all the way to the basement, relieved that it is only a bad dream. "He suddenly heard a creak, the ceiling cracked, and down came Delbert, bed and all. . . . " Clearly, the bad dream is about to become reality.

Other Devices:
Foreshadow; Internal Rhyme; Understatement

Bang, Molly. *Dawn.* New York: William Morrow, 1983.
In this folktale-like story, a shipbuilder rescues a Canadian goose and marries a mysterious woman who makes him promise never to look at her while she weaves sail cloth.

Examples:
After rescuing the wounded Canadian goose and nursing it back to health, a young woman shows up at the shipbuilder's door dressed oddly in a "brown cloak over a rosy pink-as-cheeks dress." She has a long slender neck and a scar on her arm; apparently, she is the goose reincarnated.

Berger, Barbara Helen. *The Donkey's Dream.* New York: Philomel, 1985.
A donkey has fantastic dreams while crossing the desert. At the end of the day, the lady who has been riding on his back gives birth in a cave to a very special baby.

Examples:
The donkey dreams he is carrying "a lady full of heaven." "They came to a place that smelled of hay. . . and a cave for a stable". When the donkey drank, "one star above him shone in the watering trough below." Invited to view the newborn baby, the donkey sees the "cave was full of light." Though unnamed, the reader knows that the donkey is part of the Christmas message.

Blake, Quentin. *Mrs. Armitage on Wheels.* New York: Alfred A. Knopf, 1987.
The misadventures of Mrs. Armitage, who makes increasingly complicated modifications of her bicyle.

Examples:
After the bicycle becomes too laden and crashes, Mrs. Armitage goes off on the relative freedom of roller skates. But the last thing she says is, "What these roller skates need is. . . ." implying she's off again to repeat her previous mistakes all over again.

Brighton, Catherine. *Five Secrets in a Box.* New York: E.P. Dutton, 1987.
Galileo's small daughter relates, in her simple and innocent way, the magical world she observes in her father's scientific lab.

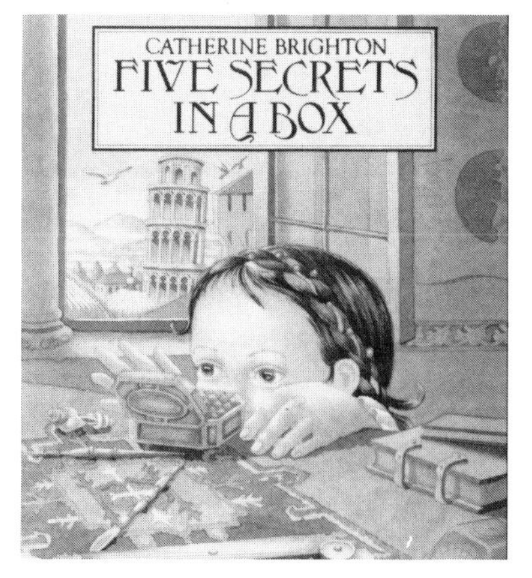

Examples:
From her simple observations, the reader infers the uses of things that Galileo's daughter finds in his study: magnifying glass, telescopic glass, and glass filters. She discovers "one piece [of glass] makes things bigger. . . . The countryside comes toward me. . . . The world turns to night."

Other Devices:
Allusion; Point of View

Christelow, Eileen. *Mr. Murphy's Marvelous Inventions.* Boston: Houghton Mifflin Co., 1983.
Cornelius Murphy, a pig inventor, makes a unique housekeeping machine for his wife's birthday, but the entire family is shocked when they discover what the machine actually does.

Examples:
A tall unsteady figure with floppy hat, glasses, and mustache tries to buy the invention. Mr. Murphy peers at the stranger suspiciously before it collapses into the two children. Later when father invents a replacement gift, a revolving vase, he declares the housecleaning machine was sold to a Professor Mortimer—then he winks at the children.

Other Devices:
Foreshadow; Understatement

Cohen, Barbara. *Gooseberries to Oranges.* Illus. by Beverly Brodsky. New York: Lothrop, Lee, & Shepard, 1982.
A young girl reminisces about the journey from her cholera-ravaged village in Russia to the U.S., where she is reunited with her father.

Examples:
The reader infers that the girl's background is Jewish when soldiers in her home country tear the Mezzuzah off the door jamb and her father reads a Yiddish newspaper. The strange search that the girl undergoes at Ellis Island during which her hair is snipped and examined for lice, is the traditional immigrant examination. The spots found on her skin which detain her at the infirmary can be inferred to be measles. Compare with Riki Levinson's *Watch the Stars Come Out.*

Other Devices:
Point of View; Symbol

Cole, Babette. *The Trouble with Granddad.* New York: G.P. Putnam's Sons, 1988.
Granddad's enormous vegetables get him in trouble with the local police.

Examples:
When a jealous gardener offers Granddad a tomato plant, the man is wearing a hat suspiciously like that belonging to witches, and his nails are painted black. Trouble is bound to come from such a "gift."

Other Devices:
Hyperbole

de Paola, Tomie. *The Knight and the Dragon.* New York: G.P. Putnam's Sons, 1980.
Pictures combine with text to show how a novice dragon and knight prepare to do battle for the first time. When it doesn't work out very well they plan a different activity, and the illustrations show who gives them the idea.

de Poala, Tomie. *Mariana May and Nursey.* New York: Holiday House, 1983.
Some thoughtful friends figure out a way that a sad little girl can enjoy her summer without worrying about getting her white dresses dirty. The illustrations provide the clues.

Douglass, Barbara. *The Chocolate Chip Cookie Contest.* Illus. by Eric Jon Nones. New York: Lothrop, Lee, & Shepard, 1985.
A boy and his young helper prepare to enter a cookie baking contest. The winner is a surprise to everyone—except the reader.

Examples:
As the story progresses, the cookie helper's efforts to create a winning cookie for the contest are clearly better than the contest entrant's efforts. The helper's victory is inferred on the last page. Step-by-step dressing of the clown implies his involvement in the coming circus event.

Other Devices:
Allusion

Fleischman, Sid. *The Scarebird.* Illus. by Peter Sis. New York: Greenwillow Books, William Morrow, 1987.
A lonely old farmer realizes the value of human friendship when a young man comes to help him and his scarecrow with their farm.

Examples:
At first, Lonesome John tells the boy who stops by for a job, "I get along by myself." But the reader infers that maybe he wouldn't mind some companionship. He sees how foot-weary the boy seems: "You legged it all these miles? Didn't they tell you it's so far to my place that crows pack a lunch before setting out?" He offers the boy bread and sidemeat. As an afterthought he adds, "And open a can of peaches while you're at it."

Other Devices:
Simile; Tone

Flournoy, Valerie. *The Patchwork Quilt.* Illus. by Jerry Pinkney. New York: Dial, 1985.
Mother's attitude about Grandma as someone who only requires custodial care and is not worthy in her own right changes to respect and enthusiasm when Grandma's masterpiece quilt creation begins to involve the whole family.

Examples:
When Grandma's quilt scraps litter the floor, Mama's impatience shows. "I just cleaned this room, and now it's a mess." Later, with daughter Tanya's enthusiasm about the quilt as incentive, Mama talks with Grandma about the family quilt. Tanya "saw Mama pick up a piece of fabric, rub it with her fingers, and smile." Soon both women "spent their evenings working on the quilt."

Other Devices:
Foreshadow; Theme; Tone

Galbraith, Kathryn. *Waiting for Jennifer.* Illus. by Irene Trivas. New York: Macmillan, Margaret K. McElderry Books, 1987.
Nan and Thea eagerly await the arrival of a new baby in their family, confident that it will be a girl.

Examples:
Passage of time before the baby's birth is implied by the seasonal activities Halloween, Thanksgiving, Christmas, George Washington's Birthday, etc.

Gammell, Stephen. *Once Upon MacDonald's Farm.* New York: Four Winds, 1981.
A farmer who has no animals on his farm gets some: an elephant, a baboon, and a lion. He puts them to farm chores, but they don't plow well or provide eggs or milk. After they run away, a neighbor gives him proper farm animals: a cow, horse, and chicken. However, MacDonald is not likely to fare any better this time. The closing picture shows him hitching the chicken to a plow.

Other Devices:
Parody

Gerstein, Mordicai. *The Mountains of Tibet.* New York: Harper & Row, 1987.
After dying, a Tibetan woodcutter is given the choice of going to heaven or living another life anywhere in the universe.

Examples:
When the woodcutter chooses a "pinwheel-shaped galaxy that looked like a great splash of milk;" when one "warm and golden" star catches his eye; when from among its nine planets he chooses one like a "blue-green marble"; it is clear he wishes to return to live on Earth.

Other Devices:
Foreshadow; Irony

Graham, Bob. *Crusher Is Coming!* New York: Viking Kestrel, 1988.
Crusher is coming and everything had better be just right. Pete wants to impress the school football hero. Claire, Pete's baby sister, must stay out of the way.

Examples:
Crusher has no sooner arrived than he pokes Claire playfully and thereby sets up events to follow. He clearly prefers babies, tea things, playing "horsey," and pushing her in the stroller rather than macho stuff.

Other Devices:
Irony

Haseley, Dennis. *My Father Doesn't Know About the Woods and Me.* Illus. by Michael Hays. New York: Atheneum, 1988.
As a child walks in the woods with his father, he seems to be transformed into other animals enjoying the freedom of nature.

Examples:
While the boy imagines himself a wolf, a hawk, and a fish, he assumes his father knows nothing of these changes. But he meets a deer that stands in a familiar, special way watching him just before his father steps out of the woods where something tall like deer antlers has hooked the high branches and left them swaying. Maybe his father knows more about changing into woodland creatures than he has thought.

Other Devices:
Simile

Haywood, Carolyn. *The King's Monster.* Illus. by Victor Ambrus. New York: William Morrow, 1980.
Only one man in the kingdom is willing to face the king's monster for the hand of the princess.

Examples:
Early on, there is an explanation for the 'monster's' bad smell: garbage in the moat. Those who work for the king have never seen the monster. Letters to the king protesting the monster draw from him a huge laugh. When one suitor agrees to face the monster, the king is momentarily at a loss as to where to tell him the creature is kept. The reader suspects that there really is no monster.

Other Devices:
Symbol

Houston, Gloria. *The Year of the Perfect Christmas Tree: An Appalachian Story.* Illus. by Barbara Cooney. New York: Dial, 1988.
Since Papa has left the Appalachian area to go to war, Ruthie and her mother wonder how they will fulfill his obligation of getting the perfect Christmas tree to the town for the holiday celebration.

Examples:
When Mama and Ruthie go after the tree, they sing carols. Later when the preacher visits, he mentions folks hearing angels singing high on the ridge. Mama and Ruthie exchange a smile when they hear this. From her wedding dress Mama fashions a tiny doll dress; for its body she uses a silk stocking. Ruthie later notes that the Christmas doll feels soft as the stockings Papa had sent for Mama's Christmas gift.

Other Devices:
Tone

Innocenti, Roberto. *Rose Blanche.* Mankato, MN: Creative Education, 1985.
Matter-of-fact reporting of the effect upon one German village and one little girl living there during World War II.

Examples:
The reader assumes that Rose has accidentally been killed by the very soldiers expected to protect her. When she visits the prisoners' camp for the last time, she discovers it has been dismantled. Nervous German soldiers "see the enemy everywhere in the fog." A shot is fired, and Rose Blanche's mother waits and waits for her return.

Other Devices:
Atmosphere; Point of View; Symbol; Tone

Kennedy, Richard. *Song of the Horse.* Illus. by Marcia Sewall. New York: E.P. Dutton, 1981.
Girl describes her ride on her horse.

Examples:
She says, "He loves me to be on his back"; "He loves the feel of my hands on his neck, the weight of my body, and the touch of my heels"; "I don't understand how he can love me so much." But the reader infers that it is clearly she who adores her horse, "O, my lovely, heavenly horse; O, my God who made my horse and me!"

Other Devices:
Imagery; Personification; Point of View; Simile; Tone; Understatement

King-Smith, Dick. *Farmer Bungle Forgets.* Illus. by Martin Honeysett. New York: Atheneum, 1987.
A forgetful farmer has a miserable day not remembering any of his wife's instructions, but he readily remembers his name, or does he?

Examples:
The illustrations show unexpressed examples of the farmer's forgetfulness: milking on the barn floor instead of into the pail, leaving the sink water running, drying his hands on the curtain rather than the nearby towel, trying to hitch the horse backwards to its cart. Even his name implies his nature.

Other Devices:
Irony

Kraus, Robert. *Come Out and Play, Little Mouse.* Illus. by Jose Aruego and Arianne Dewey. New York: Greenwillow Books, 1987.
Little Mouse is busy helping his family five days a week, but he gets to play with them on weekends.

Examples:
It is emphasized that older brother is expected to look after little brother. When little brother is lured out of the family mousehole by a cat who wishes to "play" with him, a funny-looking blue creature which looks like a dog heads off the outcome of this dangerous game. The reader is not surprised when the blue animal unzips, and big brother mouse steps out of the costume.

Other Devices:
Foreshadow

Lindbergh, Anne. *Next Time, Take Care.* Illus. by Susan Hoguet. San Diego, CA: Harcourt Brace Jovanovich, 1988.
While making friends outdoors, Ralph manages to lose all the caps made for him by his constantly knitting Aunt Millicent.

Examples:
Through Ralph's influence, the reader infers that stern, no-nonsense Aunt Millicent becomes more caring and softer toward those around her. Ralph "saw a twinkle in Millicent Meeker's eye." She says she will knit things in holly green, cranberry red, sparrow wing speckle, and squirrel fur gray, all descriptive colors Ralph has taught her to see.

Other Devices:
Aphorism; Foreshadow; Pun; Stereotype/Reverse Stereotype

Lobel, Arnold. *The Rose in My Garden.* Illus. by Anita Lobel. New York: Greenwillow Books, 1984.
A variety of flowers and creatures grow near a rose with a sleeping bee on it. Disruption sets in on this peaceful cumulative tale when a mouse and cat enter the scene.

Examples:
When the cat chases the mouse into the garden and upsets the scene, the bee "wakes up on the rose in my garden." The bee is shown resting on the cat's nose; the next picture shows a bandage on the cat's nose and no bee resting on the rose.

Other Devices:
Alliteration; Imagery

Locker, Thomas. *The Boy Who Held Back the Sea.* Retold by Lenny Hort. New York: Dial, 1987.
A boy banished to his room for a misdeed hears from his grandmother a tale about a misbehaving lad like himself who saved his town from a flood.

Examples:
"Pieter had just been sent to his room and now there was a knock. He expected to see Papa, and maybe Papa's belt" implying punishment is due for some crime committed.

Other Devices:
Allusion

Low, Joseph. *Mice Twice.* New York: Atheneum, 1980.
A devious hungry cat expects to feast on two mice when Mouse asks if she can bring a guest with her to Cat's invitational dinner.

Examples:
The reader knows what the cat really means when he says, "I was just thinking, 'How nice to have a friend for supper!'" Cat is pleased when Mouse asks if she can bring along a friend. Cat thinks, "Mice Twice!"

Other Devices:
Irony; Poetic Justice

Macaulay, David. *Why the Chicken Crossed the Road.* Boston: Houghton Miffin, 1987.
By crossing the road, a chicken sets off a series of wild reactions which eventually return full circle and threaten to repeat the process.

Examples:
When all the reactions finally resolve, the characters are in a restaurant beside the railroad track celebrating the capture of jewel thieves. One of the celebrants requests chicken. The chef is seen with an axe chasing after a fleeing chicken which is about to cross the road. Now the reader knows why a chicken was crossing the road when all the trouble started in the first place. It seems that conditions are again present for a repetition of all the pandemonium.

Other Devices:
Flashback; Pun; Understatement

McPhail, David. *Adam's Smile.* New York: E.P. Dutton, 1987.
The night that his bicycle is struck by a car seems to be the longest in Adam's life; then he learns of the strange and wonderful power of his smile.

Examples:
Adam's accident leaves him in a semi-concious state and immobile. The reader infers his condition through his own interpretations: the night seemed like "the longest of his life. It seemed to go on forever." In his dream, Adam can't move his legs. He believes that the creatures in his dreams have tied him down. The turning point in his recovery is signalled

by his smile, an effort that appears to release him from the dream hold on him. "'You are free to go' . . . as the ropes fell away."

Mahy, Margaret. *Jam, a True Story.* Illus. by Helen Craig. Boston: Atlantic Monthly Press, 1985.
When Mrs. Castle finds a job as an atomic scientist, it's Mr. Castle who stays home to look after the children and make plum jam.

Examples:
After using up the last of a very large batch of plum jam, the family goes out on the lawn. While at play, "Mr. Castle heard a soft thud on the roof. The plums were ripe again." It seems they will soon go through the great jam-making fiasco again.

Other Devices:
Allusion

Maiorano, Robert. *A Little Interlude.* Illus. by Rachel Isadora. New York: Coward, McCann, & Geoghegan, 1980.
In the interlude before Bobby's important ballet appearance, he sees a man called Jiminy Cricket playing a piano.

Examples:
Bobby assumes the piano player is from the orchestra until the man tells him he isn't; the reader then sees him standing with a tool box in his hand, apparently a member of the stage crew.

Other Devices:
Allusion; Atmosphere

Marshall, James. *The Cut-Ups.* New York: Viking Kestrel, 1984.
Two practical jokers get away with every trick in the book until Mr. Spurgle, the man whose flower bed they destroy, turns out to be their school principal in the fall, and he never forgets a face.

Examples:
"School starts soon and we can really cut loose. But little did they know. . . " Spurgle sees them coming and trouble for them is assured.

Other Devices:
Poetic Justice; Tone

Marshall, James. *The Cut-Ups Cut Loose.* New York: Viking Kestrel, 1987.
At the end of summer Spud and Joe eagerly return to school for more practical jokes, unaware that Principal Lamar J. Spurgle is out of retirement and awaiting them.

Examples:
The reader infers that Spud and Joe are a pain in the neck because, "their mothers were beside themselves with joy" when they head back to school in the fall. Although the boys promise to behave, the reader suspects they may not because "unfortunately, some habits are hard to break."

Other Devices:
Irony; Tone; Understatement

Marshall, James. *Wings, a Tale of Two Chickens.* New York: Viking Kestrel, 1986.
Sensible Harriet Chicken must devise an escape for air-head Winnie, who never reads and doesn't realize her danger at the hand of Mr. Johnson, the fox.

Examples:
Making an unscheduled stop, Mr. Johnson picks up a package of instant dumplings. He offers Winnie a raspberry tart because "plump is nice." After accidentally losing and then regaining her he announces, "If at first you don't succeed. . . ." and "nothing worse than picking soggy feathers" which implies the fox plans to eat the chicken.

Mattingley, Christobel. *The Angel With a Mouth-Organ.* Illus. by Astra Lacia. New York: Holiday House, 1986.

Just before the glass angel is put on the Christmas tree, Mother describes her experiences as a little girl during World War II, when she and her family were refugees, and how the glass angel came to symbolize a new beginning in their lives.

Examples:

Poignant comments illustrate stark reality. "Father wasn't taken into service because he had only one arm. But he could hug almost as hard as he used to before the planes came." The reader infers that the shelling from passing planes disabled this civilian father. Later, as displaced refugees, the family walks until "our neighbor and our last cheese disappears one night." Then they see someone wearing the neighbor's boots and her shawl. The reader infers that life evens out small cruelties. One day there is an empty place between the two sisters on the cart where grandma had been riding. The reader infers her death.

Other Devices:

Flashback; Metaphor; Point of View; Understatement

Mattingley, Christobel. *The Miracle Tree.* Illus. by Marianne Yamaguchi. San Diego, CA: Harcourt Brace Jovanovich, Gulliver Books, 1985.

Separated by the explosion of the atomic bomb, a husband, wife, and mother carry on with their lives in the ruins of Nagasaki. They are eventually reunited one Christmas by a very special tree.

Examples:

Three people converge at the site of a newly planted tree. The reader infers through descriptions of them and their behavior that they are a missing wife, husband, and mother who were separated during the war. They have been searching unsuccessfully for twenty years for one another. Their mutual appreciation of the fir tree seems to be the focal point which will bring about disclosure of their identities.

Other Devices:

Atmosphere; Irony; Metaphor; Simile; Symbol

Murphy, Jill. *Five Minutes' Peace.* New York: G.P. Putnam's Sons, 1986.

All Mrs. Large, the elephant, wants is five minutes' peace from her wonderful, rambunctious children. But chaos follows her all the way from the kitchen to the bathroom and back again.

Examples:

"'Can I play you my tune?' Mrs. Large opened one eye. 'Must you?'" Again, a child interferes by wanting to read to her. Mrs. Large agrees: "'Go on then. Just one page.' So Laura read. She read four and a half pages. . . ." It is obvious that she is not getting the peace that she wants.

Other Devices:

Atmosphere; Understatement

Neville, Emily Cheney. *The Bridge.* Illus. by Ronald Himler. New York: Harper & Row, 1988.

When the old wooden bridge collapses, a young boy is delighted to be able to watch the many different machines at work building the new bridge.

Examples:

Though the process of constructing the bridge pleases the boy, the reader infers that the parents worry about the unexpected cost. Mom doesn't answer Ben's rapid-fire questions; Dad says "great" without really meaning it when Ben excitedly relates how the bridge fell; Dad makes many phone calls and "frowns" a lot.

Other Devices:

Foreshadow

Nixon, Joan Lowery. *Fat Chance, Claude.* Illus. by Tracey Campbell Pearson. New York: Viking Kestrel, 1987.
Two zany Texans, Shirley and Claude, grow up and meet out in the gold mining hills of Colorado

Examples:
After Claude works hard to put his two brothers through school, his widowed mother marries a man with six sons who are all "smart as whips and eager for learning." Claude sees the handwriting on the wall, does not want to work to support more brothers, and suddenly decides to go west to look for gold.

Other Devices:
Flashback; Irony; Satire; Simile; Stereotype/Reverse Stereotype; Understatement

Parker, Nancy Winslow. *The Christmas Camel.* New York: Dodd, Mead, 1983.
A child receives a letter describing the unusual gift of a camel with a special talent which arrives at Christmas time. The illustrations support the letter and extend it.

Examples:
Visually, the enchanting mysterious quality about this camel shows that it can take its rider back to the event of the Holy birth.

Other Devices:
Allusion

Pinkwater, Daniel. *Devil in the Drain.* New York: E.P. Dutton, 1984.
A boy talks down the kitchen sink drain to the "devil." He comes to terms with the loss of his pet goldfish.

Examples:
The reader suspects that the 'devil,' who isn't any bigger than the goldfish the boy accidentally dropped down the drain, and who is the goldfish's color, is really the boy's conscience expressing shame and responsibility for the pet's demise. When he asks the devil if it remembers his fish, the devil says, "Sure I do . . . You murdered him."

Other Devices:
Tone

Pinkwater, Daniel. *Roger's Umbrella.* Illus. by James Marshall. New York: E.P. Dutton, 1982.
Roger's umbrella has a mind of its own. Everyone has advice for him to get it to behave.

Examples:
Advice from people has no effect on Roger's recalcitrant umbrella until three particular ladies start saying the right things to the umbrella, words like "Bloogie! Hoop! Dup!" The reader suspects these advice-givers are witches because their cookies are shaped like lizards and shoes, and their house is "full of all sorts of odd things."

Rogers, Paul. *From Me to You.* Illus. by Jane Johnson. New York: Orchard Books, Franklin Watts, 1987.
A grandmother shares her memories of three generations with a young granddaughter and presents her with a precious gift.

Examples:
Grandma says to the child, "She [your mother] was asleep beneath a tree when Grandad went away." He is shown in uniform and no mention is made of his return. We infer that he died in the war.

Other Devices:
Atmosphere; Point of View; Theme

Sadler, Marilyn. *Alistair's Elephant.* Illus. by Roger Bollen. Englewood Cliffs, NJ: Prentice-Hall, 1983.
Alistair's life is never quite the same again after the elephant follows him home from the zoo.

Examples:
Pictures enlarge upon what isn't said: 'rain' comes from the elephant's trunk; the elephant, who wakens early, also awakens Alistair by laying his trunk on Alistair; the elephant gives Alistair some privacy, by turning his huge back to the window. Alistair may think he'll get back to his stuffy peaceful world after the elephant is returned to the zoo, but the illustration shows him being followed home by a giraffe.

Other Devices:
Stereotype; Understatement

Say, Allen. *The Lost Lake.* Boston: Houghton Mifflin, 1989.
A young boy and his father become closer during a camping trip in the mountains.

Examples:
Though his gern father seems preoccupied with work and not very talkative, he does notice the many pictures of camping and lakes which the son has pinned to his wall. The next day they go to the mountains to camp. When the boy later tells his father that he seems different on the trip, more friendly and inclined to talk, the father tells him he will talk more then. The reserved father wants very much to be a good father.

Other Devices:
Ambiguity

Schwartz, Amy. *Her Majesty, Aunt Essie.* Scarsdale, NY: Bradbury Press, 1984.
A little girl makes a bet with her friend that her Aunt Essie is really a queen because of Essie's "Imperial" behavior. Everything works to indicate the truth of her belief but doesn't prove it definitely until the evening of Aunt Essie's date.

Examples:
"You should have seen the way she talked to Daddy when we washed dishes. I could tell she was used to giving orders." Essie's "queenly" behavior comes off as merely pompous.

Other Devices:
Point of View

Schwartz, Amy. *Oma and Bobo.* New York: Bradbury Press, 1987.
Bobo the dog learns to stay, sit, and with the help of Grandma Oma, to fetch.

Examples:
Oma's behavior belies her distaste for dogs. When no one is around she rubs Bobo's tummy with the tip of her black shoe, takes him for a walk in case he's not getting enough exercise, feeds him scrambled eggs in case he's not eating right, and is the first one in the car to go to the dog obedience contest. The reader infers that she really does like dogs.

Other Devices:
Allusion; Foreshadow: Stereotype

Snyder, Dianne. *The Boy of the Three-Year Nap.* Illus. by Allen Say. Boston: Houghton Mifflin Co., 1988.
A poor Japanese woman maneuvers events to change the lazy habits of her son.

Examples:
The peasant son dresses up to look as fierce as a Samurai warrior. Suddenly, a rich merchant is stopped by just such a fierce scowling warrior. While the merchant wails his fate, (the warrior has just ordered him to permit the peasant to marry his daughter) this fierce "god" warrior disappears, showing clothes on under his costume similar to the peasant's.

We infer that the peasant son is implementing his plan to marry the rich merchant's daughter.

Other Devices:
Poetic Justice

Snyder, Zilpha Keatley. *The Changing Maze.* Illus. by Charles Mikolaycak. New York: Macmillan, 1985.
A shepherd boy braves the evil magic of a wizard's maze to save his pet lamb.

Examples:
Hugh "traveled the paths of everywhere and the years he had never known" on wintry evenings at the cottage with his granny, implying that he listens to her tell stories. Hugh almost touches the chest of gold, but his lamb's bleat calls him back though "his hands are bent and numb," implying that he was nearly destroyed by the lure of the evil gold.

Other Devices:
Aphorism; Atmosphere; Flash-forward; Imagery; Personification; Symbol

Solotareff, Grégoire. *Never Trust an Ogre.* New York: Greenwillow Books, 1988.
A hungry, lazy ogre tries to trick the forest animals into coming over to his house for dinner.

Examples:
The ogre remarks how "plump" and "juicy" everyone looks. While they're eating vegetables, he doesn't. He will be "eating later." They see the hunting knife in his pocket. All this causes them to conclude that he really means no friendship after all.

Other Devices:
Pun

Stolz, Mary. *Storm in the Night.* Illus. by Pat Cummings. New York: Harper & Row, 1988.
While sitting through a fearsome thunderstorm that has put the lights out, Thomas hears a story from Grandfather's boyhood, when Grandfather was afraid of thunderstorms.

Examples:
"'I'm not afraid of anything,'" Thomas says, holding his cat close," implying that he is indeed afraid.

Other Devices:
Ambiguity; Hyperbole; Imagery; Pun; Simile

Switzer, Ellen. *Lily Boop.* Illus. by Lillian Hoban. New York: Crown, 1986.
A young girl describes her adventures with her unusual friend who keeps a pet slug and eats raw eggs for lunch.

Examples:
As the story unfolds, the reader recognizes that Lily is not a human child. By the end, an educated guess partly confirmed by text and pictures would be that Lily and her family are badgers.

Other Devices:
Theme

Townson, Hazel. *Terrible Tuesday.* Pictures by Tony Ross. New York: William Morrow, 1985.
When Terry overhears his mother predicting Terrible Tuesday, he dreams up all kinds of hilarious disasters.

Examples:
When "Terrible Tuesday" brings only a fun day with his cousins, Terry can't imagine what his mother thought would be so terrible. The picture on the last page clarifies the messy fun that made Mom dread the day.

Turkle, Brinton. *Do Not Open.* New York; E.P. Dutton, 1981.
Living by the sea, an old woman and her cat find an intriguing bottle washed up on the beach after a storm. They ignore the warning on it: "Do not open."

Examples:
Miss Moody dispenses with the evil genie, and when she returns to her cottage, finds the banjo clock working. Her unspoken wish has been fulfilled, perhaps because the genie was overpowered by goodness.

Other Devices:
Foreshadow; Parody

Turner, Ann. *Dakota Dugout.* Illus. by Ronald Himler. New York: Macmillan, 1985.
A woman describes her experiences living with her husband in a sod house on the Dakota prairie.

Examples:
The loneliness of the empty prairie is inferred from the woman's comments, "The birds visited me, there was no one else, with Matt all day in the fields. . . a sparrow jabbered. . . on a gray fence post. I jabbered back." The frustration of losing hard fought gains when the corn dries up is inferred by her comment, "Matt sat and looked two whole days, silent and long." But her deep love of this stark, primitive life is also inferred when she says, "Talking brings it near again, the sweet taste of new bread in a Dakota dugout, how the grass whispered like an old friend, how the earth kept us warm."

Other Devices:
Aphorism; Atmosphere; Flashback; Imagery; Metaphor; Simile

Van Allsburg, Chris. *Jumanji.* Boston: Houghton Mifflin Co., 1981.
Left on their own for an afternoon, two bored and restless children find more excitement than they bargained for in a mysterious and mystical jungle adventure board game.

Examples:
After enduring fearsome adventures to get to the end of the game, the children return the game to the park where they found it. One of their parents' guests casually remark to them that her two sons never read directions to games. The children then watch out the window as the guest's two boys are seen running off with the game. The experiences awaiting them can be inferred.

Other Devices:
Pun

Van Allsburg, Chris. *The Wreck of the Zephyr.* Boston: Houghton Mifflin Co., 1983.
An old story-teller tells of a youth who ignored advice and attempted alone a skill he had not mastered, much to his sorrow.

Examples:
As the story concludes, it is apparent that the old story-teller is the boy sailor in the story's events.

Other Devices:
Allusion; Flashback; Foreshadow; Theme

INTERNAL RHYME

Two or more words rhyme within a single line.

Example: I bring fresh showers to the thirsting flowers.—Shelley

Sources

Allison, Diane Worfolk. *In Window Eight, the Moon is Late.* Boston: Little, Brown, 1988.
At the end of a summer day, a little girl goes through the house saying good-night to the various members of her family.

Examples:
Tumbling/crumbling; sliding/hiding; squealing/wheeling; blue in window two; window three, weeping tree; window six, the glass plays tricks; faces alive in window five; swallows soar in window four; window eight, the moon is late; heaven in window seven; sun in window one.

Other Devices:
Alliteration

Arnold, Tedd. *No Jumping on the Bed!* New York: Dial, 1987.
Walter lives near the top floor of a tall apartment building, where one night his habit of jumping on his bed leads to a tumultuous fall through floor after floor, collecting occupants all the way down.

Examples:
All the characters' names in the story end in the sound "-atty": Miss Hattie, Mr. Matty, Aunt Batty, Patty and Natty, Fatty Cat, Mr. Hanratty, Maestro Ferlingatti.

Other Devices:
Foreshadow; Inference; Understatement

Carlstrom, Nancy White. *Wild Wild Sunflower Child Anna.* Illus. by Jerry Pinkney. New York: Macmillan, 1987.
Spending a day outdoors, Anna revels in the joys of sun, sky, grass, flowers, berries, frogs, ants, and beetles.

Examples:
Kneeling/leaning; talking/walking; picking/licking; skipping/slipping.

Other Devices:
Alliteration; Atmosphere; Imagery

Mayne, William. *The Patchwork Cat.* Illus. by Nicola Bayley. New York: Knopf, 1981.

Examples:
A cat braves frightening experiences to retrieve her favorite sleeping quilt, which her mistress has unthinkingly decided to throw away.

Examples:
Snatchwork on Tabby's patchwork quilt may call for angry scratchwork; engines are shaking and quaking; rats gnash their teeth and flash their eyes.

Other Devices:
Alliteration; Metaphor; Point of View

Snyder, Zilpha Keatley. *The Changing Maze.* Illus. by Charles Mikolaycak. New York: Macmillan, 1985.
A shepherd boy braves the evil magic of a wizard's maze to save his pet lamb.

Examples:
Stood alone. . . of the great gray stones; old and gray. . . who loved to play; if sheep could speak; when the day and their play were done; granny's chair and . . . paths of everywhere; from their westward crest. . . Hugh knew the rest; of the Ragged Lands prepared a secret evil plan; the gardeners slept, the wizard-king a vigil kept; wondrous fast. . . when at last; secret, too. . . still knew. . . still grew.

Other Devices:
Aphorism; Atmosphere; Flash-forward; Imagery; Inference; Personification; Symbol

Stevenson, James. *What's Under My Bed?* New York: Greenwillow Books, 1983.
Grandpa tells his two young houseguests a story about his own childhood when he was scared at bedtime.

Examples:
Grandpa describes the many creatures after him at night: scratchers and catchers; growlers and howlers.

Other Devices:
Alliteration; Theme

Willard, Nancy. *The Voyage of the Ludgate Hill.* Illus. by Alice and Martin Provensen. New York: Harcourt Brace Jovanovich, 1987.
A poem inspired by Robert Louis Stevenson's letters describes how the author and his wife survived a stormy ocean voyage with a cargo of exotic animals.

Examples:
Carried a crew of sixty and two; now eat your porridge, and I'll sing you the voyage; I sailed with my wife, the light of my life; but an ape in a squall made fools of us all; cold mutton pie was in such short supply.

Other Devices:
Alliteration; Imagery

IRONY

Contrast between expected outcomes or what appears to be and the actual way things turn out; useful to humorously comment upon the unpredictable nature of life. Three main literary forms of irony:

Verbal. Saying one thing and meaning its opposite.
Example: As you come in from a raging blizzard you say, "Nice day, huh?"

Situation. Events turn out opposite to what is expected to happen or to what seems appropriate under the circumstances.
Example: A man believes he is the only human left on earth; in despair he swallows sleeping tablets; just as he slips into unconsciousness, the telephone rings.

Dramatic. Reader perceives something which the characters in the story don't see or know. In picture books this may often be shown through illustrations.

Sources

Baker, Keith. *The Dove's Letter.* New York: Harcourt Brace Jovanovich, 1988.
A dove tries to deliver an unaddressed letter it finds to the letter's rightful owner. In the process, it brings great pleasure to each person who receives the letter.

Examples:
Because each person who receives the letter wants it to be from a loved one, all find 'proof' in the unsigned note convincing them it is from a particular person.

Bang, Molly. *Delphine.* New York: Morrow, 1988.
Anxious about her ability to handle the new bicycle that is waiting at the post office for her, Delphine worriedly goes to retrieve it.

Examples:
All the skills needed to ride her new bike are used as Delphine steers a baby carriage around sharp bends, balances on a narrow bridge, and negotiates treacherous rapids on her way to pick up the gift. She is already using skills more difficult than riding a bike.

Other Devices:
Theme

Blos, Joan W. *Old Henry.* Illus. by Stephen Gammell. New York: William Morrow, 1987.
Henry's neighbors are scandalized that he ignores them and lets his property get run down, until they drive him away and find themselves missing him.

Examples:
Though seemingly pleased to be rid of each other after their false expectations and confrontations, the townspeople and Henry grow to miss the presence of each other in spite of their differences.

Other Devices:
Aphorism; Paradox

Burningham, John. *John Patrick Norman McHennessy: The Boy Who Was Always Late.* New York: Crown, 1987.
A teacher comes to regret his decision to disbelieve a student's outlandish excuses for being tardy.

Examples:
A teacher punishes a child for his unbelievable excuses and then falls victim himself to one of these unbelievable occurrences.

Other Devices:
Poetic Justice

Coleridge, Ann. *The Friends of Emily Culpepper.* Illus. by Roland Harvey. New York: G.P. Putnam's Sons, 1987.
Seeking companionship, a lonely old lady miniaturizes the mail carrier, milk delivery person, and plumber, then places them in jars around the house.

Examples:
Forced by the town policeman to allow her friends to return to their careers in the village, Emily is not left bereft because she now lets the policeman out of the jar each day at noon to eat his lunch, play in the old doll's house, and to hunt him as he tries to escape. He has now taken the place of her former companions.

Demarest, Chris L. *Morton and Sidney.* New York: Macmillan, 1987.
Sidney, one of the monsters who lives in Morton's closet, has been kicked out by the other monsters. Morton must figure out a scheme to get him reinstated so that at night "everything was back to normal."

Examples:
This is a turn-about of the monster-in-the-dark theme. The 'victim' not only welcomes monsters in his closet but must restore harmony to their world so that they can continue to do their monster thing.

Other Devices:
Satire

Friedman, Ina R. *How My Parents Learned to Eat.* Illus. by Allen Say. Boston: Houghton Mifflin Co., 1984.
A young mixed ethnic couple each supposes that the other is not interested in marriage, since they are unable to eat in one another's style. Unbeknownst to each, the other practices eating properly in the unfamiliar style. Eventually they share eating styles and their daughter grows up using each style naturally.

Other Devices:
Flashback

Gerstein, Mordicai. *The Mountains of Tibet.* New York: Harper & Row, 1987.
After dying, a Tibetan woodcutter is given the choice of going to heaven or living another life anywhere in the universe.

Examples:
Though we long for change and variety, what we are familiar with is what we prefer most. The woodcutter longed to travel and see the world, but when given the opportunity for a second life, he chooses to repeat the first one.

Other Devices:
Foreshadow; Inference

Goode, Diane. *I Hear a Noise.* New York: E.P. Dutton, 1988.
A little boy, hearing noises at his window at bedtime, calls for his mother. His worst fears are realized, but he learns that monsters have mothers too.

Examples:
Though the boy and his mother are captured by monsters and carried off to monsterland, a mother monster reprimands the young thieves who have stolen the humans and orders them to quit fighting over the victims. She makes the monster children return the boy and his mother "right back where you found them."

Gordon, Margaret. *The Supermarket Mice.* New York: E.P. Dutton, 1984.
Mice living in a grocery store must cope with a cat out to eliminate them.

Examples:
The mice work a guard cat to their own advantage so that they may continue to prowl the food market at night to their heart's content without leaving tell-tale crumbs for the manager to find.

Graham, Bob. *Crusher Is Coming!* New York: Viking Kestrel, 1988.
Crusher is coming and everything had better be just right. Pete wants to impress the school football hero. Claire, Pete's baby sister, must stay out of the way.

Examples:
Clearly the tough guy is really a softie. He likes baby sitting and animal tea-parties better than "Raiders of the Universe."

Other Devices:
Inference

Hearn, Michael Patrick. *The Porcelain Cat.* Illus. by Leo and Diane Dillon. Boston: Little, Brown, 1987.
A sorcerer's apprentice has to complete several difficult tasks before dawn in order to obtain a missing ingredient for one of his master's spells.

Examples:
A sorcerer's apprentice struggles to obtain a rare ingredient for his master to use in a potion that will turn a porcelain cat into a live cat that will rid the sorcerer of annoying rats. The cat makes one leap and crashes, breaking into glass shards. The sorcerer gives up in disgust but the apprentice, given the task of sweeping up the pieces, is privileged to witness a beautiful porcelain bird fly up from the mess.

Other Devices:
Allusion; Pun

Howe, James. *I Wish I Were a Butterfly.* Illus. by Ed Young. San Diego, CA: Harcourt Brace Jovanovich, Gulliver Books, 1987.
A wise spider helps a despondent cricket realize that he is special in his own way.

Examples:
A cricket who has always admired the appearance of butterflies doesn't realize that a butterfly wishes he could be a cricket because he admires the cricket's beautiful music.

Other Devices:
Imagery

Hutchins, Pat. *The Very Worst Monster.* New York: Greenwillow Books, 1985.
Hazel sets out to prove that she, not her baby brother, is the worst monster anywhere.

Examples:
No one will notice Hazel's efforts to be the worst monster in the world until she gives away her baby brother. This earns her the title, but the baby is still the worst baby monster because his new owners don't want him: he is too awful.

Other Devices:
Hyperbole

Kasza, Keiko. *The Wolf's Chicken Stew.* New York: G.P. Putnam's Sons, 1987.
A hungry wolf's attempts to fatten a chicken for his stew pot have unexpected results.

Examples:
While a wolf believes his culinary gifts left at Mrs. Chicken's door are fattening her up for his pot, he discovers that her multitude of children are appreciative of 'Uncle' Wolf's presents. They kiss him and declare him the best cook in the world. He doesn't have chicken stew after all. He decides he'll bake the little critters a hundred scrumptious cookies.

King-Smith, Dick. *Farmer Bungle Forgets.* Illus. by Martin Honeysett. New York: Atheneum, 1987.
A forgetful farmer has a miserable day not remembering any of his wife's instructions, but he still remembers his name, or does he?

Examples:
All the way through the story Farmer Bungle promises to remember, "or his name isn't Bill Bungle." After his day of forgetfulness, his exasperated wife admonishes him, "One of these fine days you're going to forget your own name, *Henry* Bungle." He has, indeed, forgotten even his own name.

Other Devices:
Inference

Lewis, Rob. *Hello, Mr. Scarecrow.* New York: Farrar, Straus, & Giroux, 1987.
Simple text about a year in the life of a scarecrow.

Examples:
All the animals meant to be deterred by the scarecrow actually enjoy his presence and move about and on him freely without harm. It is the human children who end his existence in their rough play.

Low, Joseph. *Mice Twice.* New York: Atheneum, 1980.
Cat plans for a mouse meal, maybe two mice. He ends up losing his chance at dinner and, nearly, his life. He is outwitted by the mice who use his own strategy against him when they bring along the fiercest "guest" of all.

Other Devices:
Inference; Poetic Justice

McPhail, David. *Fix-It.* New York: E.P. Dutton, 1984.
Emma comes down early one morning to watch TV, but it doesn't work. Her parents and the repairman all try to fix it to no avail. Eventually Emma is distracted with a story book and her dolls; when the true cause for the broken TV is found, she no longer wants to watch it.

Marshall, James. *The Cut-Ups Cut Loose.* New York: Viking Kestrel, 1987.
At the end of summer Spud and Joe eagerly return to school for more practical jokes, unaware that Principal Lamar J. Spurgle is out of retirement and awaiting them.

Examples:
Spurgle, who frustrates the efforts of kids, is frustrated himself by his own former teacher as he commits the same sins he did in grade school.

Other Devices:
Inference; Tone; Understatement

Mattingley, Christobel. *The Miracle Tree.* Illus. by Marianne Yamaguchi. San Diego, CA: Harcourt Brace Jovanovich, Gulliver Books, 1985.
Separated by the explosion of the atomic bomb, a husband, wife, and mother carry on with their lives in the ruins of Nagasaki. They are eventually reunited on Christmas by a very special tree.

Examples:
A mother, angry because her daughter sidestepped tradition by marrying without parental permission, comes to bitterly regret burning her daughter's letters unread. She does not now know the name of her daughter's husband and has, thus, lost an avenue to help locate the missing girl. She admires a newly planted tree without realizing that the gardener, who lovingly tends it, is her daughter's husband.

Other Devices:
Atmosphere; Inference; Metaphor; Simile; Symbol

Modell, Frank. *Tooley! Tooley!* New York: Greenwillow Books, 1979.
None of Marvin's ideas for finding movie money sound anything but silly to Milton. But when it comes to finding a lost dog for the reward money, Marvin is the one with logic that works.

Nixon, Joan Lowery. *Fat Chance, Claude.* Illus. by Tracey Campbell Pearson. New York: Viking Kestrel, 1987.

Two zany Texans, Shirley and Claude, grow up and meet out in the gold mining hills of Colorado.

Examples:

Claude tells Shirley not to do something a woman can't do and not to be a nuisance on a man's wagon train. But it's Shirley who saves Claude's life by dumping hot stew on a snake.

Other Devices:

Flashback; Inference; Satire; Simile; Stereotype/Reverse Stereotype; Understatement

Perrault, Charles. *Cinderella.* Illus. by Roberto Innocenti. Creative Education, 1983.

At the end of this 1920s version of Cinderella, the reader wonders whether Cinderella does live happily ever after because the final illustration shows her with dyed hair sitting bored and alone at 4 pm on a rainy day with a cigarette drooping from her lips, a drink in her hand, empty liquor bottles around the floor, and a vase of spent flowers.

Pittman, Helena Clare. *A Grain of Rice.* New York: Hastings House, 1986.

A clever, cheerful, hard working farmer's son wins the hand of a Chinese princess by outwitting her father the Emperor, who treasures his daughter more than all the rice in China.

Examples:

Asking the emperor for what seems an absurdly small reward, only one grain of rice doubled every day for 100 days, the farmer's son becomes rich enough to be a nobleman. His lack of a noble title was what had kept him from marrying the princess in the first place.

Other Devices:

Foreshadow; Paradox

Rogers, Paul. *Tumbledown.* Illus. by Robin Bill Corfield. New York: Atheneum, 1988.

In the village of Tumbledown, where everything is broken down, an announcement that the Prince is coming to visit creates a flurry of fixing-up.

Examples:

A special effort is made to fix up all the places where the Prince is sure to visit. The one place missed is the site which pleases the Price most, because now he knows why the town is called Tumbledown.

Rose, David S. *It Hardly Seems Like Halloween.* New York: Lothrop, Lee, & Shepard Books, 1983.

A child talks about the things he expects to see at Halloween. Mournfully, he laments their absence. But he doesn't turn around or he would see all of the ghosts and monsters behind him. He is oblivious to the strange creatures who seem to take on his gloomy mood as they listen to his complaints concerning how this Halloween is very dull.

Steig, William. *Doctor De Soto.* New York: Farrar, Straus, & Giroux, 1982.

Although only a diminutive mouse, the resourceful dentist Dr. De Soto is able to treat patients of all shapes and sizes, except animals dangerous to mice. One day his kind nature gets him into danger with a fox.

Examples:

A dentist at the mercy of his patient turns potential disaster to his own advantage, a fox out-foxed by a mouse.

Other Devices:

Theme

Stevens, Kathleen. *Molly McCullough and Tom the Rogue.* Illus. by Margot Zemach. New York: Thomas Y. Crowell, 1982.
Tom Devlin roams the countryside charming the farmers' wives and tricking the farmers out of fruits and vegetables until he meets his match in a plain-faced, sharp-tongued farmer's daughter.

Examples:
The Rogue, expecting to pull his scam on yet another dumb, greedy farmer finds he's the victim this time.

Other Devices:
Aphorism; Foreshadow; Poetic Justice; Theme

Testa, Fulvio. *Never Satisfied.* London: Abelard/ North-South, 1982.
In this story, much like Ellen Raskin's *Nothing Ever Happens on My Block,* David Rose's *It Hardly Seems Like Halloween,* and Harriet Ziefert's *My Sister Says Nothing Ever Happens When We Go Sailing,* two boys bemoan the dullness of their life while their unobservant eyes miss the drama around them.

Examples:
Illustrations show a house being vandalized, a woman balancing on a clothesline as she hangs the wash, a huge snake they must step over, a panther leaning on a tree. All the while the two boys wish they were having dangerous adventures in the Amazon.

Titherington, Jeanne. *A Place for Ben.* New York: Greenwillow Books, 1987.
When his baby brother is moved into his bedroom, Ben goes elsewhere in search of a place of his own but finds himself longing for company of some kind.

Examples:
Initially, Ben wishes to separate himself from his brother because he no longer feels he has a place for himself. By the story's conclusion the only person who has time to visit him in his new place is his baby brother.

Willis, Jeanne. *The Monster Bed.* New York: Lothrop, Lee, & Shepard, 1986.
A little monster is afraid to go to bed because he thinks humans will get him while he is asleep,.

Examples:
The little monster sleeps under his bed because he thinks humans won't be apt to look for him underneath it. When a lost human child enters the monster cave to rest, he first looks under the bed in case the cave might have monsters. He sees the monster child, and each frightens the other away.

Wood, Audrey. *King Bidgood's in the Bathtub.* Illus. by Don Wood. New York: Harcourt Brace Jovanovich, 1985.
Despite pleas from his court, a fun-loving king refuses to get out of his bathtub to rule his kingdom.

Examples:
A lowly Page calls for help from his "betters" to dislodge the stubborn King. The Knight, the Queen, the Duke, and the Court all fail to convince the King to leave his tub. The Page succeeds by relying on his own resources. He pulls the plug.

Other Devices:
Poetic Justice

Yorinks, Arthur. *It Happened in Pinsk.* New York: Farrar, Straus, & Giroux, 1983.
A complaining man, wishing always to be someone else, suddenly loses his head and becomes mistaken for other people after his wife makes a pillow-case head for him.

Examples:
Irv constantly wishes he were other members of the community. But after being fitted with a pillowcase head, he is now mistaken for a variety of persons, none of whom he would like to be.

Other Devices:
Allusion; Ambiguity; Satire; Understatement

Ziefert, Harriet. *My Sister Says Nothing Ever Happens When We Go Sailing.* Illus. by Seymour Chwast. New York: Harper & Row, 1986.
When the wind dies down on a family sailing trip, Sister gets bored and falls asleep. She snoozes through a rain squall and a rescue at sea and doesn't wake until the boat docks. Sister has missed all the fun; no wonder she says nothing ever happens when they go sailing. This story is similar in concept to Ellen Raskin's *Nothing Ever Happens on My Block*, David Rose's *It Hardly Seems Like Halloween*, and Fulvio Testa's *Never Satisfied.*

Other Devices:
Stereotype

METAPHOR

A suggested comparison between two unlike things for the purpose of pointing out an implied similarity of some sort between them; suggests that the thing is this other thing.

Example: Tumbleweeds are the lost children of the desert.

Sources

Fleischman, Paul. *Rondo in C.* Illus. by Janet Wentworth. New York: Harper & Row, 1988.
As a young piano student plays Beethoven's "Rondo in C" at her recital, each member of the audience is stirred by memories.

Examples:
The music becomes for each listener a scene from their respective experiences, transporting them to vivid personal images from their past.

Other Devices:
Atmosphere

Goffstein, M.B. *A Writer.* New York: Harper & Row, 1984.
A writer is compared to a gardener as she cuts, prunes, plans, and shapes words, never sure of her ground or which seeds are rooting there.

Other Devices:
Analogy

McNulty, Faith. *The Lady and the Spider.* Illus. by Bob Marstall. New York: Harper & Row, 1986.
A spider who lives in a head of lettuce is saved when the lady who finds her puts her back into the garden.

Examples:
A lettuce is compared to hills, valleys, a green cave, a den; dew on leaves becomes a tiny pool; footsteps become an earthquake to the spider.

Martin, Bill and Archambault, John. *Knots on a Counting Rope.* Illus. by Ted Rand. New York: Henry Holt, 1987.
One cool dark night an Indian boy sits with his grandfather, bathed in the glow of a campfire as they reminisce about the night he was born. A poignant story of love, hope, and courage.

Examples:
The counting rope is a metaphor for the passage of time and for the boy's emerging confidence in facing his greatest challenge, his blindness.

Other Devices:
Foreshadow; Imagery; Symbol

Mattingley, Christobel. *The Angel with a Mouth-Organ.* Illus. by Astra Lacie. New York: Holiday House, 1986.
Just before the glass angel is put on the Christmas tree, Mother describes her experiences as a little girl during World War II, when she and her family were refugees. The glass angel came to symbolize a new beginning in their lives.

Examples:
The village is likened to a garden: fire "flowers" turn haystacks into "poppies"; church spires into "scarlet salvia"; "petals" of flame result from the bombs; and "seeds" of fear, hate, courage, and love exist.

Other Devices:
Flashback; Inference; Point of View; Understatement

Mattingley, Christobel. *The Miracle Tree.* Illus. by Marianne Yamaguchi. San Diego, CA: Harcourt Brace Jovanovich, Gulliver Books, 1985.
Separated by the explosion of the atomic bomb, a husband, wife, and mother carry on with their lives in the ruins of Nagasaki. They are eventually reunited one Christmas by a very special tree.

Examples:
The old woman says that Hanako, her daughter, is "my precious flower." Hanako describes herself as a "withered leaf." The "ice" in Hanako's heart "thaws." Pigeons "spun in whirring wheels." When Taro, her husband, sees Hanako, "a hundred thousand seeds were springing into bloom in his brain." The old woman sees her daughter after twenty years and "tears extinguished the embers of unhappiness in her heart."

Other Devices:
Atmosphere; Inference; Irony; Simile; Symbol

Mayne, William. *The Patchwork Cat.* Illus. by Nicola Bayley. New York: Knopf, 1981.
A cat braves frightening experiences to retrieve her favorite sleeping quilt, which her mistress has unthinkingly decided to throw away.

Examples:
The garbage truck is likened to a cat: "it lifted its back and hissed."

Other Devices:
Alliteration; Point of View

Pittman, Helena Clare. *Once When I Was Scared.* Illus. by Ted Rand. New York: E.P. Dutton, 1988.
Grandfather tells how, when he was a child, he coped with fear during a journey alone through a dark wood to get coals to start a fire in the family cook range.

Examples:
As the boy runs in the dark, he becomes a fox springing gracefully off slippery rocks and tangles. He becomes a bobcat bounding with balance through roots and fallen logs. He turns into a fierce loud eagle that screams and lifts to frighten away a bear.

Other Devices:
Symbol

Turner, Ann. *Dakota Dugout.* Illus. by Ronald Himler. New York: Macmillan, 1985.
A woman describes her experiences living with her husband in a sod house on the Dakota prairie.

Examples:
"We saw dresses, buggies, gold in that grain." "The ground was iron."

Other Devices:
Aphorism; Atmosphere; Flashback; Imagery; Inference; Simile

Yolen, Jane. *Owl Moon.* Illus. by John Schoenherr. New York: Philomel Books, 1987.
One winter's night under a full moon, a father and daughter trek into the woods to see a Great Horned Owl.

Examples:
"The moon made his face into a silver mask"; "I was a shadow as we walked home."

Other Devices:
Imagery; Simile

PARADOX

A statement that reveals a kind of unlikely truth although it seems at first to be self-contradictory and untrue.

Example: Good fences make good neighbors. (Fences do separate people, but since they define limits of people's property, fences prevent conflicts.)

Sources

Arnold, Tedd. *Ollie Forgot.* New York: Dial, 1988.
Ollie's rather unreliable memory, which loses whatever he has in mind whenever he hears something new, gets him into all kinds of trouble on the way to the market.

Examples:
Each time Ollie makes a mindless repetition of the last phrase he's heard, he speaks it accidentally to a situation which it fits by chance.

Other Devices:
Parody

Baring, Maurice. *The Blue Rose.* Illus. by Anne Dalton. Kingswood, England: Kay & Ward, The Windmill Press, 1982.
Wise Emperor of China sets a condition that only he who can find the Blue Rose may marry his accomplished, beautiful daughter. Less than desirable suitors respond to the condition and are rejected. The successful suitor achieves her acceptance in the time-honored method of earning her love.

Examples:
Although the successful suitor actually brings a white rose in response to the request for a blue one, the Emperor accepts it because his daughter says it is blue and her perception is known to be more acute than anyone's in the kingdom.

Other Devices:
Imagery; Theme; Tone

Blos, Joan W. *Old Henry.* Illus. by Stephen Gammell. New York: William Morrow, 1987.
Henry's neighbors are scandalized that he ignores them and lets his property get run down. They drive him away but find they miss him.

Examples:
Their differences first separate, then join them. The townspeople think, "His house looks so empty, so dark in the night. And having him gone doesn't make us more right." Meanwhile, "to his great surprise," Henry "was missing the neighbors who brought him the pies. . . . He really did care for them and their street."

Other Devices:
Aphorism; Irony

Brinckloe, Julie. *Playing Marbles.* New York: William Morrow, 1988.
A little girl proves her skill in a game of marbles with two boys.

Examples:
Fierce competitors end up being fast friends. Their skill earns mutual respect and admiration from one another surmounting children's antipathy and jealousy between the sexes.

Other Devices:
Stereotype/Reverse Stereotype

Domanska, Janina. *What Happens Next?* New York: Greenwillow books, 1983.
A baron who loves tall tales promises to free the peasant who can tell him a tale that will surprise him.

Examples:
The peasant who wins his freedom concocts a wild tale which does not surprise the baron until he says that he met an old herdsman tending his flocks. He greeted the man saying, "Good morning, dear herdsman!" and said that he received for a reply, "I am not a herdsman; I am the baron's father." This bit of effrontery, logical and sane as it is compared to the ridiculous tall tales the peasant has just spouted, catches the baron off guard. "Impossible!" he says. "My father tending sheep! That would surprise me!" The only sane part of his story surprises the baron more than all the illogical events.

Other Devices:
Hyperbole

Gedin, Birgitta. *The Little House from the Sea.* Illus. by Petter Pettersson. Trans. by Elisabeth Dyssegaard. New York: Farrar, Straus, & Giroux, 1988.
A little house on a rocky island never moves but longs to be a ship that can travel over the ocean to see the Other Side.

Examples:
A small island house claims it is a boat. Actually, it *was* built from a ship that was beached in a storm.

Other Devices:
Aphorism; Personification

Jukes, Mavis. *Lights Around the Palm.* Illus. by Stacey Schuett. New York: Knopf, 1987.
Seven-year-old Emma tries to convince her disbelieving older brother that she is teaching their farm animals to read the English they already appear to speak.

Examples:
Bob knows animals don't speak, yet Emma can show him out there in the special evening atmosphere that they obviously do.

McAfee, Annalena. *The Visitors Who Came to Stay.* Illus. by Anthony Browne. New York: Viking Kestrel, 1984.
A small girl's calm, predictable life is upended when her father brings home a zany woman and her practical joker son to share their lives.

Examples:
Although Katy dislikes their uncomfortable intrusion into her world, she finds that after the visitors have gone she is no longer content with her humdrum life; she actually needs their kooky presence to feel happy again.

Other Devices:
Atmosphere; Pun

Morris, Winifred. *The Magic Leaf.* Illus. by Ju-Hong Chen. New York: Atheneum, 1987.
When a foolish man believes he has become invisible by possessing a magic leaf, he sneaks into the mayor's private garden to view the peonies.

Examples:
It is only after Lee Foo begins to think that he's not so very clever that he actually becomes a bit smarter than he had been before.

Other Devices:
Aphorism; Satire

Peet, Bill. *No Such Things.* Boston: Houghton Mifflin Co., 1983.
Describes in rhyme a variety of fantastic creatures such as the blue-snouted Twumps, pie-faced Pazeeks, and the fancy Fandangos.

Examples:
One of the invented sea creatures is part plant and part animal. It loves to catch fish, but it can't eat them since it doesn't have a gullet. Therefore, the frightened fish "cannot possibly know that they will not be eaten, until they're let go."

Other Devices:
Allusion; Pun

Pittman, Helena Clare. *A Grain of Rice.* New York: Hastings House, 1986.
A clever, cheerful hard-working farmer's son wins the hand of a Chinese princess by outwitting her father the emperor, who treasures his daughter more than all the rice in China.

Examples:
A seemingly insignificant and tiny reward request, one grain of rice doubled every day for 100 days, enables a poor peasant to realize his heart's desire: to become rich enough to become a nobleman and thus deserve to marry the princess.

Other Devices:
Foreshadow; Irony

Rylant, Cynthia. *All I See.* Illus. by Peter Catalanotto. New York: Orchard Books, Franklin Watts, 1988.
A child paints with an artist friend who sees and paints only whales.

Examples:
Although he is at a lake, an artist paints whales as though they are out frolicking in plain view. Charlie likes the artist. His faith and respect for Gregory enable him to know that for Gregory the whales are there somewhere. Friendship has made it possible for him to believe that there will be something interesting for him waiting there to be painted too. Imaginative vistas opened by the sensitive painter are possible for a budding artist to emulate.

PARALLEL STORY

A narrative or picture story enclosed within another story upon which equal or primary interest is centered.

Sources

Ahlberg, Janet and Allan Ahlberg. *The Cinderella Show.* New York: Viking Kestrel, 1986.
A school play is shown on and off stage in two side-by-side stories, the story of Cinderella and a behind-the-scenes look at the production.

Grifalconi, Ann. *The Village of Round and Square Houses.* Boston: Little, Brown, 1986.
A grandmother explains to her listeners why in their village on the side of a volcano the men live in square houses and the women in round ones.

Examples:
A woman tells about the custom of her culture: that men lived in square houses and women in round and all was harmony. Then she tells the tale her grandmother told her of how this all came about.

Other Devices:
Theme

Kitamura, Satoshi. *Lily Takes a Walk.* New York: E.P. Dutton, 1987.
Lily enjoys walks with her dog Nicky, not realizing he is fending off unseen monsters all along the way.

Examples:
While Lily observes the usual city sights, Nicky sees a snake crawling down a tree, a tree leering at him, a mail box opened in toothy-mouthed danger, a set of eyes on tunnel lamps, a clock tower and moon staring at him, a giant man looming out of a window at him, a canal monster, and garbage can creatures. While Lily tells her parents about her sights, Nicky barks his sights. Even as the day's events end for Lily, Nicky is being beseiged by mice crawling into his basket.

McAfee, Annalena. *Kirsty Knows Best.* Illus. by Anthony Browne. New York: Knopf, 1987.
A child's daydreams turn her ordinary life into a much more interesting one.

Examples:
Kirsty's imaginative world parallels the real experiences she lives and make for a more vivid and pleasant existence than does reality. When a bully tries to intrude with cruel reality, Kirsty knows how to fix her.

Ormerod, Jan. *The Story of Chicken Licken.* New York: Lothrop, Lee, & Shepard, 1985.
"Chicken Licken" is retold in drama form by school children with an audience of parents and family watching.

Examples:
While the stage story is going on, in the audience a baby escapes its basket and crawls about doing mischief before finally ending up on stage with the performers.

Peters, Lisa Westberg. *The Sun, The Wind and the Rain.* Illus. by Ted Rand. New York: Henry Holt, 1988.
This is a side-by-side narration of the earth's making of a mountain, shaping it with sun, wind, and rain, and a child's efforts at the beach to make a tall sand mountain which is also affected by the elements.

Prater, John. *The Perfect Day.* New York: E.P. Dutton, 1986.
A family sets out to enjoy all that a day at the beach offers for amusement.

Examples:
The narrative describes a day at the beach. But Kevin's version of the day is entirely at odds with the text. At the amusement park "Kevin and his sister ride on nearly everything (My bottom hurts. This seat is really hard!) and they both win a prize (I wanted a red balloon. Can we go home now?)" At the story's conclusion, Kevin's interpretation of events, again, doesn't mesh with the text. "A sudden storm sends the family rushing for their car. (Wow! This is great! Look at those waves.)"

PARODY

A humorous but recognizable imitation of another literary work for the sake of amusement or gentle ridicule; the copied work's language, style, characters, plot, or theme can be mimicked.

Example: This humorous imitation of the plot in Edgar Allan Poe's gothic story "The Fall of the House of Usher" is a poem by Reed Whittemore:

"It was big boxy wreck of a house
Owned by a classmate of mine named Rod Usher,
Who lived in the thing with his twin sister.
He was a louse and she was a souse."

Sources

Arnold, Tedd. *Ollie Forgot.* New York: Dial, 1988.
Ollie's rather unreliable memory, which loses whatever he has in mind whenever he hears something new, gets him into all kinds of trouble on the way to the market.

Examples:
In this medieval version of the cumulative Epaminondas folktale, Ollie starts with his mother's original admonition to go to market to buy "a joint of beef, a wedge of cheese, a loaf of bread too, if you please." He forgets this when it begins to rain. An old rhyme pops into his head: "Rain, rain, go away. Come again another day." A farmer hears him and is angry because rain is desired for his crops. He shouts at the boy, "I hope it rains a long, long while, and as it rains I'll sing and smile." This unfortunate chant is heard by a homeowner whose house is being flooded. And so it goes as he manages to enrage everyone he meets. Eventually luck is with him and he stumbles upon the beef, cheese, and bread Mother wanted—if only he can recall the way home now.

Other Devices:
Paradox

Berson, Harold. *Charles and Claudine.* New York: Macmillan, 1980.
The witch Grisnel helps Charles, a handsome young man, and Claudine, an exquisite little frog, overcome their differences and live happily ever after.

Examples:
Rather than be separated from his friend, the young man, in this reversal of the "Frog Prince" tale, decides to be changed into a frog to enjoy life in frog world.

Cole, Babette. *Prince Cinders.* New York: G.P. Putnam's Sons 1987.
A fairy grants a small skinny prince a change in appearance and the chance to go to the palace disco.

Examples:
Like Cinderella, teasing siblings make the younger child a slave to their needs while they go off to have fun. Prince Cinders has a visit from a dirty fairy who gets the magic all wrong. He accidentally frightens a princess by his changed appearance. When the clock strikes 12 and he becomes himself again, the princess thinks he frightened away the other fellow. Her shy hero loses his pants as he flees. She has them tried on all the eligible princes until she is united happily every after with Prince Cinders.

Other Devices:
Poetic Justice

Cole, Brock. *The Giant's Toe.* New York: Farrar, Strauss, & Giroux, 1986.
A giant chops off his toe while hoeing cabbages in his garden. The toe meddles in his affairs, but each time he tries to dispose of it, it manages to outwit him, until one day the toe saves him from Jack the giant killer.

Examples:
The "toe" inadvertently bakes into a pie the hen that laid the golden eggs and throws away the golden harp that sings and plays by itself. But all turns out well when the "toe" also saves the giant from being chopped up by *Jack the Giant Killer,* the tale from which these incidents are borrowed.

French, Fiona. *Snow White in New York.* Oxford: Oxford University Press, 1986.
A modern version of the "Snow White" story.

Examples:
Stepmother is queen of the underworld. She likes to see herself in the *New York Mirror* newspaper until she reads about Snow White and begins plotting her demise. Snow White is taken by goons to the inner city and abandoned. She finds seven jazzmen and sings in their club. A news reporter sees her and writes about her admiringly in the *Mirror.* Stepmother plots her death with a poisoned cherry in a cocktail. As the jazzmen carry her coffin up church steps, the cherry is dislodged from her throat and she opens her eyes to see the reporter, who marries her and takes her on a cruise.

Gammell, Stephen. *Once Upon MacDonald's Farm.* New York: Four Winds Press, 1981.
In this version of "Old McDonald's Farm," the farmer had no animals so he got some: an elephant, a baboon, and a lion. He put them to farm chores, but they didn't plow well or provide eggs, and they ran away. A neighbor gave him proper farm animals: a cow, horse, and chicken. However, Mac-

Donald is not likely to fare any better this time, since the closing picture shows him hitching the chicken to a plow.

Other Devices:
Inference

Garfield, Leon. *King Nimrod's Tower.* Illus. by Michael Bragg. New York: Lothrop, Lee, & Shepard, 1982.
This is a play on the biblical "Tower of Babel" story but places a boy who is trying to make friends with a stray puppy in the foreground of the story. God is more interested in them than in the effrontery of King Nimrod and his tower. To avoid harming the boy and dog, God mixes languages instead of casting down the tower.

Other Devices:
Aphorism

Kellogg, Steven. *Chicken Little.* New York: William Morrow, 1985.
The traditional characters are alarmed that the sky is falling and are easy prey for the fox who poses as a police officer in hopes of tricking them into his truck. He doesn't count on a patrol helicopter.

Other Devices:
Alliteration

Lorenz, Lee. *Big Gus and Little Gus.* Englewood Cliffs, NJ: Prentice-Hall, 1982.
When two friends go out into the world to seek their fortune, Big Gus is rewarded despite his foolishness.

Examples:
As in the cumulative tales of "Epaminondas" and "Lazy Jack," a dreamy dull-witted character always follows precisely all the advice he is given regardless of how unsuitable it may be. Little Gus is "full of schemes for getting rich." Big Gus "was just big." While Little Gus works on plans, Big Gus earns wages on which they can live. Big Gus receives goods for his wages and manages to carry them home in inappropriate ways. On the day that he carries a donkey home on his back, a rich girl, unable to talk, sees him and bursts out laughing. Her father is grateful to him for curing her and invites Big Gus to come live with them. Little Gus comes along because "he probably could use someone like me to manage his affairs."

Other Devices:
Poetic Justice; Understatement

Marshall, James. *Red Riding Hood.* New York: Dial, 1987.
Embellished familiar tale has irreverent flourishes.

Examples:
Red Riding Hood's mother says, "Granny isn't feeling up to snuff today." The wolf says to himself when he meets Red Riding Hood in the woods, "No reason why I can't eat them both." He asks to escort her to Granny's: "You're too kind," she responds. When the wolf meets Granny she says, "Get out of here, you horrid thing!" As Red Riding Hood comes to the door, the wolf says, "Here comes dessert." After gobbling up his victims, "having enjoyed such a heavy meal, he was soon snoring away." When the hunter rescues them, Granny says, "It was so dark in there I couldn't read a word."

Martin, Rafe. *Foolish Rabbit's Big Mistake.* Illus. by Ed Young. New York: G.P. Putnam's Sons, 1985.
This is a jungle version of "Chicken Little."

Examples:
". . .a foolish thought crossed his mind. What if the earth broke up?. . . Crash! He heard a loud sound behind him. . . 'The earth is breaking up!'" Soon the foolish rabbit has panicked several other gullible jungle animals into believing him. They race madly in fear until a lion forces them to investigate the truth of the incident. A falling apple from the apple tree has been the cause of the fright. The angry animals want to tear the rabbit to

pieces until the lion explains with a roar how they contributed to the madness. The rabbit sighs contentedly and munches the apple.

Other Devices:
Aphorism

Myers, Bernice. *Sidney Rella and the Glass Sneaker.* New York: Macmillan, 1985.
In this humorous twist on the "Cinderella" story, Sidney Rella becomes a football player with a little help from his fairy godfather.

Other Devices:
Pun

Pinkwater, Daniel. *Ducks!* Boston: Little, Brown, 1984.
In a candy store, a boy encounters a duck who claims to be an angel and, in return for granting it its freedom, endures some bizarre adventures with a chariot and other duck angels. A parody of Greek myths.

Other Devices:
Satire

Ross, Tony. *The Three Pigs.* New York: Pantheon Books, 1982.
Three little pigs leave a cramped high-rise apartment in the city to seek their fortune in the country.

Examples:
When the wolf finally comes down the brick chimney and lands in the pot of boiling water, the pig "gobbled the wolf up with some asparagus tips and potato puffs." With the wolf gone "more and more people moved from their apartments and built houses around Pig's house. . . . Sometimes it feels like I am back on the 39th floor," he says.

Other Devices:
Pun

Rounds, Glen. *Washday on Noah's Ark.* New York: Holiday House, 1985.
When the forty-first day on the ark dawns bright and clear, Mrs. Noah decides to do the wash and, having no rope long enough, devises an ingenious clothesline. This spoof on the biblical story reflects what life with the animals may have been like.

Other Devices:
Caricature

Turkle, Brinton. *Do Not Open.* New York: E.P. Dutton, 1981.
Living by the sea an old woman and her cat find an intriguing bottle washed up on the beach after a storm. They ignore the warning on it, "Do not open."

Examples:
An old woman is tricked by an evil genie in a bottle into releasing it. Fortunately, she exhibits the presence of mind to render it ineffective before it goes to "work" starting "a nice little war." She tells the genie that she fears only mice. Of course the genie changes into a mouse to frighten her, but her cat pounces so quickly "it didn't have time to squeak." When the woman asks her cat if he is ok, he "burps contentedly." A parody on the traditional "genie in a bottle" story.

Vesey, A. *The Princess and the Frog.* Boston: The Atlantic Monthly Press, 1985.
Set in a European court in the early 1900s, this story is about a frog who retrieves a princess's ball and is invited by the scheming mother to live at the palace, where she is sure he will turn into the handsome prince for her daughter. The frog remains a frog and is a demanding guest besides. Even kissing him fails to do the trick. Instead, he announces that he is already married and plans to move his children into the palace, too. A parody on the traditional "frog turns into a prince" story.

PERSONIFICATION

A figure of speech that assigns human qualities, actions, characteristics, or personality to an animal, an object, a natural force, or an idea.

Example: The two stores held a tête-à-tête across Main Street.

Sources

Bunting, Eve. *Ghost's Hour, Spook's Hour.* Illus. by Donald Carrick. New York: Ticknor & Fields, 1987.
Scary incidents at midnight give Biff the dog and his master a frightening time, but all turn out to have good explanations.

Examples:
"Our table seemed monstrously big. Chairs, humpbacked, clawed and crouched around it."

Other Devices:
Imagery

Carrick, Carol. *Dark and Full of Secrets.* Illus. by Donald Carrick. New York: Clarion Books, 1984.
A boy's first tentative experiences with pond life are described.

Examples:
In text and pictures, the shore cedar trees are described as having drowned and fallen into the water.

Other Devices:
Foreshadow; Imagery; Simile

Cole, Brock. *The Winter Wren.* New York: Farrar, Straus, & Giroux, 1984.
Two children set out to find spring because winter is hanging on too long.

Examples:
Spring was "a princess dressed all in green and gold"; "Spring's asleep at Winter's farm and can't wake up"; "Winter, striding back and forth over his field, sowing the earth with sleet"; "He gave a great roar and threw a handful of ice;" "Green spikes prickled and tickled Old Winter's toes so that he danced and stamped."

Other Devices:
Alliteration; Foreshadow; Imagery; Simile

Gedin, Birgitta. *The Little House from the Sea.* Illus. by Petter Pettersson. Trans. by Elisabeth Dyssegaard. New York: Farrar, Straus, & Giroux, 1988.
A little house on a rocky island never moves but longs to be a ship that can travel over the ocean to see the Other Side.

Examples:
". . . thought the little house angrily. . . closed its eyes. . . remembered almost nothing from its early years." Bird and wind also exhibit human traits.

Other Devices:
Aphorism; Paradox

Goble, Paul. *Death of the Iron Horse.* New York: Bradbury Press, 1987.
In an act of bravery and defiance against the white men encroaching on their territory in 1867, a group of young Cheyenne braves derail and raid a freight train.

Examples:
The Indians ascribe living traits to the locomotive: it pants and screams and hisses. They shoot arrows at it and try to throw a rope over it.

Other Devices:
Foreshadow; Point of View

Goffstein, M.B. *Artists' Helpers Enjoy the Evenings.* New York: Harper & Row, 1987.
When daylight fades, the artists' helpers go out to dinner and a masquerade ball to enjoy themselves.

Examples:
Crayons pursue a lifestyle after their working hours not unlike their human counterparts. They chat business at a cafe, sing about their job, have interesting large families, go to each other's homes as dinner guests, and party.

Kennedy, Richard. *Song of the Horse.* Illus. by Marcia Sewall. New York: E.P. Dutton, 1981.
Girl describes her ride on her horse.

Examples:
"Fence posts are struck dumb by our speed;" "Sheep argue our existence;" "Chickens think we're supernatural;" "Dust tells stories of our passing."

Other Devices:
Imagery; Inference; Point of View; Simile; Tone; Understatement

McKissack, Patricia. *Flossie and the Fox.* Illus. by Rachel Isadora. New York: Dial, 1986.
A wily fox, notorious for stealing eggs, meets his match when he encounters a bold little girl in the woods who insists upon proof that he is a fox before she will be frightened. This is an excellent book to read aloud!

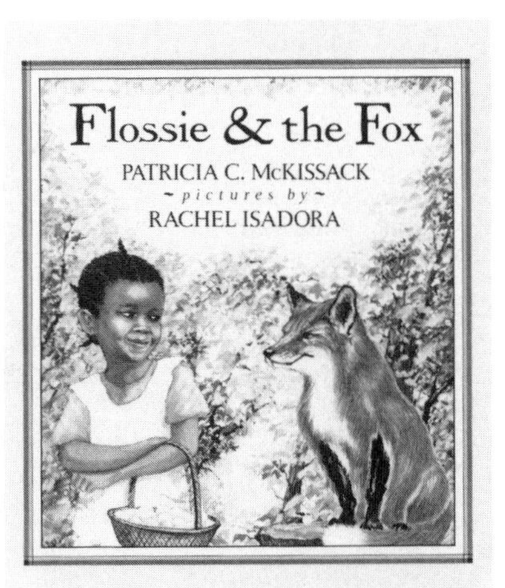

Examples:
Fox speaks like a well-bred human as he deals with Flossie, the little girl. "My dear child. . . of course I'm a fox. A little girl like you should be simply terrified of me. Whatever do they teach children these days?"

Other Devices:
Poetic Justice; Pun

Parnall, Peter. *Apple Tree.* New York: Macmillan, 1987.
Describes the many ways an apple tree interacts with insects, birds, and other animals during a full year of its development.

Examples:
Apple tree is accorded human characteristics: "Cold finally got into their bones"; "winds tear at the fingertips of our old brittle tree"; "snow finally comes, burying. . . beneath its cloak. . . ."

Other Devices:
Imagery; Simile

Parnall, Peter. *Winter Barn.* New York: Macmillan, 1986.
A dilapidated old barn shelters a wide variety of animals during the sub-zero winter temperatures in Maine while they wait for the first signs of spring.

Examples:
"Icy breeze that darts through cracks and holes"; "wooden fibers wince and complain. . . they play their own music"; "The barn sings its own songs"; "An old cracked board has been a friend"; "new ice will steal the chance"; "arms of the winter barn"; "great sockets that hold together the barn's huge bones."

Other Devices:
Atmosphere; Imagery; Simile

Skofield, James. *All Wet! All Wet!* Illus. by Diane Stanley. New York: Harper & Row, 1984.
A child's walk on a rainy summer day is described.

Examples:
Whispering rain; thunder roars its name; sleeping meadow; crows' scolding taunts; skunk dreams of suppertime; green-deep voice of summer night.

Other Devices:
Simile

Snyder, Zilpha Keatley. *The Changing Maze.* Illus. by Charles Mikolaycak. New York: Macmillan, 1985.
A shepherd boy braves the evil magic of a wizard's maze to save his pet lamb.

Examples:
Lost winds sigh and worry; gray stones weep.

Other Devices:
Aphorism; Atmosphere; Flash-forward; Imagery; Inference; Symbol

Steig, William. *Yellow & Pink.* New York: Farrar, Straus, & Giroux, 1984.
Two wooden marionettes lying on a newspaper begin to speculate about how they came to be and invent a logical story for their existence which is, nevertheless, quite wrong.

Examples:
"It was hot and quiet, and they were both wondering." They question, they think, they argue. When the man who made them picks them up they ask each other, "Who is this guy?"

Other Devices:
Analogy; Satire

Tennyson, Noel. *The Lady's Chair and the Ottoman.* New York: Lothrop, Lee, & Shepard, 1987.
An ottoman has spent as long as he can remember trying to get close to a lady's chair, and though fortune separates them and they seem to come to unhappy ends, a marvelous coincidence reunites them in a very happy way.

Other Devices:
Allusion; Pun; Simile

POETIC JUSTICE

An outcome to a situation in which vice is punished and virtue is rewarded, usually in a manner appropriate to the situation.

Example: A bunch of hungry animals, each bent upon eating the one beneath him in strength and size, are all frightened away from their purpose by an army of tiny red ants whom everyone had ignored until these ants spoil their opportunity for a snack.

Sources

Allen, Jeffrey. *Nosey Mrs. Rat.* Illus. by James Marshall. New York: Viking Kestrel, 1985.

Mrs. Rat makes a career out of spying on her neighbors, but the tables are unexpectedly turned on her.

Examples:
After spying on all her neighbors, Shirley ends up watching a movie of herself spying as all her neighbors witness her humiliation.

Other Devices:
Inference; Understatement

Blaustein, Muriel. *Lola Koala and the Ten Times Worse Than Anything.* New York: Harper & Row, 1987.

Two sisters realize they can be brave about different things when Lola, the younger sister, is timid about scary movies and high places and her big sister is terrified of amusement park rides.

Examples:
The older sister chides the younger one for her fear of ordinary experiences and teases her about how she'll act when they go to the amusement park. Once there, the younger girl breezes through the rides while the older sister experiences terror.

Browne, Anthony. *Look What I've Got!* New York: Knopf, 1980.

Jeremy keeps trying to impress Sam by boasting about all his belongings and activities, but on each occasion, it's Sam who comes out on top with the last word and the last laugh.

Other Devices:
Satire

Bunting, Eve. *The Man Who Could Call Down Owls.* Illus. by Charles Mikolaycak. New York: Macmillan, 1984.

A stranger, thinking he can call down owls by wearing the owl caller's clothing, kills the owl caller and tries to assume his position. But the very creatures who responded lovingly to the owl caller turn on the interloper and drive him off, just as he turned on the owl caller.

Other Devices:
Atmosphere; Foreshadow; Simile; Symbol; Theme

Burningham, John. *John Patrick Norman McHennessy: The Boy Who Was Always Late.* New York: Crown, 1987.

A teacher comes to regret his decision to disbelieve a student's outlandish excuses for being tardy.

Examples:
After being late because of a crocodile, a lion, and a tidal wave, and being punished for those excuses, a boy comes to school on time one day to find the teacher being held up to the roof by a big hairy gorilla, at which point the boy reminds his teacher there are no such creatures around here. Then he walks away.

Other Devices:
Irony

Cazet, Denys. *Lucky Me.* New York: Bradbury Press, 1983.

Beginning with the lucky chicken who finds a donut, each subsequent animal feels he's found a tasty morsel until the army of red ants spoils everyone's "snack."

Examples:
The attempt to eat animals smaller than themselves is muffed when the smallest animal of all drives all of them off.

Cole, Babette. *Prince Cinders.* New York: G.P. Putnam's Sons, 1987.
A fairy grants a small skinny prince a change in appearance and the chance to go to the palace disco.

Examples:
The mean brothers, who had kept Prince Cinders slaving to clean up their messes, are turned into house fairies who must forever flit around the palace doing housework.

Other Devices:
Parody

Demi. *Chen Ping and His Magic Axe.* New York: Dodd, Mead, 1987.
Chen Ping's honesty in his encounter with a stranger causes his axe to acquire magic powers, while his greedy master's attempt to reap the same reward comes to a different end.

Other Devices:
Atmosphere

Hutchins, Pat. *One-Eyed Jake.* New York: Greenwillow Books, 1979.
A greedy pirate who overfills his ship with the spoils of war must lighten the load or lose his ill-gotten gains.

Examples:
To relieve the boat of weight, the pirate throws overboard his various crew members who are actually delighted to leave his employ and go where their talents can be better appreciated. Jake, the pirate, also gets his appropriate "reward."

Kroll, Steven. *Friday the 13th.* Illus. by Dick Gackenbach. New York: Holiday House, 1981.
Unlucky Harold's tidy sister constantly chides him for being a walking disaster. On Friday the 13th she gets her just reward by ending up making a mess to match any that Harold ever made.

Lorenz, Lee. *Big Gus and Little Gus.* Englewood Cliffs, NJ: Prentice-Hall, 1982.
Big Gus, who did all the work while Little Gus schemed money-making ideas, gets to marry the rich princess.

Other Devices:
Parody; Understatement

Low, Joseph. *Mice Twice.* New York: Atheneum, 1980.
Each animal invited by the next smaller one to be a "dinner guest" expects to feast on his host, but each is foiled in his desire by a worse threat to himself. In the end, the mouse enjoys a fine meal unhampered by anyone trying to eat him by inviting the most menacing guest of all.

Other Devices:
Inference; Irony

McKissack, Patricia. *Flossie and the Fox.* Illus. by Rachel Isadora. New York: Dial, 1986.
A wily fox, notorious for stealing eggs, meets his match when he encounters a bold little girl in the woods who insists upon proof that he is a fox before she will be frightened.

Examples:
The fox spends so much effort trying to convince Flossie that he is a fox and should be feared that he neglects to be cautious. Flossie tells him, "There's one of Mr. J.W. McCutchin's hounds behind you. He's got sharp teeth and can run fast too."

Other Devices:
Personification; Pun

Marshall, James. *The Cut-Ups.* New York: Viking Kestrel, 1984.
Two practical jokers get away with every trick in the book until Mr. Spurgle, the man whose flower bed they destroy, turns out to be their school principal in the fall, and he never forgets a face.

Other Devices:
Inference; Tone

Snyder, Dianne. *The Boy of the Three-Year Nap.* Illus. by Allen Say. Boston: Houghton Mifflin Co., 1988.
A poor Japanese woman maneuvers events to change the lazy habits of her son.

Examples:
The boy connives to engineer marriage to a rich man's daughter. His mother does some conniving too so that along with the marriage will come a job for her lazy son.

Other Devices:
Inference

Stevens, Kathleen. *Molly McCullough and Tom the Rogue.* Illus. by Margot Zemach. New York: Thomas Crowell, 1982.
Tom Devlin roams the countryside, charming the farmers' wives and tricking the farmers out of fruits and vegetables until he meets his match in a plain-faced, sharp-tongued, farmer's daughter.

Examples:
The clever trickster himself gets tricked out of his bonus vegetables and into marrying the one who bested him at his own game.

Other Devices:
Aphorism; Foreshadow; Irony; Theme

POINT OF VIEW

The perspective from which the story is seen and told; three principal vantage points are most commonly employed.

Omniscient. Ability to see into minds and record thoughts of characters and make comments about either one or several of them so that the reader may come to know more of their situation than does any single character in it.

Example: George, anxiously hoping that no one was watching him, placed a carefully wrapped package on an empty park bench. But Molly, who was walking home, saw him and couldn't help thinking that he was acting strangely.

Third Person. Central observer of the story who limits interpretation to what is seen or heard without additional comment about character motive or thoughts; thus limits the knowledge available to the reader.

Example: As George placed the carefully wrapped package on the park bench, he looked up and saw Molly walking across the street.

First Person. View and thoughts solely through one character telling the story, (I); can only reveal what the character sees and is told by others.

Example: As I placed the carefully wrapped package on the park bench, I looked up and saw Molly walking across the street. I hoped that she hadn't seen me.

Sources

Blegvad, Lenore. *Anna Banana and Me.* Illus. by Erik Blegvad. New York: Atheneum, 1985.

Anna Banana's fearlessness inspires a playmate to face his own fears.

Examples:

Without explanatory comment, the first-person narrator gets across his female friend's intrepidness as well as his own sensitivity and timidness as the two explore a city park together.

Other Devices:

Stereotype/Reverse Stereotype; Theme; Tone

Brighton, Catherine. *Five Secrets in a Box.* New York: E.P. Dutton, 1987.

Galileo's small daughter simply relates the magical world she observes in her father's scientific lab. There are good accurate pictures of Renaissance life here. Older students familiar with Galileo's work will benefit from the information shown.

Examples:

The child's perspective is conveyed through her comments about the magnifying glass, the telescopic glass, the glass filter, and her father's experiments in weight and gravity. She says, "One piece makes things bigger. . . . I hold the first piece next to the second. The countryside comes toward me. . . . The world turns to night." When she wakes her father, "his book slips to the floor. The feather floats after it. He says the feather is important to his work."

Other Devices:

Allusion; Inference

Cohen, Barbara. *Gooseberries to Oranges.* Illus. by Beverly Brodsky. New York: Lothrop, Lee, & Shepard, 1982.

A young girl reminisces about the journey from her cholera-ravaged village in Russia to the U.S., where she is reunited with her father.

Examples:

History is seen as an intensely personal series of events. Events are interpreted by an eight-year-old girl: the trip to America and the strange city life in New York as well as the reasons behind the need for the trip to a new land. See also Riki Levinson's *Watch the Stars Come Out.*

Other Devices:

Inference; Symbol

Dunrea, Olivier. *Eddy B., Pigboy.* New York: Atheneum, 1983.

After mama pig wanders off to have her babies, it is Eddy B's job to find them and bring them safely back to the pigsty on his father's farm.

Examples:

The direct and easy-to-follow pictures and text show simply how a boy goes about his chores and how he's paid.

Edwards, Linda Strauss. *The Downtown Day.* New York: Pantheon Books, 1983.

Linda describes her day shopping for school clothes with her two tiresome aunts. Her record shows the teasing that goes on between the three and the family love and understanding as well.

Goble, Paul. *Death of the Iron Horse.* New York: Bradbury Press, 1987.

In an act of bravery and defiance against the white men encroaching on their territory in 1867, a group of young Cheyenne braves derail and raid a freight train.

Examples:

The Indians speculate about what kind of creature "Iron Horse" could be and the trail it has left. They hack apart the iron bands binding Mother Earth to set her free. They gallop up to the steam engine, and it chases them with belches of black smoke and screams and hisses. They try to lasso it and shoot arrows into it. After it jumps track they check out the contents of the wagons. They take coins to use in necklaces but toss the useless green paper bits into the air.

Other Devices:
Foreshadow; Personification

Guthrie, Donna. *The Witch Who Lives Down the Hall.* Illus. by Amy Schwartz. San Diego, CA: Harcourt Brace Jovanovich, 1985.
A child narrates the activities of the "witch" neighbor; the pictures and mother's explanations are juxtaposed with his own interpretation of events. The reader sees the truth of mother's views until the last page casts a doubt on all things logical.

Innocenti, Roberto. *Rose Blanche.* Mankato, MN: Creative Education, 1985.
Matter-of-fact reporting of the effect upon one German village and one little girl living there during World War II.

Examples:
The story begins in first-person narration. "My name is Rose Blanche. I live in a small town in Germany with narrow streets. . . ." But in the middle of the story, the narration style switches to third person because the child does not survive. " Rose Blanche was getting thinner. . . Rose Blanche hid her food in her school bag and sneaked out of school early."

Other Devices:
Atmosphere; Inference; Symbol; Tone

Kennedy, Richard. *Song of the Horse.* Illus. by Marcia Sewall. New York: E.P. Dutton, 1981.
A girl's poetic view of her horse and her passionate riding experience puts thoughts into her horse's mind as well as reactions from farm animals, clouds, fence posts, birds, and other non-human objects.

Other Devices:
Imagery; Inference; Personification; Simile; Tone; Understatement

Mattingley, Christobel. *The Angel with a Mouth-Organ.* Illus. by Astra Lacie. New York: Holiday House, 1986.
Just before the glass angel is put on the Christmas tree, Mother describes her experiences as a little girl during World War II when she and her family were refugees.

Examples:
Mother's narration is through her view as a child. She reports but does not judge. When a spray of bullets from a plane sent the family to cover, she says, "My father pushed us into a ditch. Me and my doll. My sister on top. My mother on her. I felt the breath go out of me and my doll squeaked as Father threw himself across my mother. The cuckoo clock called, but I couldn't laugh because my mouth was full of doll's hair."

Other Devices:
Flashback; Inference; Metaphor; Understatement

Mayne, William. *The Patchwork Cat.* Illus. by Nicola Bayley. New York: Knopf, 1981.
A cat braves frightening experiences to retrieve her favorite sleeping quilt, which her mistress has unthinkingly decided to throw away.

Other Devices:
Alliteration; Metaphor

Nesbit, E. *The Town in the Library.* Illus. by Shirley Tourret. New York: Dial, 1988.
Playing in the library in their home, Rosamund and Fabian build a huge town out of books only to find themselves trapped when they go inside.

Examples:
Third person narrative style is personalized by the author's occasional asides to her readers. As she describes the furnishings in the house, she

says, "Perhaps you don't know what a bureau is—children learn very little at school nowadays, so I will tell you. . . . "

Parker, Nancy Winslow. *Poofy Loves Company.* New York: Dodd, Mead, 1980.
Sally is overwhelmed by a large, over-friendly dog when she and her mother visit a friend for afternoon tea.

Examples:
The text is a monologue by the hostess. Her comments are contrasted, humorously, with what is happening in the illustrations. When she gives Sally a cookie for herself and a puppy biscuit to give to Poofy, she says, "Hold the cookie up, Sally! Oh well, Poofy loves cookies." The pictures show Poofy has tackled Sally, is holding her down, and walks off with the cookie in his mouth.

Petroski, Catherine. *Beautiful My Mane in the Wind.* Illus. by Robert Andrew Parker. Boston: Houghton, Mifflin Co., 1983.
Imagining herself to be a horse, a young girl escapes from the loneliness and frustrations of everyday life into the smooth green windy world of horses.

Examples:
Girl describes her behavior as a horse and why she prefers being a Mustang to being a "girlygirl."

Rogers, Paul. *From Me to You.* Illus. by Jane Johnson. New York: Orchard Books, Franklin Watts, 1987.
A grandmother shares her memories of three generations with a young granddaughter and presents her with a precious gift.

Other Devices:
Atmosphere; Inference; Theme

Ryder, Joanne. *The Snail's Spell.* Illus. by Lynne Cherry. New York: Frederick Warne, 1982.
The reader is invited to imagine how it feels to be a snail.

Examples:
"Imagine you are soft and have no bones inside you. . . . You are soft and small and slow gliding up and down and upside down." Pictures illustrate size perspective in this imaginative journey.

Say, Allen. *The Bicycle Man.* Boston: Houghton, Mifflin Co., 1982.
The amazing tricks two American soldiers perform on a borrowed bicycle are a fitting finale for the school sports day festivities in a small rural Japanese village after World War II.

Examples:
The narrator, a Japanese student, describes the peculiar-looking Americans from an uncommon perspective.

Other Devices:
Simile

Schwartz, Amy. *Her Majesty, Aunt Essie.* Scarsdale, New York: Bradbury Press, 1984.
A little girl makes a bet with her friend that her Aunt Essie is really a queen because her behavior is so 'Imperial.' Everything works to indicate the truth of her belief but doesn't prove it definitively until the evening of Aunt Essie's date.

Examples:
"She was wearing a long satin gown. She had a fur stole over her shoulders. She was wearing those long dangling earrings, and—you can have everything I own, if I'm lying—there was a gold crown on her head." The reader sees a gaudy hair band.

Other Devices:
Inference

Talbott, Hudson. *We're Back! A Dinosaur's Story.* New York: Crown, 1987.
In this very funny picture book, creatures from prehistoric time travel to the twentieth century and create excitement at New York's Museum of Natural History.

Examples:
The confusion of being plunked down in a strange environment is expressed humorously by Rex the dinosaur, who only wants to ask a friend where to get a bite to eat.

Other Devices:
Allusion; Tone; Understatement

Willis, Jeanne. *Earthlets as Explained by Professor Xargle.* Illus. by Tony Ross. New York: E.P. Dutton, 1989.
A professor on another planet lectures his class about the nature of earth babies before they put on their human disguises for their spaceship field trip to earth.

Examples:
"Earthlets are born without fangs. At first, they drink only milk through a hole in their faces called a mouth. When they finish the milk, they are patted and squeezed so they won't explode."

PUN

A humorous use of a word or phrase to suggest two or more meanings at the same time; involves three kinds of word play.

1. Words spelled or pronounced the same but with different meanings.

   Example: "Now we must all *hang* together or we will surely *hang* separately." —Ben Franklin (If the revolutionaries did not remain united, their individual lives would be in danger.)

2. Words based on homonyms.
   Example:
   lone/loan

3. Words based on close similarities in sound or meaning.
   Example: Teacher to Child: You're a disturbing element today, Mike.
   Child to Mother: She called me a scurvy elephant today!

Sources

Agee, Jon. *The Incredible Painting of Felix Clousseau.* New York: Farrar, Straus, & Giroux, 1988.
Who would dare enter a portrait of a duck in the Grand Contest of Art? But when the painting quacks, Clousseau is hailed a genius. And that is only half of it.

Examples:
Felix Clousseau's paintings are alive with excitement. When the story concludes, Clousseau goes back to his studio and "returns to his painting." The illustration shows him physically walking into a framed painting.

Other Devices:
Foreshadow

Allard, Harry. *Miss Nelson Has a Field Day.* Illus. by James Marshall. Boston: Houghton, Mifflin Co., 1985.
The notorious Miss Swamp reappears at the Horace B. Smedley School, this time to shape up the football team and make them win at least one game.

Examples:
The term "field day"in the title refers to Viola Swamp's fun whipping the mediocre football team into shape. The wimpy principal is Mr. *Blands*worth. The team's fullback tried to "pussy foot" (take mincing steps) away as the Swamp slammed him with a thunderous tackle."

Other Devices:
Foreshadow; Inference; Understatement

Berger, Barbara Helen. *When the Sun Rose.* New York: Philomel Books, 1986.
An imaginative little girl spends a happy day with her playmate who arrives with a pet lion.

Examples:
The sun "rose" on a special day in the life of a little girl whose pleasure is accompanied by the rose motif throughout: a huge yellow cabbage rose of a rising sun, a carriage shaped like a rose, her new friend's dress of huge roses, and finally the roses that lay scattered on the playroom floor after the friend leaves.

Other Devices:
Atmosphere; Symbol

Blos, Joan. *Martin's Hats.* Illus. by Marc Simont. New York: William Morrow, 1984.
A variety of hats affords an imaginative boy many play experiences.

Examples:
At the end of his busy day, he goes to his room and finds on his bedpost one last appropriate cap to top off his day fittingly, a nightcap.

Hearn, Michael Patrick. *The Porcelain Cat.* Illus. by Leo and Diane Dillon. Boston: Little, Brown, 1987.
A sorcerer's apprentice has to complete several difficult tasks before dawn in order to obtain a missing ingredient for one of his master's spells.

Examples:
An insensitive sorcerer rouses his sleeping apprentice to fetch a "*vial* of basilisk blood this very instant." The drowsy boy wants to say something about how "*vile*" he thinks the request is!

Other Devices:
Allusion; Irony

Kellogg, Steven. *A Rose for Pinkerton.* New York: Dial, 1981.
The title implies that this dog will receive a flower. The "Rose" he receives turns out to be a kitten by that name.

Other Devices:
Stereotype/Reverse Stereotype

Kraus, Robert. *Another Mouse to Feed.* Illus. by Jose Aruego and Ariane Dewey. New York: Windmill Wanderer, 1980.
Mr. and Mrs. Mouse, exhausted from overwork, are invited to rest as their 31 children take over.

Examples:
The play on "mouth/mouse" is made in the book's title.

Lindbergh, Anne. *Next Time, Take Care.* Illus. by Susan Hoguet. San Diego, CA: Harcourt Brace Jovanovich, 1988.
While making friends outdoors, Ralph manages to lose all the caps made for him by his constantly knitting Aunt Millicent.

Examples:
"How do *you do*" said Ralph when he arrived. "It's how *you do* that counts," said Millicent Meeker. Ralph is merely making a polite customary

greeting. The no-nonsense Millicent refers directly to his expected good conduct while he visits.

Other Devices:
Aphorism; Foreshadow; Inference; Stereotype

McAfee, Annalena. *The Visitors Who Came to Stay.* Illus. by Anthony Browne. New York: Viking Kestrel, 1984.
A young girl's simple world is invaded by her father's lady friend and her son.

Examples:
Visual puns, somewhat surrealistic, literally illustrate a bed with tulips growing in it; fried eggs on a stalk which compose an "egg" plant; a bathtub with birds soaking in a "bird bath"; a man's smoking pipe poking out of a roof chimney; a carpenter's nail among regular fingernails on a Halloween monster's rubber hand gag; "ears" listening at a wall.

Other Devices:
Atmosphere; Paradox

Macaulay, David. *Why the Chicken Crossed the Road.* Boston: Houghton Mifflin Co., 1987.
By crossing the road a chicken sets off a series of wild reactions which eventually return full circle. At the end, it seems the chicken will repeat it all.

Examples:
Names of story characters are a play on their behavior or occupation. Mel Toom, the garbage collector, throws trash into the "tomb" of his closed vehicle. Lulu Thump, the retired teacher, "thumps" people with her cane to improve their behavior. Officer Goode is the "good" guy who captures thieves.

Other Devices:
Flashback; Inference; Understatement

McKissack, Patricia. *Flossie and the Fox.* Illus. by Rachel Isadora. New York: Dial, 1986.
A wily fox notorious for stealing eggs meets his match when he encounters a bold little girl in the woods who insists upon proof that he is a fox before she will be frightened.

Examples:
Says the fox "I may never recover my confidence." Says Flossie: "That's just what I been saying. You just an ol' confidencer." Flossie is deliberately twisting the meaning of "confidence" as she chides the fox his penchant for swindling.

Other Devices:
Personification; Poetic Justice

Meddaugh, Susan. *Maude and Claude Go Aboard.* Boston: Houghton Mifflin Co., 1980.
Two young foxes travel alone on a ship to visit relatives far away. On their journey they save a whale from harpooners.

Examples:
The two foxes are going to visit Phox-En-Ville in France.

Other Devices:
Theme

Miller, Moira. *The Proverbial Mouse.* Illus. by Ian Deuchar. New York: Dial, 1987.
During his nightly quests for food in a toy shop, a hungry mouse learns a number of proverbs from the toys and eventually devises one himself for the cat that tries to catch him.

Examples:
The mouse in this story, as the title suggests, is the object of a number of proverbs. In one instance, he thinks he sees a suger-iced cake but finds,

instead, that it is a drum. He is told, "You cannot have your cake and *beat* it," a slight play on a familiar proverb.

Other Devices:
Aphorism

Myers, Bernice. *Sidney Rella and the Glass Sneaker.* New York: Macmillan, 1985.
Sidney Rella becomes a football player with a little help from his fairy godfather.

Examples:
Sidney's fairy godfather misunderstands when Sidney states that he wants to play on the "football team." Godfather thinks that the wish is for a "milking machine." Sidney eventually becomes president of a large corporation that manufactures laces for footballs; on the wall is a plaque with "First Lace" on it. Fairy godfather was there to help Sidney go to the "ball": the foot"ball" tryouts.

Other Devices:
Parody

Peet, Bill. *No Such Things.* Boston: Houghton, Mifflin Co., 1983.
Describes in rhyme a variety of fantastic creatures such as the blue-snouted Twumps, pie-face Pazeeks, and the fancy Fandangos.

Examples:
Referring to weeds sprouting on their backs upon which young ones feed, the author says that the creatures support their young as both "fodder" and mother. Pie-face Pazeeks feed on cherries and are shaped like slices of cherry pie complete with fork feet. Each creature has a pun shape.

Other Devices:
Allusion; Paradox

Pomerantz, Charlotte. *The Half-Birthday.* Illus. by DyAnne DiSalvo-Ryan. New York: Clarion Books, 1984.
Daniel can't think of a *half*-gift for his little sister's six-month birthday until he spots the half moon outside his window and offers her that half moon. Mom asks him if he knew all along that was the gift he had planned for her. He says it is "*half*-true."

Other Devices:
Ambiguity

Ross, Tony. *The Three Pigs.* New York: Pantheon Books, 1983.
Three little pigs leave a cramped high-rise apartment in a city to seek their fortune in the country.

Examples:
The three pigs attempt to borrow money at the bank in order to buy a house; the manager refuses to loan them a penny. He tells them, "We're not a *piggy bank.*"

Other Devices:
Parody

Solotareff, Grégoire, *Never Trust an Ogre.* New York: Greenwillow Books, 1988.
A hungry, lazy ogre tries to trick the forest animals into coming over to his house for dinner.

Examples:
"He wants to *have us all for dinner.*" "I'll bet he does." The ogre intends to invite the forest animals not *to* his dinner but *as* his dinner.

Other Devices:
Inference

Stolz, Mary. *Storm in the Night.* Illus. by Pat Cummings. New York: Harper & Row, 1988.
While sitting through a fearsome thunderstorm that has put the lights out, Thomas hears a story from Grandfather's boyhood, when Grandfather was afraid of thunderstorms.

Examples:
Referring to both himself and his dog, Grandfather says, "When Melvin and I were pups together. . . . "

Other Devices:
Ambiguity; Hyperbole; Imagery; Inference; Simile

Tennyson, Noel. *The Lady's Chair and the Ottoman.* New York: Lothrop, Lee, & Shepard, 1987.
An ottoman has spent as long as he can remember trying to get close to a lady's chair, and though fortune separates them and they seem to come to unhappy ends, a marvelous coincidence reunites them in a very happy way.

Examples:
There is a "secretary" next to her, but the ottoman considers him a snoop because he was always taking "notes." Said the packing crate to the ottoman: "Get rid of those legs altogether, and you'll really be 'squared away.'"

Other Devices:
Allusion; Personification; Simile

Van Allsburg, Chris. *Jumanji.* Boston: Houghton, Mifflin Co., 1981.
Left on their own for an afternoon, two *bored* and restless children find more excitement than they bargained for in a mysterious and mystical jungle adventure *board* game.

Examples:
Here the situation is punned on: "bored" and "board."

Other Devices:
Inference

Wild, Jocelyn. *Florence and Eric Take the Cake.* New York: Dial, 1987.
A brother and sister lamb accidentally cause a major mix-up between a delicious cake and a beautiful hat.

Examples:
In the title is a play on words since the characters do pick up an actual cake as well as cause a situation of chaos.

Other Devices:
Allusion; Ambiguity

SATIRE

Act of criticizing or ridiculing weaknesses, characteristics, and wrongdoings of humans (clothing, fads, political problems, etc.), groups, and institutions; exaggerating faults for the purpose of showing how absurd they are. Can be in a tone of scorn, amusement or contempt to get across the point.

Sources

Browne, Anthony. *Look What I've Got!* New York: Knopf, 1980.
Jeremy keeps trying to impress Sam by boasting of all his belongings and activities, but it's always Sam who comes out on top with the last word and the last laugh.

Examples:
The author points out through Jeremy's selfishness that his posturing only results in his looking very foolish and not a bit enviable. Regardless of the amount of money financing his pleasures, wealth is no guarantee of happiness. It is his "have not" friend Sam who is able, without money, to appreciate some of life's more subtle rewards.

Other Devices:
Poetic Justice

Demarest, Chris L. *Morton and Sidney.* New York: Macmillan, 1987.
Sidney, one of the monsters who lives in Morton's closet, has been kicked out by the other monsters. Morton must figure out a scheme to get him reinstated so that at night everything will be back to normal.

Examples:
The fear of having monsters in one's closet has been much overdramatized. This story points out the worse trouble that can result from *not* having a monster in your closet.

Other Devices:
Irony

Gerrard, Roy. *The Favershams.* New York: Farrar, Straus, & Giroux, 1983.
Born more than 130 years ago in England, Charles Agustus Faversham's life is depicted in whimsical, Victorian style as he goes to school, joins the army, is wounded, meets wife Gwen, serves in India, and retires to become an author and family man.

Examples:
The heyday of the British empire, with allegiance to queen and country, regimental balls, large country houses, cultivation of stiff upper lip and appropriate convention, doggerel poetry and stumpy squat red and brown figures all serve to make the era laughable.

Keeping, Charles. *Sammy Streetsinger.* Oxford: Oxford University Press, 1984.
The foolish quest for stardom is examined from its humble beginnings, through its heights, into its inevitable decline, and finally back to its original state of happy simplicity, as the career of a rock star is catalogued.

Other Devices:
Atmosphere; Flashback

Kent, Jack. *Joey.* Englewood Cliffs, NJ: Prentice-Hall, 1984.
Parent and child relations are spoofed when a bored child gets permission to invite his friends over to play. Mrs. Kangaroo soon regrets her invitation.

Examples:
A careful, concerned parent, Mrs. Kangaroo suggests that her son invite his friends *here* to play rather than let him out of her pouch into the dangerous world where he might come to harm. The children's cacophonous racket finally forces her to fling the whole lot of them out. Good parenting becomes impossible to endure.

Morris, Winifred. *The Magic Leaf.* Illus. by Ju-Hong Chen. New York: Atheneum, 1987.
When a foolish man believes he has become invisible by possessing a magic leaf, he sneaks into the mayor's private garden to view the peonies.

Examples:
Those who put stock in their own brilliance and power because they are "scholars" who read large heavy books, or because they possess a fine sword, are brought to humility and reality soon enough.

Other Devices:
Aphorism; Paradox

Nixon, Joan Lowery. *Fat Chance, Claude.* Illus. by Tracey Campbell Pearson. New York: Viking Kestrel, 1987.
Two zany Texans, Shirley and Claude, grow up and meet out in the gold mining hills of Colorado.

Examples:
Claude works hard to send one brother to Havard and the other one to Yale. A few years after they graduate, they get so rich they no longer need to send their dirty laudry home to get it washed. When his mother remarries there are several new stepbrothers who are described as "bright and eager to learn." At this point, Claude suddenly sees the merit in going West!

Other Devices:
Flashback; Inference; Irony; Simile; Stereotype/Reverse Stereotype; Understatement

Pinkwater, Daniel. *Ducks!* Boston: Little, Brown, 1984.
In a candy store, a boy encounters a duck who claims to be an angel; in return for granting it its freedom, he endures some bizarre adventures with a chariot and other duck angels.

Examples:
Parental truth and accuracy are under attack as the boy questions the ducks who tell him that parents aren't to be trusted.

Other Devices:
Parody

Pinkwater, Daniel. *I Was a Second Grade Werewolf.* New York: E.P. Dutton, 1983.
Though he has turned into a werewolf, his parents, teacher, and classmates still don't really see him as anything but Lawrence Talbot, second grader.

Pinkwater, Daniel. *Roger's Umbrella.* Illus. by James Marshall. New York: E.P. Dutton, 1982.
Roger's very real troubles with a recalcitrant umbrella to unheeded by the "good" people. Not until he accidentally meets some folks out of society's mainstream do his problems get addressed and solved.

Other Devices:
Inference

Snow, Pegeen. *Mrs. Periwinkle's Groceries.* Illus. by Jerry Warshaw. Chicago: Children's Press, 1981.
Several well-meaning younger folk try to 'help' an older lady carry her groceries home. She doesn't need any help and is more than able to do for herself. The so-called helpful people end up hindering.

Other Devices:
Stereotype/Reverse Stereotype

Steig, William. *Yellow & Pink.* New York: Farrar, Straus, & Giroux, 1984.
Two wooden marionette dolls lying on newspaper begin to speculate about how they came to be and invent a logical story for their existence. The futility of humans' poking into their reason for being is illustrated.

Examples:
The causes of life are ridiculed and shown as puny, foolish speculations that are hopelessly off-base, just like the carefully considered reasoning of the wooden-headed dolls.

Other Devices:
Analogy; Personification

Stolz, Mary. *Zekmet, the Stone Carver: A Tale of Ancient Egypt.* Illus. by Deborah Lattimore. New York: Harcourt Brace Jovanovich, 1988.
Chosen to design a magnificent monument for a vain and demanding Pharaoh, an Egyptian stone carver conceives and begins work on the Sphinx, which still stands in the Egyptian desert today.

Examples:
"Peasants and pharaohs had but one thing in common. None could stay the moment of death." That which we revere may not be worthy of the pomp and majesty accorded it. In this case, the face of the particular pharaoh on the Sphinx may not even be a representation of his countenance.

Willard, Nancy. *The Marzipan Moon.* Illus. by Marcia Sewall. New York: Harcourt Brace Jovanovich, 1981.
The almonds in an old, mended, but magic crock produce a delicious, nourishing marzipan moon nightly for a poor parish priest until a visiting bishop decides the miraculous almonds need a more fitting home.

Examples:
Story spoofs the church hierarchy for its grasping ways. The box built especially to house the magical almonds is decorated with likenesses of "all the best people in heaven."

Other Devices:
Allusion; Tone

Yorinks, Arthur. *Company's Coming.* Illus. by David Small. New York: Crown, 1988.
Chaos erupts when Moe and Shirley invite some visitors from outer space to stay for dinner with the relatives.

Examples:
A nation's overeager penchant for seeing enemies everywhere is the focus of ridicule in this tale. The FBI, pentagon, army, air force, and marines arrive to oversee a gift which the aliens say will "knock you out." The suspicious gift turns out to be a kitchen blender which the aliens say they hope Shirley does not already own. Luckily, Shirley has prepared enough food so that the soldiers, pilots, marines, and FBI agents can all stay for dinner.

Yorinks, Arthur. *It Happened in Pinsk.* New York: Farrar, Straus, & Giroux, 1983.
A complaining man wishing always to be someone else suddenly loses his head and becomes mistaken for other people after his wife makes a pillowcase head for him.

Other Devices:
Allusion; Ambiguity; Irony; Pun; Understatement

SIMILE

Explicit comparison from one unlike thing to another which shares some common recognizable similarity; uses "like," "as," "such as," and "than" to set them off.

Example: Mad as a hornet; laughed like a hyena; lower than a snake's belly in a wagon rut.

Sources

Bunting, Eve. *The Man Who Could Call Down Owls.* Illus. by Charles Mikolaycak. New York: Macmillan, 1984.
A stranger, thinking he can call down owls by wearing the owl caller's clothing, finds the owls unwilling.

Examples:
Cloak drifting about him "like marsh mist"; stranger's smile "as cold as death."

Other Devices:
Atmosphere; Foreshadow; Poetic Justice; Theme

Carrick, Carol. *Dark and Full of Secrets.* Illus. by Donald Carrick. New York: Clarion Books, 1984.
A boy's first tentative experiences with pond life are explored.

Examples:
Early morning mist rose from pond like steam from a witch's brew. In the ocean the waves rose clear green like glass. School of tiny fish hung together like the mobile in his classroom. Trees had fallen into the water sinking like ancient ships. Pond was like a dark mirror.

Other Devices:
Foreshadow; Imagery; Inference; Personification

Cole, Brock. *The Winter Wren.* New York: Farrar, Straus, & Giroux, 1984.
Two children set out to find spring after winter hangs on longer than it should.

Examples:
At the end of story, spring rolled before them like a great green wave.

Other Devices:
Alliteration; Foreshadow; Imagery; Personification

Collins, Meghan. *The Willow Maiden.* Illus. by Laszlo Gal. New York: Dial Books, 1985.
A young farmer falls in love with a beautiful princess but must accept that she lives as a willow tree during the spring and summer months.

Examples:
Air warm as milk; pitiless stare like a fox; pain tightened like a strong belt around his chest; like trying to catch trout with bare hands; parting was for each of them like a tearing of roots; new moon was slow as apples growing.

Other Devices:
Foreshadow

Dragonwagon, Crescent. *Jemima Remembers.* Illus. by Troy Howell. New York: Macmillan, 1984.
Just before leaving for the winter, Jemima visits one last time her favorite places on the farm, recalling the wonderful summer she spent there with her aunt.

Examples:
Small tomato hard as a marble; fat zucchini lying like crocodiles in the shade; hair floated like seaweed; crow circled the sky like a splash of spilled paint; pond like a still black mirror.

Other Devices:
Atmosphere; Imagery

Fields, Julia. *The Green Lion of Zion Street.* Illus. by Jerry Pinkney. New York: Margaret K. McElderry Books, 1988.
The stone lion on Zion Street, proud and fierce, instills fear and admiration in those who see it in the cold city fog.

Examples:
Weather ten times colder than a roller skate; fog jumps the bridge like a big gray hog; melting out quick like some sly shark; fly like a space-flight demon in a rush-hour car; bittered-in like a winter lemon; higher than gold; trample the street like pounding grain; courage shattering like a summer window pane.

Other Devices:
Atmosphere; Imagery

Fleischman, Sid. *The Scarebird.* Illus. by Peter Sis. New York: Greenwillow Books, William Morrow, 1987.
A lonely old farmer realizes the value of human friendship when a young man comes to help him and his scarecrow with their farm.

Examples:
You look like sunshine on stilts with them yeller-paint eyes; slept like a pine log; windows chattering like baby rattles; steady as a rock; meaner than fishhooks; like an itch that needed scratching; like a bird's wing.

Other Devices:
Inference; Tone

Haseley, Dennis. *My Father Doesn't Know About the Woods and Me.* Illus. by Michael Hays. New York: Atheneum, 1988.
As a child walks in the woods with his father, he seems to become other animals enjoying the freedom of nature.

Examples:
Howl crashes into the moon like it's hitting a frying pan; grin that shows all my teeth; trees that look like broccoli below; my tail like a silver light.

Other Devices:
Inference

Kennedy, Richard. *Song of the Horse.* Illus. by Marcia Sewell. New York: E.P. Dutton, 1981.
Girl describes her ride on her horse.

Examples:
Sides like breathing mountains; blows through his nose like a locomotive; legs like mighty wheels; tail like spouting steam; eyes like shining lights; nerves like trembling strings of a great instrument; hoofs like diamonds; lick the earth like a dark flame.

Other Devices:
Imagery; Inference; Personification; Point of View; Tone; Understatement

Mattingley, Christobel. *The Miracle Tree.* Illus. by Marianne Yamaguchi. San Diego, CA: Harcourt Brace Jovanovich, Gulliver Books, 1985.
Separated by the explosion of the atomic bomb, a husband, wife, and mother carry on with their lives in the ruins of Nagasaki. They are eventually reunited on Christmas by a very special tree.

Examples:
Skin as smooth as a camellia petal; hair as shiny as a crow's wing; eyes sparkled like pools in the sun; voice as sweet as a nightingale's; tree needles like the first-cut locks of a child's hair; pigeons speed like single arrows; tree's beauty as subtle as a silk painting, as haunting as a poem; small fluttering shape like a star; voice rang like a bell.

Other Devices:
Atmosphere; Inference; Irony; Metaphor; Symbol

Nesbit, Edith. *The Deliverers of Their Country.* Illus. by Lisbeth Zwerger. Natick, MA: Picture Book Studio, 1985.
Two children set out to rid their land of nasty dragons.

Examples:
The dragons stuck fast "as flies and wasps do on sticky papers in the kitchen"; wings pale, half-transparent yellow like "gear-cases on bicycles"; rat-

tling like a "third class carriage"; dragons running all sorts of ways like "ants if you are cruel enough to pour water into an ant-heap"; labeled with china labels like "you see in baths."

Other Devices:
Allusion; Imagery; Stereotype/Reverse Stereotype; Tone

Nixon, Joan Lowery. *Fat Chance, Claude.* Illus. by Tracey Campbell Pearson. New York: Viking Kestrel, 1987.
Two zany Texans, Shirley and Claude, grow up and meet out in the gold mining hills of Colorado.

Examples:
"Faster than a dragonfly on the way to becoming a fish's dinner"; coyotes howling like "ghosts in the hills"; enough vittles to "choke a cow"; frisky as a "half-growed hound"; nuggets the "size of a horsefly"; as helpless as a "burro in a blizzard."

Other Devices:
Caricature; Flashback; Inference; Irony; Satire; Stereotype/Reverse Stereotype; Understatement

Parnall, Peter. *Apple Tree.* New York: Macmillan, 1987.
Describes the many ways an apple tree interacts with insects, birds and other animals during a full year of its development.

Examples:
Branches seem like "witches' claws"; stumps remain looking like "skeletons, twisted like a mass of melted wire."

Other Devices:
Imagery; Personification

Parnall, Peter. *Winter Barn.* New York: Macmillan, 1986.
A dilapidated old barn shelters a wide variety of animals during the sub-zero winter temperatures in Maine while they wait for the first signs of spring.

Examples:
"Like a great woolly mammoth frozen in the Arctic ice the winter barn waits. . . . "

Other Devices:
Atmosphere; Imagery; Personification

Say, Allen. *The Bicycle Man.* Boston: Houghton, Mifflin Co., 1982.
The amazing tricks two American soldiers do on a borrowed bicycle are a fitting finale for the school sports day festivities in a small village in Japan.

Examples:
Trees made the sound of waves; building creaked like an old sailing ship; mountains echoed like rumbling thunder; white man with bright hair like fire; face as black as the earth; shoes shone like polished metal; legs like a huge dancing spider; cruising like an enormous dragonfly.

Other Devices:
Simile

Skofield, James. *All Wet! All Wet!* Illus. by Diane Stanley. New York: Harper & Row, 1984.
A child's rainy summer day walk in the woods is described.

Examples:
Grass flashing like a jewel; spider-like black stars.

Other Devices:
Personification

Stolz, Mary. *Storm in the Night.* Illus. by Pat Cummings. New York: Harper & Row, 1988.
While sitting through a fearsome thunderstorm that has put the lights out, Thomas hears a story from Grandfather's boyhood, when Grandfather was afraid of thunderstorms.

Examples:
Thunder like mountains blowing up; chin as smooth as a peach; voice like a tuba; Thomas's voice like a penny whistle; clattered on the roof like a million tacks; face like a crack in the ice.

Other Devices:
Ambiguity; Hyperbole; Imagery; Inference; Pun

Tennyson, Noel. *The Lady's Chair and the Ottoman.* New York: Lothrop, Lee, & Shepard, 1987.
An ottoman has spent as long as he can remember trying to get close to a lady's chair, and though fortune separates them and they seem to come to unhappy ends, a marvelous coincidence reunites them in a very happy way.

Examples:
"The ottoman felt like a birthday cake with nine candles on a tenth birthday, or a roller skate with three wheels."

Other Devices:
Allusion; Personfication; Pun

Turner, Ann. *Dakota Dugout.* Illus. by Ronald Himler. New York: Macmillan, 1985.
A woman describes her experiences living with her husband in a sod house on the Dakota prairie.

Examples:
Geese like "yarn in the sky"; heron flapped by with "wings like sails"; snugged like "beavers in our burrow"; with windows like suns; grass "whispered like an old friend."

Other Devices:
Aphorism; Atmosphere; Flashback; Imagery; Inference

Turner, Ann. *Nettie's Trip South.* Illus. by Ronald Himler. New York: Macmillan, 1987.
A ten-year-old northern girl encounters the ugly realities of slavery when she visits Richmond, Virginia, and sees a slave auction.

Examples:
Trees like "old men with tattered gray coats"; face so "black it could've been fired from a cannon in war"; "someone called out a price and she was gone, like a sack of flour pushed across a store counter"' face like the "oak in our yard."

Other Devices:
Ambiguity; Atmosphere

Yolen, Jane. *Owl Moon.* Illus. by John Schoenherr. New York: Philomel Books, 1987.
One winter's night under a full moon, a father and daughter trek into the woods to see a Great Horned Owl.

Examples:
Trees stood still as "giant statues"; train whistle blew like a "sad sad song"; it was quiet as a "dream"; cold as if "someone's icy hand was palm-down on my back"; whiter than the "milk in a cereal bowl"; like a "shadow without sound."

Other Devices:
Imagery; Metaphor

STEREOTYPE/REVERSE STEREOTYPE

Fixed generalized ideas about characters and situations such as plots of predictable formula or recognizable pattern; persons typed rather than unique, denied full range of qualities and characteristics.

Reversed stereotype is opposite of the expected.

Example: Instead of a lady's group creating a winning quilt at the fair, a man's group takes honors for the winning quilt.

Sources

Aylesworth, Jim. *Hush Up!* Illus. by Glen Rounds. New York: Holt, Rinehart, & Winston, 1980.
Jasper is rudely awakened from his nap through a chain of events set off by a mean horsefly.

Examples:
The mountain people and animals are portrayed as lazy and shiftless.

Other Devices:
Caricature

Blegvad, Lenore. *Anna Banana and Me.* Illus. by Erik Blegvad. New York: Atheneum, 1985.
Anna Banana's fearlessness inspires a playmate to face his own fears.

Examples:
In a reversal of male/female stereotypes, a girl and boy of dissimilar temperaments delve into the offerings of an urban park. He is content to be a step or two behind and marvels at her intrepidness.

Other Devices:
Point of View; Theme; Tone

Brinckloe, Julie. *Playing Marbles.* New York: William Morrow, 1988.
A little girl proves her skill in a game of marbles with two boys.

Examples:
The myth that girls can't compete successfully against boys at their games is dispelled in this story.

Other Devices:
Paradox

Browne, Anthony. *Piggybook.* New York: Knopf, 1986.
When Mrs. Piggott unexpectedly leaves one day, her demanding family begins to realize just how much she did for them.

Examples:
Though the males in the house watch Mother cook, wash dishes, wash clothes, vacuum, and make beds, they never offer to help and, when left on their own, seem unable to do these tasks. After the mother makes her point about their selfishness, they swiftly learn together to do housework. Mom goes out to fix the car.

Other Devices:
Theme

Hayes, Sarah. *Eat Up, Gemma.* Illus. by Jan Ormerod. New York: Lothrop, Lee, & Shepard, 1988.
Baby Gemma refuses to eat, throwing her breakfast on the floor and squashing her grapes, until her brother gets an inspired idea.

Examples:
Typically, the baby won't eat good food offered to her but will madly go after inedible, unsuitable things.

Kellogg, Steven. *A Rose for Pinkerton.* New York: Dial, 1981.
A tiny kitten takes over giant dog Pinkerton's world commandeering his sunny spot, eating his dinner, chewing his bone. Pinkerton in turn begins to act like a kitten, drinking milk and sitting on laps. Illustrations show Pinkerton as a kitten and Rose as a tiger-striped dog.

Other Devices:
Pun

Kesselman, Wendy. *Emma.* Illus. by Barbara Cooney. Garden City, NJ: Doubleday, 1980.
Motivated by a birthday gift, a 72-year-old woman begins to paint.

Examples:
When an old lady tries to reminisce about her memory of the past, her family mistakenly assumes she must be "getting old" and senile. She finds a way to express herself by painting her memories. This earns respect from her family at last. Being old does not mean losing viability.

Lindbergh, Anne. *Next Time, Take Care.* Illus. by Susan Hoguet. San Diego, CA: Harcourt Brace Jovanovich, 1988.
While making friends outdoors, Ralph manages to lose all the caps made for him by his constantly knitting Aunt Millicent.

Examples:
Aunt Millicent is shown as the typical spinster: an eccentric, practical woman who lives an orderly life alone. She grows in this story and learns some lighthearted ways from the boy.

Other Devices:
Aphorism; Foreshadow; Inference; Pun

Lionni, Leo. *Nicolas, Where Have You Been?* New York: Knopf, 1987.
Nicolas and his mouse friends are angry because birds have taken the best berries. When he sets off to get berries that the birds haven't found, Nicolas's adventure leads him to see that not all birds are his enemies.

Examples:
From one bad experience Nicolas and his friends conclude that all birds are enemies, until this stereotypical view is changed through experiences.

Other Devices:
Aphorism; Theme

Nesbit, Edith. *The Deliverers of Their Country.* Illus. by Lisbeth Zwerger. Natick, MA: Picture Book Studio, 1985.
Two children set out to rid their land of nasty dragons.

Examples:
In stereotypical fashion it is the girl who wails in fear that she wants to go home and her brother who tells her not to be silly. But incidents of reverse stereotype occur when the girl behaves resourcefully to free her brother and herself from the dragon's claws and figures out the handles that control weather. St. George, the famous dragonslayer, does not rush to his nation's defense but rather decries that "I can't do anything. Things have changed since my time."

Other Devices:
Allusion; Imagery; Simile; Tone

Nixon, Joan Lowry. *Fat Chance, Claude.* Illus. by Tracey Campbell Pearson. New York: Viking Kestrel, 1987.
Two zany Texans, Shirley and Claude, grow up and meet out in the gold mining hills of Colorado.

Examples:
Unconventional Shirley is told she shouldn't be an old maid. Claude tells her she needs a husband to take care of her or she'll be helpless if she runs into trouble. She ought to be "tending a house so she won't be a nuisance to all men folk on the wagon train." In a reversal of roles, Claude makes biscuits for Shirley's stew, and she braces his broken wheel spoke with her best wooden stirring spoon.

Other Devices:
Caricature; Flashback; Inference; Irony; Satire; Simile; Understatement

Sadler, Marilyn. *Alistair's Elephant.* Illus. by Roger Bollen. Englewood Cliffs, NJ: Prentice-Hall, 1983.
Alistair's life is never quite the same again after the elephant follows him home from the zoo.

Examples:
Alistair is depicted as the classic stuffy little Goody-Two-Shoes. He studies all the time, loves to take arithmetic tests, is super neat, challenges body and mind, never wastes time, and loves vegetables best.

Other Devices:
Inference; Understatement

Schwartz, Amy. *Oma and Bobo.* New York: Bradbury Press, 1987.
Bobo the dog learns to stay, sit, and with the help of Oma, to fetch.

Examples:
At dog obedience school, pictures show the kind of dogs chosen by particular persons. The tough man has two poodle puppies. The skinny scholarly boy has a huge doberman.

Other Devices:
Allusion; Foreshadow; Inference

Sharmat, Marjorie Weinman. *Gila Monsters Meet You at the Airport.* Illus. by Byron Barton. New York: Macmillan, 1980.
A boy traveling from an eastern city to a new home out west has some misconceptions about the West that eventually change when he meets a boy heading East who has equally awful misconceptions about the East.

Snow, Pegeen. *Mrs. Periwinkle's Groceries.* Illus. by Jerry Warshaw. Chicago: Children's Press, 1981.
A boy precipitates comic confusion when he attempts to aid an old lady by carrying her groceries.

Examples:
The older person in this story is a physical fitness teacher and ends up helping all her would-be "helpers."

Other Devices:
Satire

Ziefert, Harriet. *My Sister Says Nothing Ever Happens When We Go Sailing.* Illus. by Seymour Chwast. New York: Harper & Row, 1986.
A family leaves the marina, goes under a bridge out on to the ocean, but when the wind dies down, Sister gets bored and falls asleep. She snoozes through a rain squall and a rescue at sea and doesn't wake until the boat docks. Sister has missed all the fun; no wonder she says nothing ever happens when they go sailing.

Examples:
Perpetuates the view that girls aren't athletic and dislike adventurous activities: "My sister didn't want to be on the boat."

Other Devices:
Irony

SYMBOL

Any person, object, or action that has additional meaning beyond itself to represent or stand for a more abstract emotion or idea.

Example: Great Conestogas, white against the sky:
Listen to the rumble as the East goes by. . . from Jessamyn West's "Conestoga Wagons"

Sources

Alexander, Sue. *There's More. . . Much More.* Illus. by Patience Brewster. San Diego, CA: Harcourt Brace Jovanovich, Gulliver Books, 1987.
Squirrel and Sherri celebrate spring by collecting it in their May baskets.

Examples:
All the sensory images stand for spring: flowers, sap running, new leaves, butterflies.

Other Devices:
Imagery

Asch, Frank and Vladimer Vagin. *Here Comes the Cat!* New York: Scholastic, 1989.
A mouse spying a cat on the horizon spreads the word throughout the land. As the mice become galvanized to the danger, they all take up the chant until the huge shadow of the feline causes them to fall silent. The object of all the fear comes bearing a huge wheel of cheese.

Examples:
This joint Soviet-American literary effort has created the "cat," which represents an international enemy. The "mice" represent home defenders.

Other Devices:
Theme

Berger, Barbara Helen. *When the Sun Rose.* New York: Philomel Books, 1986.
An imaginative little girl spends a happy day with her playmate who arrives with a pet lion.

Examples:
The huge yellow cabbage rose ties together the start of the day (sunrise) with the arrival of the guest (in a rose carriage) with the costume of the guest (rose-studded dress) and finally with the exit of the guest (leaving behind an armload of roses scattered on the floor). The rose is associated with this lonely child's sunny pleasure.

Other Devices:
Atmosphere; Pun

Bunting, Eve. *The Man Who Could Call Down Owls.* Illus. by Charles Mikolaycak. New York: Macmillan, 1984.
A stranger thinking he can call down owls by wearing the owl caller's clothing, kills the owl caller and tries to assume his position of power. The owls drive him off.

Examples:
The white cape and white Snowy Owl stand for purity and goodness; the owl caller's assistant, the youth, stands for innocence; the hard-faced stranger stands for evil.

Other Devices:
Atmosphere; Foreshadow; Poetic Justice; Simile; Theme

Cohen, Barbara. *Gooseberries to Oranges.* Illus. by Beverly Brodsky. New York: Lothrop, Lee, & Shepard, 1982.
A young girl reminisces about the journey from her cholera-ravaged village in Russia to the U.S., where she is reunited with her father.

Examples:
When the young girl embraces her new country's fruit, the orange, and sets aside her former preference for goosberries, the fruit of her old country, the reader understands that she has accepted the new land as home.

Other Devices:
Inference; Point of View

Haywood, Carolyn. *The King's Monster.* Illus. by Victor Ambrus. New York: William Morrow, 1980.
Only one man in the kingdom is willing to face the king's monster for the hand of the princess.

Examples:
In this allegory, the unseen "monster" stands for the irrational fears perpetuated by people's imaginations.

Other Devices:
Inference

Heine, Helme. *The Pearl.* New York: Atheneum, 1985.
As Beaver finds a pearl mussel, he is overjoyed at the prospective wealth it undoubtedly holds. He dozes off and dreams about its effect, learning the other side of supposed good fortune.

Examples:
The pearl stands for the greed engendered when jealousy among the haves and have-nots disrupts peaceful harmony. Older students might profit from this picture book before taking on Steinbeck's *The Pearl.*

Innocenti, Roberto. *Rose Blanche.* Mankato, MN: Creative Education, 1985.
Matter-of-fact reporting of the effect upon one German village and one little girl living there during World War II.

Examples:
Drab green and brown military hues are interruped by two bright spots of discordant red, the Nazi swastika and the child's hair bow. The ribbons represent intensely opposite values: calculated deliberate cruelty and kindly innocence.

Other Devices:
Atmosphere; Inference; Point of View; Tone

Johnston, Tony. *Yonder.* Illus. by Lloyd Bloom. New York: Dial, 1988.
As the plum tree changes in the passing seasons, so do the lives of a three-generation farm family.

Examples:
The plum trees planted in a ceremony of each birth and death in the family and tended through each session stand for life's continuity and progression and faith in the future of the family's generations.

Other Devices:
Theme; Tone

Lionni, Leo. *Cornelius, a Fable.* New York: Pantheon Books, 1983.
A crocodile named Cornelius was different. He walked upright. Eventually his unimpressed family was moved by tricks a monkey taught him.

Examples:
Cornelius serves as a symbol for the inventive new voice, the instigator of change and progress, which is embraced by others only reluctantly and without proper recognition accorded to its source.

Martin, Bill and John Archambault. *Knots on a Counting Rope.* Illus. by Ted Rand. New York: Henry Holt, 1987.
One cool dark night an Indian boy sits with his grandfather as they reminisce about the night the boy was born. A poignant story of love, hope, and courage.

Examples:
Crossing the "dark mountains" refers to the obstacles the blind child must face during his life growing up and as an adult in a seeing world.

Other Devices:
Foreshadow; Imagery; Metaphor

Mattingley, Christobel. *The Miracle Tree.* Illus. by Marianne Yamaguchi. San Diego, CA: Harcourt Brace Jovanovich, 1985.
Separated by the explosion of the atomic bomb, a husband, wife, and mother carry on with their lives in the ruins of Nagasaki. They are eventually reunited one Christmas by a very special tree.

Examples:
The pine tree represents rebirth, restoration of confidence in the continuation of life, and recovery of shattered mental and physical health.

Other Devices:
Atmosphere; Inference; Irony; Metaphor; Simile

Paterson, Banjo. *Clancy of the Overflow.* Illus. by Robert Ingpen. New York: Rigby, 1982.
The ballad contrasts the life of the author/city dweller with the outback cowboy. The author longs for the country and decries the city.

Examples:
Clancy is the epitome many men would wish to be, the symbol of perfect "manhood," the free independent spirit galloping through the wide open spaces, vigorous, hearty, self-reliant, scornful of society, and free from city hassles. In their dreams, many men are cowboys at heart.

Other Devices:
Imagery; Theme

Pittman, Helena Clare. *Once When I Was Scared.* Illus. by Ted Rand. New York: E.P. Dutton, 1988.
Grandfather tells how when he was a child he coped with fear during a journey alone through a dark wood to get coals to start a fire in the family cook range.

Examples:
The feathers, supposedly from the eagle which a boy became in order to frighten away a bear, stand for the courage one needs when faced with fearful situations.

Other Devices:
Metaphor

Snyder, Zilpha Keatley. *The Changing Maze.* Illus. by Charles Mikolaycak. New York: Macmillan, 1985.
A shepherd boy braves the evil magic of a wizard's maze to save his pet lamb.

Examples:
The boy and his lamb represent simple innocence untarnished by greed. This is the only combination that can break the evil spell. The green maze is the lure of easy wealth. Granny is possibly the wisdom of conscience. The wizard is evil.

Other Devices:
Aphorism; Atmosphere; Flash-forward; Imagery; Inference; Internal Rhyme; Personification

THEME

The underlying meaning of a literary work, a particular truth about life or humanity which the author is trying to make the reader see; plot is a pattern of events—what happens, but theme is the meaning—what it's about.

Example: Plot—Young soldier during his first battle.
Theme—War is futile; fighting solves nothing.

Sources

Allen, Pamela. *Hidden Treasure.* New York: G.P. Putnam's Sons, 1987.
After claiming the treasure that he and his brother haul out of the ocean, Herbert spends the rest of his life fearfully guarding it from possible thieves.

Examples:
Greed leads one to a lonely and unfulfilled life. Real treasure is not in the chest.

Other Devices:
Inference

Aruego, Jose. *Rockaby Crocodile.* Illus. by Arianne Dewey. New York: Greenwillow Books, 1988.
Two elderly boars with contrasting dispositions take turns caring for a baby crocodile and find that their attitudes determine how they are paid.

Asch, Frank and Vladimir Vagin. *Here Comes the Cat!* New York: Scholastic, 1989.
A mouse spying a cat on the horizon spreads the word throughout the land. As the mice become galvanized to the danger, they all take up the chant until the huge shadow of the feline causes them to fall silent. The object of all the fear comes bearing a huge wheel of cheese.

Examples:
Rather than permit sterotypical labels of "enemy" to paralyze and prevent normal relationships, individuals should allow communication to determine responses.

Other Devices:
Symbol

Baker, Jeannie. *Where the Forest Meets the Sea.* New York: Greenwillow Books, William Morrow, 1987.
On a camping trip in an Australian rain forest with his father, a young boy thinks about the history of the plant and animal life around him and wonders about the future of the environment.

Examples:
The need for preservation of natural ecology is pervasive. The boy fears that when he wishes to return to the unspoiled rain forest, it will be altered by real estate development. He imagines kids sitting on a beach patio watching TV with their backs to the remaining natural beauty.

Other Devices:
Allusion

Bang, Molly. *Delphine.* New York: Morrow, 1988.
Anxious about her ability to handle a mysterious gift (a bicycle) awaiting her at the post office, Delphine is unaware of her amazing feats of courage and skill as she journeys down a steep slope, across a narrow bridge, and through treacherous rapids to pick it up.

Examples:
We have the necessary coping skills within us and only need to draw upon them to apply them to new situations.

Other Devices:
Irony

Baring, Maurice. *The Blue Rose.* Illus. by Anne Dalton. Kingswood, England: Kaye & Ward, The Windmill Press, 1982.
A wise Emperor of China set a condition that the one who can find the Blue Rose may marry his accomplished, beautiful daughter. Less-than-desirable suitors attempt to meet the condition and are rejected. The one successful suitor achieved her acceptance in the time-honored method of earning her love.

Examples:
The best method of selecting mates is still mutual respect and love. Such an approach beats artificial means of "earning" a spouse.

Other Devices:
Imagery; Paradox; Tone

Blegvad, Lenore. *Anna Banana and Me.* Illus. by Erik Blegvad. New York: Atheneum, 1985.
Anna Banana's fearlessness inspires a playmate to face his own fears.

Examples:
Daily chance meetings with a jaunty friend enables a timid child to finally face his restricting inhibitions and fears as he is forced to call upon his resources and find that he can be just as brave as Anna Banana. It is not necessary to wait for another person to supply us with bravery; it's present to cultivate and tap whenever needed.

Other Devices:
Point of View; Stereotype; Tone

Brandenberg, Franz. *Otto Is Different.* Illus. by James Stevenson. New York: Greenwillow Books, 1985.
Otto Octopus learns the advantages of having eight arms instead of only two like everyone else.

Examples:
Learning to appreciate one's own abilities rather than wishing always to be like others.

Other Devices:
Hyperbole

Browne, Anthony. *Piggybook.* New York: Knopf, 1986.
When Mrs. Piggott unexpectedly leaves one day, her demanding family begins to realize just how much she did for them.

Examples:
One's gender ought not to dictate the dimensions of one's skills or responsibilities.

Other Devices:
Stereotype/Reverse Stereotype

Browne, Anthony. *Willy the Wimp.* New York: Knopf, 1984.
A young chimpanzee, tired of being bullied by the suburban gorilla gang, decides to build up his muscles so he won't be a wimp anymore.

Examples:
Although Willy goes through all the accepted routines to build up his body, and although he does look powerful, his personality doesn't change. The new Willy is only skin-deep. Changing appearances doesn't necessarily change internal reality.

Bunting, Eve. *The Man Who Could Call Down Owls.* Illus. by Charles Mikolaycak. New York: Macmillan, 1984.
When a stranger takes away the powers of an old man who has befriended owls, the vengeance wrecked on him is swift and fitting.

Examples:
Reminder of the struggle between good and evil.

Other Devices:
Atmosphere; Foreshadow; Poetic Justice; Simile; Tone

Carrick, Donald. *Harald and the Great Stag.* New York: Clarion, Ticknor & Fields, 1988.
When Harald, who lives in England during the Middle Ages, hears that the Baron and his royal guests are planning to hunt the legendary Great Stag, he devises a clever sheme to protect the animal.

Examples:
A strong environmental message against hunting for sport is evident as the boy finds a soul-mate in the old hunter who has also worked to sabotage the killing of the stag.

Other Devices:
Foreshadow

Catley, Alison. *Jack's Basket.* New York: E.P. Dutton, 1987.
Baby Jack sleeps in a basket until he outgrows it. But it is still valuable to him and his sister for several years. Finally, a mouse recycles it as a nursery for her little ones.

Examples:
The cycle of life is illustrated as one object runs its length of usefulness and returns to its original purpose.

Cazet, Denys. *Frosted Glass.* New York: Bradbury Press, 1987.
Gregory the dog's vivid imagination gets him in trouble at school, leading him to draw cities and spaceships when he should be doing something else. But his artistic ability does not go unrecognized.

Examples:
It's okay to be unconventional; sometimes it even leads to the accomplishment of something better than the standard acceptable product.

Christian, Mary Blount. *The Devil Take You, Barnabas Beane!* Illus. by Anne Burgess. New York: Thomas Crowell, 1980.
The similarity between the footprints of a long-tailed mouse and the traditional descriptions of the devil's cloven hooves frightens a miser out of his ways.

Examples:
Wit triumphs over greed: the metamorphosis of a lonely miser into a convivial host.

Clement, Claude. *The Painter and the Wild Swans.* Illus. by Frederic Clement. New York: Dial, 1986.
Transfixed by the beauty of a passing flock of white swans, a Japanese painter finds that he can't work until he sees them again.

Examples:
The painter realizes that such beauty is impossible to capture, but it is enough to experience it.

Flournoy, Valerie. *The Patchwork Quilt.* Illus. by Jerry Pinkney. New York: Dial, 1985.
A grandmother's determination to create a quilt for her granddaughter finally rouses the whole family to support the project.

Examples:
Intergenerational awareness develops through the story's progress. Role individuality is expressed.

Other Devices:
Foreshadow; Inference; Tone

Frascino, Edward. *My Cousin the King.* Englewood Cliffs, NJ: Prentice-Hall, 1985.
A snobbish cat brags about being related to the King of the Beasts. The 'King's' visit is more than the barnyard animals bargain for.

Examples:
The cat learns a lesson in brotherly love and humility.

Gackenbach, Dick. *Little Bug.* New York: Houghton Mifflin Co., Clarion Books, 1981.
Along with all the dangers, the world is filled with pleasure. Little Bug happily discovers that the only way to experience pleasure is by taking chances.

Graham, Bob. *Pete and Roland.* New York: Viking Press, 1981.
Pete finds a sleepy blue parakeet in his back yard and enjoys keeping the bird as a pet until the day it decides to become independent again.

Examples:
Love and possession are not inextricably linked. Delight can come from casual encounters.

Grifalconi, Ann. *The Village of Round and Square Houses.* Boston: Little, Brown, 1986.
A grandmother explains to her listeners why in their village on the side of a volcano the men live in square houses and the women in round ones.

Examples:
"We live peacefully here" because each one has a place to be apart, and a time to be together.

Other Devices:
Parallel Story

Holman, Felice. *Terrible Jane.* Illus. by Irene Trivas. New York: Scribner's Sons, 1987.
In this story related in verse, a little girl is naughty just for the devilment of annoying others.

Examples:
All the things that everyone gets the urge to do are done by Jane. In the end, the last line tells us that in spite of her mischief and aggravating ways she "only wants us all to love her."

Johnston, Tony. *Yonder.* Illus. by Lloyd Bloom. New York: Dial, 1988.
As the plum tree changes in the passing seasons, so do the lives of a three-generation farm family.

Examples:
The rhythmic repetition of the language echos the continuity of life in a familiar, dependable pattern.

Other Devices:
Symbol; Tone

Jukes, Mavis. *Blackberries in the Dark.* Illus. by Thomas Allen. New York: Knopf, 1985.
A boy, keenly feeling the loss of his grandfather, learns to develop a new, different, and admiring relationship with his grandmother.

Examples:
Austin had always enjoyed fishing with Grandpa. Fishing with Grandma, surprisingly, has its pleasures too. They struggle together learning the things that Grandpa knew. Austin says, "Grandpa would like us doing this—wouldn't he? He would be happy we're learning to fly-fish at Two Rock Creek." Things change, but they don't have to end.

Other Devices:
Ambiguity

Keeping, Charles. *Sammy Streetsinger.* Oxford: Oxford University Press, 1984.
Story follows the fortunes of a musician from humble beginnings, to stardom, and back to simple humility.

Examples:
Social commentary on the ephemeral, empty success of the musical entertainment industry.

Other Devices:
Atmosphere; Flashback; Satire; Tone

Kimmel, Eric. *Why Worry?* Illus. by Elizabeth Cannon. New York: Pantheon Books, 1979.
A pessimistic cricket and an optimistic grasshopper disagree about what will happen to them during a day's busy adventures.

Examples:
Worrying won't alter events. It's best to take life as it comes and make the best of it.

Levitin, Sonia. *Nobody Stole the Pie.* Illus. by Fernando Krahn. New York: Harcourt Brace Jovanovich, 1980.
The annual lollyberry festival in Little Digby is marred because everybody sneaks a little taste of pie meant to be shared together. Everyone justifies taking a 'taste' by thinking there will be plenty left for the celebration.

Examples:
Even though each person takes only a tiny piece, in the end the whole pie is gone. Thus, the loss is caused by everyone.

Other Devices:
Aphorism

Lionni, Leo. *Nicolas, Where Have You Been?* New York: Knopf, 1987.
Nicolas and his mouse friends are angry because birds have beaten them to the best berries. When Nicholas sets off to get berries the birds haven't found, his adventure leads him to see that not all birds are his enemies.

Examples:
A case is made against judging with a prejudicial attitude.

Other Devices:
Aphorism; Stereotype

Meddaugh, Susan. *Maude and Claude Go Abroad.* Boston: Houghton Mifflin Co., 1980.
Two young foxes travel alone on a ship to visit relatives far away. Maude is first admonished to look after her brother. Then the two save a whale from a harpooner.

Examples:
Maude's concern first for her brother's safety causes her to be sensitive to the needs of others. Thus, caring must first start on a personal level before it can grow to encompass a broader environment.

Other Devices:
Pun

Moore, Inga. *Fifty Red Night Caps.* San Francisco: Chronicle Books, 1988.
When monkeys steal the nightcaps that he is carrying to market, a little boy inadvertently finds a way to get his caps back.

Examples:
Drawing upon an old truth, "monkey see, monkey do," the boy is able to work this knowledge to his advantage.

Paterson, Banjo. *Clancy of the Overflow.* Illus. by Robert Ingpen. New York: Rigby, 1982.
The ballad contrasts the life of the author/city dweller with outback cowboy. The author longs for the country and decries the city.

Examples:
The freedom of the self-reliant country life make the restrictive, unpleasant city life seem pale by comparison.

Other Devices:
Imagery; Symbol

Peet, Bill. *Pamela Camel.* Boston: Houghton Mifflin Co., 1984.
A tired and dejected circus camel finds long-sought-after recognition along a railroad track.

Examples:
This is a toast to the ornery and the ordinary who, like the camel in this story, if given a chance, can become special.

Rogers, Paul. *From Me to You.* Illus. by Jane Johnson. New York: Orchard Books, Franklin Watts, 1987.
A grandmother shares her memories of three generations with a young granddaughter and presents her with a precious gift.

Examples:
The story shows the continuity of family life and the binding of life's repetitions between generations.

Other Devices:
Atmosphere; Inference; Point of View

Stanley, Diane. *A Country Tale.* New York: Four Winds Press, 1985.
An ill-fated visit to the city home of the elegant Mrs. Snickers teaches an impressionable country cat a little about herself and the importance of being one's self when friendships are formed.

Examples:
A bit of the "City Mouse, Country Mouse" theme is presented in which simple honest life is foresaken, then reclaimed.

Other Devices:
Foreshadow

Steig, William. *Doctor De Soto.* New York: Fararr, Straus, & Giroux, 1982.
Although a diminutive mouse, the resourceful dentist Dr. De Soto was able to treat all patients of all shapes and sizes except animals dangerous to mice. One day his kind nature gets him into danger with a fox.

Examples:
Wit instead of might is used to outfox a fox.

Other Devices:
Irony

Stevens, Kathleen. *Molly McCullough, and Tom the Rogue.* Illus. by Margot Zemach. New York: Thomas Y. Crowell, 1982.
Tom Devlin roams the countryside charming the farmers' wives and tricking the farmers out of fruits and vegetables until he meets his match in a plain-faced, sharp-tongued, farmer's daughter.

Examples:
Those displaying greed always get their just desserts whether it's the stranger bilking the farmer or the farmer thinking he's besting a city fool.

Other Devices:
Aphorism; Foreshadow; Irony; Poetic Justice

Stevenson, James. *Monty.* New York: Greenwillow Books, 1979.
Everyday Monty (an alligator) took Tom, Doris, and Arthur across the river so that they could go to school. Every day they gave Monty instructions for a faster, smoother, straighter crossing. One morning Monty was not there. . . .

Examples:
Shows what can happen when friendship is taken too much for granted.

Stevenson, James. *What's Under My Bed?* New York: Greenwillow Books, 1983.
Grandpa tells his two young houseguests a story about his own childhood when he was scared at bedtime.

Examples:
Children hear a tale of fear similar to their own nighttime anxieties. They realistically account for and deflate each fearsome episode as Grandpa tells it. Thus they defuse their own fears at the same time.

Other Devices:
Alliteration; Flashback

Switzer, Ellen. *Lily Boop.* Illus. by Lillian Hoban. New York: Crown, 1986.
A young girl describes her adventures with an unusual friend who keeps a pet slug and eats raw eggs for lunch.

Examples:
Judy recognizes that her unusual friend is braver than she is. Though an outsider, Lily manages not only to live in a strange environment, but also to make friends. Judy, when offered a similar opportunity, isn't courageous enough to try the same thing. Physical differences are shown to be insignificant issues in true friendships.

Other Devices:
Inference

Tusa, Tricia. *Maebelle's Suitcase.* New York: Macmillan, 1987.
An elderly woman sacrifices a treasured prize to help her friend, a young bird, make his first flight south.

Examples:
Helping a friend is more important than winning an award, even if winning is practically a sure thing.

Van Allsburg, Chris. *The Wreck of the Zephyr.* Boston: Houghton, Mifflin Co., 1983.
Obsessive desire to be the greatest sailor leads to humbling defeat when a skill is misused.

Examples:
Those who yearn for a power they are not equipped to possess end up earning ridicule, not fame.

Other Devices:
Allusion; Flashback; Foreshadow; Inference

Wells, Rosemary. *A Lion for Lewis.* New York: Dial Press, 1982.
When Lewis plays make-believe with his older siblings, he always gets the least desirable role until a lion suit found in a corner turns him into a king.

Examples:
The resilience of a little brother who has been left out once too often is explored.

TONE

Author's attitude toward his or her subject and audience revealed by choice of words and details.

Example: "Afoot and light-hearted I take to the open road, healthy, free, the world before me. . . ." From Walt Whitman's "Song of the Open Road." (Tone is positive about life and up-beat.)

Sources

Adoff, Arnold. *Flamboyan.* Illus. by Karen Barbour. New York: Harcourt Brace Jovanovich, 1988.
One sunny afternoon while everyone is resting, Flamboyan, a young girl named after the tree whose red blossoms are the same color as her hair, dreamily flies over her Caribbean island home.

Examples:
She flies and dives and flies with pelicans; she soars and glides the air currents; she races frigate birds and hops along the beach with the sooty tern. All this exuberant celebration evokes loving memories of an idyllic paradise.

Other Devices:
Imagery

Baring, Maurice. *The Blue Rose.* Illus. by Anne Dalton. Kingswood, England: Kay & Ward, The Windmill Press, 1982.
A wise emperor of China has set a condition that only he who can find the Blue Rose may marry his accomplished, beautiful daughter. Less-than-desirable suitors respond to the condition and are rejected. The successful suitor achieves her acceptance in the time-honored method of earning her love.

Examples:
Language uses the Oriental style of being precise, straightforward, and unemotional. "The Emperor was old in years; his son was married and had begotten a son; he was, therefore, quite happy about the succession to the throne, but he wished before he died to see his daughter wedded to someone who should be worthy of her."

Other Devices:
Imagery; Paradox; Theme

Blegvad, Lenore. *Anna Banana and Me.* Illus. by Erik Blegvad. New York: Atheneum, 1985.
Anna Banana's fearlessness inspires a playmate to face his own fears.

Examples:
The boy's narration celebrates Anna's energetic effusive joy with life. He juxtaposes her abrupt actions with his own hesitant timidity and thoughtful introspection.

Other Devices:
Point of View; Stereotype; Theme

Dumas, Phillipe. *Lucie, a Tale of a Donkey.* Englewood Cliffs, NY: Prentice-Hall, 1980.
Edward's daughter Lucie befriends a small boy and runs off to Paris with him.

Examples:
A tongue-in-cheek present-tense narration talks to the reader with droll humor and understatement: "They [the boy and the donkey] visit the zoo where they come upon a colony of foreigners. . . ."

Other Devices:
Understatement

Fleischman, Sid. *The Scarebird.* Illus. by Peter Sis. New York: Greenwillow Books, William Morrow, 1987.
A lonely old farmer realizes the value of human friendship when a young man comes to help him and his scarecrow with their farm.

Examples:
The author displays a tender dignity and gentle respect for the farmer called Lonesome John by the townfolks. At first, he designs a purely functional scarecrow: no head or face. But as he sits on his porch playing

his nickle-plated harmonica, his "family gone and his old dog Sallyblue buried in the pasture," he has no one to talk to but himself. Soon the scarecrow has a pillowcase head and a face on it. "Does that face suit you, Scarebird? You look like sunshine on stilts with the yeller-paint eyes! Well make yourself at home."

Other Devices:
Inference; Simile

Flournoy, Valerie. *The Patchwork Quilt.* Illus. by Jerry Pinkney. New York: Dial Press, 1985.
A grandmother's determination to make her granddaughter a quilt wins the support of her whole family.

Examples:
Great respect for the value of the individual is gently expressed without sermonizing.

Other Devices:
Foreshadow; Inference; Theme

Hendershot, Judith. *In Coal Country.* Illus. by Thomas B. Allen. New York: Knopf, 1987.
Through the eyes of a little girl we see coal mining country.

Examples:
Illustrations show the pleasurable activities of childhood tainted by the reality of the world of mining: the hill the children play on is a smoldering pile of mine gob; the creek water is black with coal dust.

Hest, Amy. *The Crack-of-Dawn Walkers.* Illus. by Amy Schwartz. New York: Macmillan, 1984.
Every other Sunday Sadie and her grandfather go for their special early-morning walk.

Examples:
The author's tone is of quiet respect for the old man, dignity without a maudlin approach, as he expresses soft understanding toward his energetic granddaughter whose rivalry with her brother can't be hidden.

Houston, Gloria. *The Year of the Perfect Christmas Tree: An Appalachian Story.* Illus. by Barbara Cooney. New York: Dial, 1988.
Since Papa has left the Appalachian area to go to war, Ruthie and her mother wonder how they will fulfill his obligation of getting the perfect Christmas tree to the town for the holiday celebration.

Examples:
A sense of family love pervades the author's prose: Papa calls Ruthie "pretty young'un"; so does mama. He kisses the dimple in each of Ruthie's cheeks. Mama uses her silk stockings gift from papa and bits of her wedding gown to make Ruthie the Christmas doll she wants. When Papa shows up late Christmas Eve the family is so busy hugging they hardly hear the caroling.

Other Devices:
Inference

Innocenti, Roberto. *Rose Blanche.* Mankato, MN: Creative Education, 1985.
Matter-of-fact reporting of the effect upon one German village and one little girl living there during World War II.

Examples:
Terse, stark statements imply more than they say. Carefully orchestrated pictures allow the author's perception of war's random cruelty to tell itself. "Sometimes it seems things haven't really changed. But my mother wants me to be careful crossing the street between all the trucks. She says soldiers won't slow down."

Other Devices:
Atmosphere; Inference; Point of View; Symbol

Johnston, Tony. *Yonder.* Illus. by Lloyd Bloom. New York: Dial, 1988.
As the plum tree changes in the passing seasons, so do the lives of a three-generation farm family.

Examples:
This nostalgic appreciation shows a timeless rightness about the progression of farm life: "Inside is the mother by a quilting frame. Outside is the father plowing wheat fields. Children walk to school beneath a soft spring rain. Dreaming, dreaming of summer."

Other Devices:
Symbol; Theme

Keeping, Charles. *Sammy Streetsinger.* Oxford: Oxford University Press, 1984.
The fortunes of a simple street singer are shown from humble beginnings through stardom and back again.

Examples:
Author ridicules the musical entertainment industry with word choices: Big Chance Circus: Ivor Chance had a "sly idea,"; Palace of Dreams; Micky Raker the critic; the tabloid called *Daily Muck;* Syd Slicker and the Oil Slicks; Mr. Biggknob the impresario.

Other Devices:
Atmosphere; Flashback; Satire; Theme

Kennedy, Richard. *Song of the Horse.* Illus. by Marcia Sewall. New York: E.P. Dutton, 1981.
This poetic praise describes the powerful, impassioned experience of a girl's ride on her horse.

Other Devices:
Imagery; Inference; Personification; Point of View; Simile; Understatement

Khalsa, Dayal Kaur. *Tales of a Gambling Grandma.* New York: Crown, 1986.
Reminiscences of a grandmother who came to this country from Russia, married a plumber, gambled to earn extra money, and formed a strong bond with her young granddaughter.

Examples:
The bittersweet tone of loss and remembrance reveals how much more than card playing the little girl learns from her Grandma. When Grandma dies, the child hugs Grandma's clothes in the closet and checks on the treasures in her bedside table. She later finds that the ring, which she is to inherit, is paste; it is, nevertheless, worth more to her than real gold and diamonds.

Lasker, Joe. *A Tournament of Knights.* New York: Thomas Crowell, 1986.
Justin, a young knight in the Middle Ages, prepares to engage in his first tournament while an experienced challenger plans to defeat him.

Examples:
The author shows sympathy toward both characters caught up in a cultural event neither can escape. "I would rather break bread with you than cross spears." But they acknowledge, "That is how I live. I have no choice."

Marshall, James. *The Cut-Ups.* New York: Viking Kestrel, 1984.
Two boys play their pranks until they run up against someone who can pay them back.

Examples:
The author spares neither child nor adult in his riducule of prankish behavior: "Lamar J. Spurgle, who'd had enough of kids to last him a lifetime. . . had a whole room full of kid's stuff." But Mary Frances Hooley knows how to come out on top.

Other Devices:
Inference; Poetic Justice

Marshall, James. *The Cut-Ups Cut Loose.* New York: Viking Kestrel, 1987.
At the end of summer Spud and Joe eagerly return to school for more practical jokes, unaware that Principal Lamar J. Spurgle is out of retirement and awaiting them.

Examples:
No character is safe from being spoofed. Spurgle gets after the kids. Mary Frances sics Sister Aloysious after Spurgle. And finally Sister 'A' herself "gets" Mary Frances when she rides her souped-up car.

Other Devices:
Inference; Irony; Understatement

Nesbit, Edith. *The Deliverers of Their Country.* Illus. by Lisbeth Zwerger. Natick, MA: Picture Book Studio, 1985.
Two children set out to rid their land of nasty dragons.

Examples:
The dragons are discussed with understated, macabre humor: It "was not very easy to poison a dragon, because you see they ate such different things. The largest kind ate elephants as long as their were any, and then went on with horses and cows. Another size ate nothing but lilies of the valley, and a third size ate only Prime Ministers if they were to be had, and if not, would feed freely on boy's buttons."

Other Devices:
Allusion; Analogy; Imagery; Simile; Stereotype

Pinkwater, Daniel. *Devil in the Drain.* New York: E.P. Dutton, 1984.
Iconoclastic treatment in humorous, contemporary language of a devil who supposedly lives in a kitchen sink drain. Interesting visual perspectives are drawn in cartoon-like scrawl.

Other Devices:
Inference

Pinkwater, Daniel. *Ducks!* Boston: Little, Brown, 1984.
In a candy store, a boy encounters a duck who claims to be an angel; in return for granting it its freedom, he endures some bizarre adventures with a chariot and other duck angels.

Examples:
Tongue-in-cheek satire of parents and interpretation of life's situations.

Other Devices:
Parody; Satire

Rylant, Cynthia. *When I Was Young in the Mountains.* Illus. by Diane Goode. New York: E.P. Dutton, 1982.
Tender, gentle, simple reflection of life's pleasures and love of mountain living as seen through the eyes of a child in the early 1900s. The text is accompanied by delicate and detailed brown and blue-toned period pen and ink drawings.

Other Devices:
Imagery

Shefelman, Janice. *Victoria House.* Illus. by Tom Shefelman. San Diego, CA: Harcourt Brace Jovanovich, 1988.
An old Victorian house is moved from the country to its new location on a city street, where a family fixes it up and moves in.

Examples:
A reverence and loving appreciation is expressed by the author through the family's response to the house. As they hoist the home at last on to its new foundation, they stand looking at it: "Mason yawned. 'Home at last, Victoria.' Sarah waved, 'See you tomorrow.' Once again Victoria House was lived in and loved, and she sounded happy."

Other Devices:
Imagery

Talbott, Hudson. *We're Back! A Dinosaur's Story.* New York: Crown, 1987.
In this very funny picture book, creatures from prehistoric time travel to the twentieth century and create excitement at New York's Museum of Natural History.

Examples:
This is a buoyantly, whacky, boisterous, account of what happens when some "outsiders" unwittingly crash a twentieth century holiday parade in New York. The author's dead-pan, first-person narration by "Rex," a dinosaur, shows how logically it all occurs right up to the bedtime story when they are safe at last in the museum and listening to: "Once upon a time in the eary Paleozoic era, there was a little trilobite who wanted more than anything to walk on land. . . ."

Other Devices:
Allusion; Point of View

Willard, Nancy. *The Marzipan Moon.* Illus. by Marcia Sewall. New York: Harcourt Brace Jovanovich, 1981.
The almonds in an old, mended, but magic crock produce a delicious marzipan moon nightly for a poor parish priest, until a visiting bishop decides the miraculous almonds need a more fitting home.

Examples:
In this tongue-in-cheek spoof the author talks directly to the reader: "a diet likely to kill you if you stick to it long enough." "But the clay pot, now, that's the one you want to get hold of. And if you do, remember the priest's story. Wish for something sensible."

Other Devices:
Allusion; Satire

UNDERSTATEMENT

The act of presenting something as less significant than it really is.

Example: There seems to be a slight discrepancy in your bookkeeping statements.

Sources

Allard, Harry. *Miss Nelson Has a Field Day.* Illus. by James Marshall. Boston: Houghton Mifflin Co., 1985.
The notorious Miss Swamp reappears at the Horace B. Smedley School, this time to shape up the football team and make them win at least one game.

Examples:
"Coach Armstrong had cracked up." This statement about the effects of Coach's pressures is followed by Miss Nelson's bland comment, "I'll make us a pot of coffee."

Other Devices:
Foreshadow; Inference; Pun

Allen, Jeffrey. *Nosey Mrs. Rat.* Illus. by James Marshall. New York: Viking Kestrel, 1985.
Mrs. Rat makes a career out of spying on her neighbors, but the tables are unexpectedly turned on her.

Examples:
"Shirley's hobby kept her very busy." Says she of life: "There is nothing worse than a nosey neighbor," not recognizing herself!

Other Devices:
Inference; Poetic Justice

Arnold, Tedd. *No Jumping on the Bed!* New York: Dial, 1987.
Walter lives near the top floor of a tall apartment building, where one night his habit of jumping on his bed leads to a tumultuous fall through floor after floor, collecting occupants all the way down.

Examples:
As the floors of the building collapse through each other, events are characterized with such bland statements as: "dropped in unannounced" and "wished his audience would leave and so they did along with his string quartet" which belie the pandemonium that piles up with each added floor.

Other Devices:
Foreshadow; Inference; Internal Rhyme

Christelow, Eileen. *Mr. Murphy's Marvelous Invention.* New York: Houghton Mifflin Co., 1983.
Cornelius Murphy, a pig inventor, makes a unique housekeeping machine for his wife's birthday, but the entire family is shocked when they discover what the machine actually does.

Examples:
Mr. Murphy stays up late at night trying to fix the birthday machine and Mrs. Murphy stays up late "hoping he won't be able to fix it." The machine doesn't "mend very well, wash the car well, make beds or treat Mrs. Murphy well"—as the pictures clearly show!

Other Devices:
Foreshadow

Cole, Babette. *The Trouble With Gran.* New York: G.P. Putnam's Sons, 1987.
Gran, who is secretly an extraterrestrial being, livens up a trip to the seaside engineered by Teacher for a group of schoolchildren and senior citizens.

Examples:
The pictures show what the understated text does not. None of the senior citizens suspect Gran's true nature. One of her legs is green and the foot is webbed. Her antennae are hidden under her. She starts to "act up" at the amusement park.

Cole, Babette. *The Trouble With Mom.* New York: Coward-McCann, 1983.
A child describes how his mom seems to be different from other folks.

Examples:
The child says about his mom: "The trouble with Mom is the hats she wears." (They are suspiciously pointed, and live lizards and rats crawl on them.) "At first the other kids gave me funny looks when she took me to my new school." (They fly through the air on a broom.) "She didn't seem to get along with the other parents." (As Mom passes the bench they're sitting on at the PTA meeting, frogs are left sitting where they were.) When kids ask where his dad is, the boy says, "Mom says he's staying put until he stops going bowling every night:" (Dad is hunched down in a covered jar that says "Pickled Husband.")

Dumas, Phillipe. *Lucie, a Tale of a Donkey.* Englewood Cliffs, NJ: Prentice-Hall, 1980.
Edward's daughter Lucie befriends a small boy and runs off to Paris with him.

Examples:
Interpretation of sights comes by way of donkey-view. Paris offers a parade of cars alongside a parade of men on horseback for them to admire. In Paris, "certain clues" put Edward on to Lucie's trail: a street of wrecked stands and broken windows!

Other Devices:
Tone

Kennedy, Richard. *Song of the Horse.* Illus. by Marcia Sewall. New York: E.P. Dutton, 1981.
After describing a thrilling ride with her horse, a girl comes into her house answering her mother's question about how the ride was with the inadequate, "It was all right."

Other Devices:
Imagery; Inference; Personification; Point of View; Simile; Tone

Lorenz, Lee. *Big Gus and Little Gus.* Englewood Cliffs, NJ: Prentice-Hall, 1982.
Big Gus, who did all the work while Little Gus schemed, gets to marry the rich princess.

Examples:
Though Little Gus was the dreamer/schemer, "Big Gus was just big"—dense, obtuse, and slow to catch the way of things.

Other Devices:
Parody; Poetic Justice

Macaulay, David. *Why the Chicken Crossed the Road.* Boston: Houghton Mifflin Co., 1987.
By crossing the road a chicken sets off a series of wild reactions which eventually return full circle.

Examples:
"Turning to science," two boys playing with their chemistry set "substantially enlarged the bathroom" as a huge explosion ensues. Clarell Sweet "conducted a surprise inspection of Mel Toom's garbage truck": she was thrown from her bike into the dumpster.

Other Devices:
Flashback; Inference; Pun

Marshall, James. *The Cut-Ups Cut Loose.* New York: Viking Kestrel, 1987.
At the end of summer Spud and Joe eagerly return to school for more practical jokes, unaware that Principal Lamar J. Spurgle is out of retirement and awaiting them.

Examples:
The Cut-Ups had "gotten off to an early start" (picture shows them crawling from hospital nursery onto window ledge). "Cutting up was certainly challenging" (picture shows boys driving a taxi). "School was the biggest challenge of all" (picture shows teacher being hauled off on a stretcher from "The Little Darlings' Kindergarten").

Other Devices:
Inference; Irony; Tone

Mattingley, Christobel. *The Angel with a Mouth-Organ.* Illus. by Astra Lacie. New York: Holiday House, 1986.
Just before the glass angel is put on the Christmas tree, Mother describes her experiences as a little girl during World War II, when she and her family were refugees, and how the glass angel came to symbolize a new beginning in their lives.

Examples:
Narrated events underplay the stark horror of war: "We walked until the baby died, and Father scratched a hole under a birch tree and my sister and I gathered moss for its new bed and leaves for its blankets"; "We walked until a wheel fell off our cart and before Father could mend it, some other people broke it up for firewood to roast an ox which had died"; "But many of the soldiers were lying still. There was red on their uniforms and no one could wipe it away."

Other Devices:
Flashback; Inference; Metaphor; Point of View

Murphy, Jill. *Five Minutes' Peace.* New York: G.P. Putnam's Sons, 1986.
All Mrs. Large (elephant) wants is five minutes' peace from her wonderful, rambunctious children. But chaos follows her all the way from the kitchen to the bathroom and back again.

Examples:
The children were having breakfast. "This was not a pleasant sight." (Picture shows huge food mess).

Other Devices:
Atmosphere; Inference

Nixon, Joan Lowery. *Fat Chance, Claude.* Illus. by Tracey Campbell Pearson. New York: Viking Kestrel, 1987.
Two zany Texans, Shirley and Claude, grow up and meet out in the gold mining hills of Colorado.

Examples:
When Shirley saves Claude's life by dumping hot stew on the snake (and spilling some in the process on him), Claude says that though he's beholdin' to her he thought "there mighta been a more comfortable way to do it."

Other Devices:
Flashback; Inference; Irony; Satire; Simile; Stereotype/Reverse Stereotype

Noble, Trinka Hakes. *The Day Jimmy's Boa Ate the Wash.* Illus. by Steven Kellogg. New York: Dial Press, 1980.
In this cumulative tale a child offhandedly describes her class trip to Mom. Each understatement leads to more hilarious confusion about the day's really wild events.

Examples:
On the farm a wonderful chain of events is blandly explained beginning with the end. Some pigs had come on the bus to eat the children's lunches, because the children had thrown the pigs' corn at each other, because they had run out of eggs to throw at one another, because the boa constrictor had frightened the chickens causing them to fly. A nervous chicken had laid an egg on Jenny's head. It broke and she got mad and. . . .

Sadler, Marilyn. *Alistair's Elephant.* Illus. by Roger Bollen. Englewood Cliffs, NJ: Prentice-Hall, 1983.
Alistair's life is never quite the same again after the elephant follows him home from the zoo.

Examples:
"The elephant gave Alistair some privacy" (it turns its rear end around filling the bedroom window with its backside instead of its face).

Other Devices:
Inference; Stereotype

Sadler, Marilyn. *Alistair's Time Machine.* Englewood Cliffs, NJ: Prentice-Hall, 1986.
Alistair's entry in a science competition takes him to many places and eras, but unfortunately he can't prove this to the judges.

Examples:
He tells his mom not to expect him for lunch (he's about to take a trip in his time machine). He went "somewhat farther" back in time than yesterday (he ate lunch with some knights at a round table).

Other Devices:
Allusion

Talbott, Hudson. *We're Back! A Dinosaur's Story.* New York: Crown, 1987.
In this very funny picture book, creatures from prehistoric time travel to the twentieth century and create excitement at New York's Museum of Natural History.

Examples:
"One day as I was beginning a little afternoon snack" (a small dinosaur is struggling to escape the bigger dinosaur's jaws). "Just getting to the Museum should be the thrill of a lifetime!" (a parade is disrupted, the NYPD is out in full force and military tanks arrive on the scene). "They didn't understand us" (the *Daily Post* headline reads, "Monsters Hit Midtown!"). "Not having a good time?" Dr. Bleeb asks the panic-stricken dinosaurs, who wonder if it's "too late to get out of this bonus prize" trip to the twentieth century.

Other Devices:
Allusion; Point of View; Tone

Yorinks, Arthur. *It Happened in Pinsk.* New York: Farrar, Straus, & Giroux, 1983.
A complaining man wishing always to be someone else suddenly loses his head and becomes mistaken for other people after his wife makes a pillowcase head for him.

Examples:
When Irv tries to eat a roll one morning, he discovers that his head is missing. His wife says, "Every day you lose something. Your keys. Your glasses. Now this."

Other Devices:
Allusion; Ambiguity; Irony; Satire

Resource Titles and Literary Devices

- *Adam's Smile*
  McPhail, David
  Inference
- *Alistair's Elephant*
  Sadler, Marilyn
  Inference; Understatement
- *Alistair's Time Machine*
  Sadler, Marilyn
  Allusion; Understatement
- *All I See*
  Rylant, Cynthia
  Paradox
- *All Wet! All Wet!*
  Skofield, James
  Personification; Simile
- *Angel with a Mouth-Organ (The)*
  Mattingley, Christobel
  Flashback; Inference; Metaphor; Point of View; Understatement
- *Anna Banana and Me*
  Blegvad, Lenore
  Point of View; Stereotype/Reverse Stereotype; Theme; Tone
- *Annie and the Wild Animals*
  Brett, Jan
  Foreshadow
- *Another Mouse to Feed*
  Kraus, Robert
  Pun
- *Apple Tree*
  Parnall, Peter
  Imagery; Personification; Simile
- *Argyle*
  Wallace, Barbara Brooks
  Allusion
- *Artists' Helpers Enjoy the Evenings*
  Goffstein, M.B.
  Personification
- *Beautiful My Mane in the Wind*
  Petroski, Catherine
  Point of View
- *Best Town in the World (The)*
  Baylor, Byrd
  Atmosphere; Hyperbole; Imagery
- *Bicycle Man (The)*
  Say, Allen
  Point of View; Simile
- *Big Gus and Little Gus*
  Lorenz, Lee
  Parody; Poetic Justice; Understatement
- *Big Sneeze (The)*
  Brown, Ruth
  Foreshadow
- *Blackberries in the Dark*
  Jukes, Mavis
  Ambiguity; Theme
- *Blue Rose (The)*
  Baring, Maurice
  Imagery; Paradox; Theme; Tone
- *Boy of the Three-Year Nap (The)*
  Snyder, Dianne
  Inference; Poetic Justice

- *Boy Who Held Back the Sea (The)*
  Locker, Thomas
  Allusion; Inference
- *Bravo, Minski*
  Yorinks, Arthur
  Allusion
- *Bridge (The)*
  Neville, Emily Cheney
  Foreshadow; Inference
- *Changing Maze (The)*
  Snyder, Zilpha Keatley
  Aphorism; Atmosphere; Flash-forward; Imagery; Inference; Internal Rhyme; Personification; Symbol
- *Charles and Claudine*
  Berson, Harold
  Parody
- *Chen Ping and His Magic Axe*
  Demi
  Atmosphere; Poetic Justice
- *Chicken Little*
  Kellogg, Steven
  Alliteration; Parody
- *Chocolate Chip Cookie Contest (The)*
  Douglass, Barbara
  Inference
- *Christmas Camel (The)*
  Parker, Nancy Winslow
  Allusion; Inference
- *Cinderella*
  Perrault, Charles. Illus. by Roberto Innocenti
  Irony
- *Cinderella Show (The)*
  Ahlberg, Janet and Allan Ahlberg
  Parallel Story
- *Clancy of the Overflow*
  Paterson, Banjo
  Imagery; Symbol; Theme
- *Come Out and Play, Little Mouse*
  Kraus, Robert
  Foreshadow; Inference
- *Company's Coming*
  Yorinks, Arthur
  Satire
- *Cornelius*
  Lionni, Leo
  Symbol
- *Country Tale (A)*
  Stanley, Diane
  Foreshadow; Theme
- *Crack-of-Dawn Walkers (The)*
  Hest, Amy
  Tone
- *Crusher Is Coming!*
  Graham, Bob
  Inference; Irony
- *Cut-Ups (The)*
  Marshall, James
  Inference; Poetic Justice; Tone
- *Cut-Ups Cut Loose (The)*
  Marshall, James
  Inference; Irony; Tone; Understatement
- *Dakota Dugout*
  Turner, Ann
  Aphorism; Atmosphere; Flashback; Imagery; Inference; Metaphor; Simile
- *Dark and Full of Secrets*
  Carrick, Carol
  Foreshadow; Imagery; Personification; Simile
- *Dawn*
  Bang, Molly
  Inference
- *Day Jimmy's Boa Ate the Wash (The)*
  Noble, Trinka Hakes
  Understatement
- *Death of the Iron Horse*
  Goble, Paul
  Foreshadow; Personification; Point of View
- *Deliverers of Their Country (The)*
  Nesbit, Edith
  Allusion; Imagery; Simile; Stereotype/Reverse Stereotype; Tone
- *Delphine*
  Bang, Molly
  Irony; Theme
- *Devil in the Drain*
  Pinkwater, Daniel
  Inference; Tone

- *Devil Take You Barnabas Beane! (The)*
Christian, Mary Blount
Theme
- *Do Not Open*
Turkle, Brinton
Foreshadow; Inference; Parody
- *Doctor De Soto*
Steig, William
Irony; Theme
- *Donkey's Dream (The)*
Berger, Barbara Helen
Inference
- *Dove's Letter (The)*
Baker, Keith
Irony
- *Downtown Day (The)*
Edwards, Linda Strauss
Point of View
- *Ducks!*
Pinkwater, Daniel
Parody
- *Early American Christmas (An)*
de Paola, Tomie
Imagery
- *Earthlets as Explained by Professor Xargle*
Willis, Jeanne
Point of View
- *Eat Up, Gemma*
Hayes, Sarah
Stereotype
- *Eddy B., Pigboy*
Dunrea, Olivier
Point of View
- *Emma*
Kesselman, Wendy
Stereotype/Reverse Stereotype
- *Farmer Bungle Forgets*
King-Smith, Dick
Inference; Irony
- *Fat Chance, Claude*
Nixon, Joan Lowery
Caricature; Flashback; Inference; Irony; Stereotype/Reverse Stereotype; Satire; Simile; Understatement
- *Favershams (The)*
Gerrard, Roy
Satire
- *Fifty Red Night Caps*
Moore, Inga
Theme
- *Fish in His Pocket (A)*
Cazet, Denys
Atmosphere
- *Five Minutes' Peace*
Murphy, Jill
Atmosphere; Inference; Understatement
- *Five Secrets in a Box*
Brighton, Catherine
Allusion; Inference; Point of View
- *Fix-It*
McPhail, David
Irony
- *Flamboyan*
Adoff, Arnold
Imagery; Tone
- *Florence and Eric Take the Cake*
Wild, Jocelyn
Allusion; Ambiguity; Pun
- *Flossie and the Fox*
McKissack, Patricia
Personification; Poetic Justice; Pun
- *Foolish Rabbit's Big Mistake*
Martin, Rafe
Aphorism; Parody
- *Fox's Dream*
Tejima, Keizaburo
Atmosphere; Imagery
- *Friday the 13th*
Kroll, Steven
Poetic Justice
- *Friends of Emily Culpepper (The)*
Coleridge, Ann
Irony
- *From Me to You*
Rogers, Paul
Atmosphere; Inference; Point of View; Theme
- *Frosted Glass*
Cazet, Denys
Theme
- *Garden for a Ground Hog (A)*
Balian, Lorna
Foreshadow

- *Garden of Abdul Gasazi (The)*
  Van Allsburg, Chris
  Inference
- *Ghost's Hour, Spook's Hour*
  Bunting, Eve
  Imagery; Personification
- *Giant Vegetable Garden (The)*
  Westcott, Nadine Bernard
  Hyperbole
- *Giant's Toe (The)*
  Cole, Brock
  Parody
- *Gila Monsters Meet You at the Airport*
  Sharmat, Marjorie Weinman
  Stereotype/Reverse Stereotype
- *Git Along, Old Scudder*
  Gammell, Stephen
  Caricature
- *Gooseberries to Oranges*
  Cohen, Barbara
  Inference; Point of View; Symbol
- *Grain of Rice (A)*
  Pittman, Helena Clare
  Foreshadow; Irony; Paradox
- *Grandma Goes Shopping*
  Armitage, Ronda and David Armitage
  Allusion
- *Grandpa's Slide Show*
  Gould, Deborah
  Atmosphere
- *Green Lion of Zion Street (The)*
  Fields, Julia
  Atmosphere; Imagery; Simile
- *Half Birthday (The)*
  Pomerantz, Charlotte
  Ambiguity; Pun
- *Harald and the Great Stag*
  Carrick, Donald
  Foreshadow; Theme
- *Hattie and the Fox*
  Fox, Mem
  Foreshadow
- *Hello, Mr. Scarecrow*
  Lewis, Rob
  Irony
- *Her Majesty, Aunt Essie*
  Schwartz, Amy
  Point of View
- *Here Comes the Cat!*
  Asch, Frank
  Symbol; Theme
- *Hidden Treasure*
  Allen, Pamela
  Inference; Theme
- *House on Maple Street (The)*
  Pryor, Bonnie
  Flashback
- *How Many Days to America?*
  Bunting, Eve
  Imagery
- *How My Parents Learned to Eat*
  Friedman, Ina R.
  Flashback; Irony
- *Hush Up!*
  Aylesworth, Jim
  Caricature; Stereotype/Reverse Stereotype
- *I Hear a Noise*
  Goode, Diane
  Irony
- *I Was a Second Grade Werewolf*
  Pinkwater, Daniel
  Satire
- *I Wish I Were a Butterfly*
  Howe, James
  Imagery; Irony
- *In Coal Country*
  Hendershot, Judith
  Tone
- *In Window Eight, the Moon is Late*
  Allison, Diane Worfolk
  Alliteration; Internal Rhyme
- *Incredible Painting of Felix Clousseaux (The)*
  Agee, Jon
  Foreshadow; Pun
- *Island Rescue*
  Martin, Charles E.
  Flash-forward
- *It Happened in Pinsk*
  Yorinks, Arthur
  Allusion; Ambiguity; Irony; Satire; Understatement

- *It Hardly Seems Like Halloween*
  Rose, David S.
  Irony
- *Jack's Basket*
  Catley, Alison
  Theme
- *Jam, A True Story*
  Mahy, Margaret
  Allusion; Inference; Pun
- *Jemima Remembers*
  Dragonwagon, Crescent
  Atmosphere; Imagery; Simile
- *Jim and the Beanstalk*
  Briggs, Raymond
  Parody
- *Joey*
  Kent, Jack
  Satire
- *John Patrick Norman McHennessy: The Boy Who Was Always Late*
  Burningham, John
  Irony; Poetic Justice
  Irony
- *Jumanji*
  Van Allsburg, Chris
  Inference; Pun
- *Jump, Frog, Jump!*
  Kalan, Robert
  Foreshadow
- *King Bidgood's in the Bathtub*
  Wood, Audrey
  Irony; Poetic Justice
- *King Nimrod's Tower*
  Garfield, Leon
  Aphorism; Parody
- *King's Monster (The)*
  Haywood, Carolyn
  Inference; Symbol
- *Kirsty Knows Best*
  McAfee, Annalena
  Parallel Story
- *Knight and the Dragon (The)*
  de Paola, Tomie
  Inference
- *Knots on a Counting Rope*
  Martin, Bill and Archambault, John
  Foreshadow; Imagery; Metaphor; Symbol
- *Lady and the Spider (The)*
  McNulty, Faith
  Metaphor
- *Lady's Chair and the Ottoman (The)*
  Tennyson, Noel
  Allusion; Personification; Pun; Simile
- *Lights Around the Palm*
  Jukes, Mavis
  Paradox
- *Like Jake and Me*
  Jukes, Mavis
  Ambiguity
- *Lily Boop*
  Switzer, Ellen
  Inference; Theme
- *Lily Takes a Walk*
  Kitamura, Satoshi
  Parallel Story
- *Lion for Lewis (A)*
  Wells, Rosemary
  Theme
- *Little Bug*
  Gackenbach, Dick
  Theme
- *Little House from the Sea (The)*
  Gedin, Birgitta
  Aphorism; Paradox; Personification
- *Little Interlude (A)*
  Maiorano, Robert
  Allusion; Atmosphere; Inference
- *Lola Koala and the Ten Times Worse Than Anything*
  Blaustein, Muriel
  Aphorism; Poetic Justice
- *Look What I've Got!*
  Browne, Anthony
  Poetic Justice; Satire
- *Lost and Found*
  Walsh, Jill Paton
  Allusion; Aphorism; Flash-forward
- *Lost Lake (The)*
  Say, Allen
  Ambiguity; Inference
- *Lucie, a Tale of a Donkey*
  Dumas, Phillipe
  Tone; Understatement

- *Lucky Me*
  Cazet, Denys
  Poetic Justice
- *Maebelle's Suitcase*
  Tusa, Tricia
  Theme
- *Magic Leaf (The)*
  Morris, Winifred
  Aphorism; Paradox; Satire
- *Man Who Could Call Down Owls (The)*
  Bunting, Eve
  Atmosphere; Foreshadow; Poetic Justice; Simile; Symbol; Theme
- *Marianna May and Nursey*
  de Paola, Tomie
  Inference
- *Martin's Hats*
  Blos, Joan
  Pun
- *Marzipan Moon (The)*
  Willard, Nancy
  Allusion; Satire; Tone
- *Maude and Claude Go Abroad*
  Meddaugh, Susan
  Theme
- *Meanwhile Back at the Ranch*
  Noble, Trina Hakes
  Allusion
- *Meteor!*
  Polacco, Patricia
  Hyperbole
- *Mice and the Flying Basket (The)*
  Peppe, Rodney
  Allusion; Foreshadow
- *Mice Twice*
  Low, Joseph
  Inference; Irony; Poetic Justice
- *Miracle Tree (The)*
  Mattingley, Christobel
  Atmosphere; Inference; Irony; Metaphor; Simile; Symbol
- *Miss Nelson Has a Field Day*
  Allard, Harry
  Allusion; Foreshadow; Inference; Pun; Understatement
- *Miss Rumphius*
  Cooney, Barbara
  Flashback
- *Molly McCullough and Tom the Rogue*
  Stevens, Kathleen
  Aphorism; Foreshadow; Irony; Poetic Justice; Theme
- *Monster Bed (The)*
  Willis, Jeanne
  Irony
- *Monty*
  Stevenson, James
  Theme
- *Morton and Sidney*
  Demarest, Chris L.
  Irony; Satire
- *Mountains of Tibet (The)*
  Gerstein, Mordicai
  Foreshadow; Inference; Irony
- *Mr. Murphy's Marvelous Invention*
  Christelow, Eileen
  Foreshadow; Understatement
- *Mrs. Armitage on Wheels*
  Blake, Quentin
  Inference
- *Mrs. Periwinkle's Groceries*
  Snow, Pegeen
  Satire; Stereotype/Reverse Stereotype
- *My Cousin the King*
  Frascino, Edward
  Theme
- *My Father Doesn't Know About the Woods and Me*
  Haseley, Dennis
  Inference; Simile
- *My Sister Says Nothing Ever Happens When We Go Sailing*
  Ziefert, Harriet
  Irony; Stereotype/Reverse Stereotype
- *Nettie's Trip South*
  Turner, Ann
  Ambiguity; Atmosphere; Simile
- *Never Satisfied*
  Testa, Fulvio
  Irony
- *Never Trust an Ogre*
  Solotareff, Grégoire
  Inference; Pun

- *Next Time, Take Care*
  Lindbergh, Anne
  Aphorism; Foreshadow; Inference; Pun; Stereotype/Reverse Stereotype
- *Nicolas, Where Have You Been?*
  Lionni, Leo
  Aphorism; Stereotype; Theme
- *No Jumping on the Bed!*
  Arnold, Tedd
  Foreshadow; Inference; Internal Rhyme; Understatement
- *No Such Things*
  Peet, Bill
  Allusion; Paradox; Pun
- *Nobody Stole the Pie*
  Levitin, Sonia
  Aphorism; Theme
- *Nosey Mrs. Rat*
  Allen, Jeffrey
  Inference; Poetic Justice; Understatement
- *Old Henry*
  Blos, Joan W.
  Aphorism; Irony; Paradox
- *Ollie Forgot*
  Arnold, Tedd
  Paradox; Parody
- *Oma and Bobo*
  Schwartz, Amy
  Allusion; Foreshadow; Inference; Stereotype/Reverse Stereotype
- *Once Upon MacDonald's Farm*
  Gammell, Stephen
  Inference; Parody
- *Once When I Was Scared*
  Pittman, Helena Clare
  Metaphor; Symbol
- *One-Eyed Jake*
  Hutchins, Pat
  Poetic Justice
- *Otto Is Different*
  Brandenberg, Franz
  Hyperbole; Theme
- *Owl Moon*
  Yolen, Jane
  Imagery; Metaphor; Simile
- *Painter and the Wild Swans (The)*
  Clement, Claude
  Theme
- *Pamela Camel*
  Peet, Bill
  Theme
- *Patchwork Cat (The)*
  Mayne, William
  Alliteration; Internal Rhyme; Metaphor; Point of View
- *Patchwork Quilt (The)*
  Flournoy, Valerie
  Foreshadow; Inference; Theme; Tone
- *Pearl (The)*
  Heine, Helme
  Symbol
- *Perfect Day (The)*
  Prater, John
  Parallel Story
- *Pete and Roland*
  Graham, Bob
  Theme
- *Pig Pig Rides*
  McPhail, David
  Hyperbole
- *Piggins*
  Yolen, Jane
  Allusion
- *Piggybook*
  Browne, Anthony
  Stereotype/Reverse Stereotype; Theme
- *Place for Ben*
  Titherington, Jeanne
  Irony
- *Playing Marbles*
  Brinckloe, Julie
  Paradox; Stereotype/Reverse Stereotype
- *Polar Express (The)*
  Van Allsburg, Chris
  Atmosphere
- *Poofy Loves Company*
  Parker, Nancy Winslow
  Point of View
- *Porcelain Cat (The)*
  Hearn, Michael Patrick
  Allusion; Irony; Pun
- *Prince Cinders*
  Cole, Babette
  Parody; Poetic Justice

- *Princess and the Frog (The)*
  Vesey, A.
  Parody
- *Proverbial Mouse (The)*
  Miller, Moira
  Aphorism; Pun
- *Quilt Story (The)*
  Johnston, Tony
  Flash-forward
- *Ralph's Secret Weapon*
  Kellogg, Steven
  Allusion; Foreshadow
- *Rapscallion Jones*
  Marshall, James
  Allusion; Flashback
- *Red Riding Hood*
  Marshall, James
  Parody
- *Rockabye Crocodile*
  Aruego, Jose
  Theme
- *Roger's Umbrella*
  Pinkwater, Daniel
  Inference; Satire
- *Rondo in C*
  Fleischman, Paul
  Atmosphere; Metaphor
- *Rose Blanche*
  Innocenti, Roberto
  Atmosphere; Inference; Point of View; Symbol; Tone
- *Rose for Pinkerton (A)*
  Kellogg, Steven
  Pun; Stereotype/Reverse Stereotype
- *Rose in My Garden (The)*
  Lobel, Arnold
  Alliteration; Imagery; Inference
- *Rotten Island*
  Steig, William
  Imagery
- *Sammy Streetsinger*
  Keeping, Charles
  Atmosphere; Flashback; Satire; Theme; Tone
- *Scarebird (The)*
  Fleischman, Sid
  Inference; Simile; Tone
- *Secret in the Matchbox (The)*
  Willis, Val
  Foreshadow
- *Sidney Rella and the Glass Sneaker*
  Myers, Bernice
  Parody; Pun
- *Snail's Spell (The)*
  Ryder, Joanne
  Imagery; Point of View
- *Snow White in New York*
  French, Fiona
  Parody
- *Socks for Supper*
  Kent, Jack
  Irony
- *Song of the Horse*
  Kennedy, Richard
  Imagery; Inference; Personification; Point of View; Simile; Tone; Understatement
- *Soup for Supper*
  Root, Phyllis
  Alliteration; Caricature
- *Storm in the Night*
  Stolz, Mary
  Ambiguity; Hyperbole; Imagery; Inference; Pun; Simile
- *Story of Chicken Licken (The)*
  Ormerod, Jan
  Parallel Story
- *Stranger (The)*
  Van Allsburg, Chris
  Foreshadow
- *Sun, the Wind and the Rain (The)*
  Peters, Lisa Westberg
  Parallel Story
- *Supermarket Mice (The)*
  Gordon, Margaret
  Irony
- *Tales of a Gambling Grandma*
  Khalsa, Dayal Kaur
  Tone
- *Terrible Jane*
  Holman, Felice
  Theme
- *Terrible Tuesday*
  Townson, Hazel
  Inference
- *There's More. . .Much More*
  Alexander, Sue
  Imagery

- *Three Pigs (The)*
  Ross, Tony
  Parody; Pun
- *Too Many Books!*
  Bauer, Caroline
  Hyperbole
- *Tooley! Tooley!*
  Modell, Frank
  Irony
- *Tournament of Knights (A)*
  Lasker, Joe
  Tone
- *Town in the Library (The)*
  Nesbit, Edith
  Point of View
- *Trouble with Gran (The)*
  Cole, Babette
  Understatement
- *Trouble with Granddad (The)*
  Cole, Babette
  Hyperbole; Inference
- *Trouble with Mom (The)*
  Cole, Babette
  Understatement
- *Tumbledown*
  Rogers, Paul
  Irony
- *Use Your Head, Dear*
  Aliki
  Allusion; Inference
- *Very Worst Monster (The)*
  Hutchins, Pat
  Hyperbole; Irony
- *Victoria House*
  Shefelman, Janice
  Imagery
- *Village of Round and Square Houses (The)*
  Grifalconi, Ann
  Parallel Story; Theme
- *Visitors Who Came to Stay (The)*
  McAfee, Annalena
  Atmosphere; Paradox; Pun
- *Voyage of the Ludgate Hill (The)*
  Willard, Nancy
  Alliteration; Imagery; Internal Rhyme
- *Waiting for Jennifer*
  Galbraith, Kathryn
  Inference
- *Wanda's Circus*
  Aitken, Amy
  Atmosphere
- *Washday on Noah's Ark*
  Rounds, Glen
  Caricature; Parody
- *Watch the Stars Come Out*
  Levinson, Riki
  Flashback
- *We're Back! A Dinosaur's Story*
  Talbott, Hudson
  Allusion; Point of View; Tone; Understatement
- *Whale Song*
  Johnston, Tony
  Imagery
- *What Happens Next?*
  Domanska, Janina
  Hyperbole; Paradox
- *What's Under My Bed?*
  Stevenson, James
  Alliteration; Flashback; Internal Rhyme; Theme
- *When I Was Young in the Mountains*
  Rylant, Cynthia
  Imagery; Tone
- *When the Sun Rose*
  Berger, Barbara Helen
  Atmosphere; Pun; Symbol
- *Where the Forest Meets the Sea*
  Baker, Jeannie
  Allusion; Theme
- *Why the Chicken Crossed the Road*
  Macaulay, David
  Flashback; Inference; Pun; Understatement
- *Why Worry?*
  Kimmel, Eric
  Theme
- *Wild Washerwomen (The)*
  Yoeman, John
  Caricature
- *Wild Wild Sunflower Child*
  Carlstrom, Nancy White
  Alliteration; Atmosphere; Imagery; Internal Rhyme

- *Willow Maiden (The)*
  Collins, Meghan
  Foreshadow; Simile
- *Willy the Wimp*
  Browne, Anthony
  Theme
- *Wings, A Tale of Two Chickens*
  Marshall, James
  Inference
- *Winter Barn*
  Parnall, Peter
  Atmosphere; Imagery; Personification; Simile
- *Winter Wren (The)*
  Cole, Brock
  Alliteration; Foreshadow; Personification; Simile
- *Witch Got on at Paddington Station (A)*
  Sheldon, Dyan
  Atmosphere
- *Witch Who Lives Down the Hall (The)*
  Guthrie, Donna
  Point of View
- *Wolf's Chicken Stew (The)*
  Kasza, Keiko
  Irony
- *Wreck of the Zephyr (The)*
  Van Allsburg, Chris
  Allusion; Flashback; Foreshadow; Inference; Theme
- *Writer (A)*
  Goffstein, M.B.
  Analogy; Metaphor
- *Yanosh's Island*
  Abolafia, Yossi
  Flashback
- *Year of the Perfect Christmas Tree (The)*
  Houston, Gloria
  Inference; Tone
- *Yellow & Pink*
  Steig, William
  Analogy; Personification; Satire
- *Yonder*
  Johnston, Tony
  Symbol; Theme; Tone
- *You Make the Angels Cry*
  Cazet, Denys
  Ambiguity
- *Zekmet, the Stone Carver*
  Stolz, Mary
  Satire

Index

Compiled by Linda Webster

Susan Hall holds an M.A. in Library Science from the University of Northern Iowa. She has been a librarian in both school and public libraries, most recently the Tipton Public Library, Tipton, IA. She is a reporter for the *Tipton Conservative.*